FINANCE & ACCOUNTING FOR NONFINANCIAL MANAGERS

Revised & Expanded Edition

Steven A. Finkler, Ph.D., CPA

PRENTICE HALL
Paramus, New Jersey 07652

RAP 398 2792

Library of Congress Cataloging-in-Publication Data

Finkler, Steven A.
  Finance & accounting for nonfinancial managers /
  Steven A. Finkler.—Rev. and expanded ed.
      p.   cm.
  Includes index.
  ISBN 0-13-157710-7
    1. Accounting.   2. Business enterprises—Finance.   I. Title.
  HF5635.F534   1992   91-40720
  658.15—dc20   CIP

Printed in the United States of America

10   9   8   7

ISBN 0-13-157710-7

 PRENTICE HALL
Career & Personal Development
Paramus, NJ 07652
A Simon & Schuster Company

On the World Wide Web at http://www.phdirect.com

Prentice-Hall International (UK) Limited, *London*
Prentice-Hall of Australia Pty. Limited, *Sydney*
Prentice-Hall Canada Inc., *Toronto*
Prentice-Hall Hispanoamericana, S.A., *Mexico*
Prentice-Hall of India Private Limited, *New Delhi*
Prentice-Hall of Japan, Inc., *Tokyo*
Simon & Schuster Asia Pte. Ltd., *Singapore*
Editora Prentice-Hall do Brasil, Ltda., *Rio de Janeiro*

In loving memory of my mother

ABOUT THE AUTHOR

Steven A. Finkler, Ph.D., CPA, is a Professor of Financial Management at the Robert F. Wagner Graduate School, New York University. He holds a bachelor's degree with a major in Finance and a master's degree in Accounting from the Wharton School. His master's degree in Economics and Ph.D in Business Administration are from Stanford University. Before joining NYU in 1984, he was on the faculty of the Wharton School for six years.

An award winning teacher and author, he has also written a book on budgeting, and over one hundred articles on financial management. He has consulted for numerous organizations.

PREFACE

There was a time when controllers and treasurers served a clear staff function of providing information and support for line managers. Today it often seems to nonfinancial managers that the financial officers are the tail wagging the dog. It seems as if there's more money to be made by buying someone else's tax loss than by producing and selling the firm's own product or service.

Financial officers may often appear to be more preoccupied with their own ever-increasing empires than with the provision of timely, useful, understandable information for running the firm efficiently. They certainly don't seem to have the time to translate the information they do generate into a form comprehensible to the average nonfinancial manager.

Yet the nonfinancial manager can no longer avoid financial information. Profit statements, operating budgets, and project analyses are a constant part of the manager's day. This book is an introduction to the world of financial management. However, its intent is not to make the reader a financial manager. This is *not* a course in accounting. It is *not* a course in finance. Rather, it is an attempt to familiarize the nonfinancial manager with what accounting and finance are all about. This book concentrates on providing a working vocabulary for communication, so that the reader can develop an ability to ask the right questions and interpret the jargon-laden answers. Any accountant can bury any nonaccountant in debits and credits. But once you understand a few basics you can fight back and demand information that is both useful and usefully explained.

In addition to vocabulary, this book describes a variety of methods, processes, and tools of accounting and finance. They are not described in sufficient detail for the reader to fire the treasurer or controller and take over the job (how many of you really want to do that?). Instead, there is sufficient detail so that the reader can say, "So that's what LIFO-FIFO is all about? I always wondered why we changed our inventory system," or perhaps, "Hey, we never thought about those advantages of leasing rather than buying; maybe we should give leasing a closer look!"

How many managers are rewarded on the basis of return on investment (ROI) without understanding the difference between

ROI and ROE (return on equity) and ROA (return on assets), not to mention RONA (return on net assets)? There's no escaping the fact that all managers are affected by the financial decisions that every firm makes. This book clarifies in the reader's mind what questions are important to the firm's financial management and why.

Who are the nonfinancial managers this book is aimed at? They are presidents and vice-presidents and all other managers except for the accountants and other financial experts in the firm. This includes all the engineers, sales personnel, and production people who have moved up within their firm to the point at which they need more financial lingo to follow what's going on in their communications with the financial officers. They are people who have shifted career paths or who have simply grown with the firm and been promoted to more responsible positions. Sometimes managers need this book simply because the growth of their firm has been so fast that the financial complexity has increased at a more rapid rate than they have been able to keep up with.

Most of the readers of this book will not have attended business school. Surprisingly, however, many business school graduates will pick this book up as an excellent refresher. Frequently, business school graduates who majored in fields such as management, marketing, and industrial organization have commented years later that they would have paid far more attention to their accounting and finance coursework had they realized how valuable that background is to those in responsible positions in industry.

Essentially, this book is for any manager who comes into contact with elements of the financial process and feels a need for a better understanding of what's going on.

One final note. This is not a text. The structure of this book is such that the reader can sit down and read it in whole or in part. Although it is not a novel, the material is presented in a prose that should eliminate the need for intensive studying to understand the main points. A once-through reading should provide the reader with a substantial gain in knowledge. As specific financial questions come before the reader at times in the future, the book will serve as a good reference to brush up on general questions in a particular area. And, when more depth is required on any topic, the list of references following the last chapter should serve as a good source for as much detailed information as is needed.

CONTENTS

PART I   INTRODUCTION

CHAPTER ONE/AN INTRODUCTION TO FINANCIAL MANAGEMENT   3

What Is Financial Management?   3
The Goals of Financial Management   4
   Profitability   5
   Viability   6
Key Concepts   9

PART II   THE FRAMEWORK OF ACCOUNTING

CHAPTER TWO/ACCOUNTING CONCEPTS   13

Basics   14
Assets   15
Liabilities   16
Owners' Equity   16
The Accounting Equation   17
Key Concepts   18

CHAPTER THREE/AN INTRODUCTION TO THE KEY FINANCIAL STATEMENTS   19

The Balance Sheet   19
The Income Statement   22
The Statement of Cash Flows   24
Notes to Financial Statements   25
Key Concepts   26

CHAPTER FOUR/THE ROLE OF THE OUTSIDE AUDITOR   27

Generally Accepted Accounting Principles (GAAP)   28
The Audit   35

The Management Letter and Internal Control   35
Fraud and Embezzlement   36
The Auditor's Report   38
The Management Report   41
Key Concepts   41

CHAPTER FIVE/VALUATION OF ASSETS AND EQUITIES   44

Asset Valuation   45
Historical Cost or Acquisition Cost   45
Price-Level Adjusted Historical Cost   46
Net Realizable Value   48
Future Profits   49
Replacement Cost   49
Which Valuation Is Right?   50
Valuation of Liabilities   52
Valuation of Stockholders' Equity   54
Key Concepts   55

CHAPTER SIX/RECORDING FINANCIAL INFORMATION   57

Double Entry and the Accounting Equation   57
Debits and Credits: The Accountant's Secret   59
Recording the Financial Events   63
Key Concepts   71

CHAPTER SEVEN/REPORTING FINANCIAL INFORMATION   72

Ledgers   73
Executive Corporation's Financial Statements   74
The Income Statement   76
The Balance Sheet   76
The Statement of Cash Flows   80
Looking Ahead   85
Key Concepts   86

PART III   FINANCIAL DECISIONS

CHAPTER EIGHT/LEVERAGE   **89**

Financial Leverage   90
  How Much Financial Leverage Is Enough?   92
  The Rule of OPM   92
  The Collateral Factor   93
  Stability of Earnings   93
Operating Leverage   94
  Break-Even Analysis   95
Key Concepts   98

CHAPTER NINE/DEPRECIATION: HAVING YOUR CAKE AND EATING IT TOO!   **100**

Amortization   101
Asset Valuation for Depreciation   102
  The Depreciable Base   104
  Asset Life   104
Straight-Line vs. Accelerated Depreciation   105
Comparison of the Depreciation Methods   106
Modified Accelerated Cost Recovery System
  (MACRS)   109
Key Concepts   113

CHAPTER TEN/DEPRECIATION AND DEFERRED TAXES: ACCOUNTING MAGIC   **115**

A One-Asset Firm   116
Deferred Taxes for the Multi-Asset Firm   121
Summary   127
Key Concepts   128

CHAPTER ELEVEN/INVENTORY COSTING: THE ACCOUNTANT'S WORLD OF MAKE-BELIEVE 129

The Inventory Equation   129
Periodic vs. Perpetual Inventory Methods   130
The Problem of Inflation   133
Cost-Flow Assumptions   134
Comparison of the LIFO and FIFO Cost Flow
  Assumptions   136
Postscripts on LIFO   144
  Switching to LIFO   144
  The LIFO Conformity Rule   145
  Who Shouldn't Use LIFO   146
  LIFO Liquidations   146
Key Concepts   147

CHAPTER TWELVE/CAPITAL BUDGETING AND DISCOUNTED CASH FLOW ANALYSIS 149

Investment Opportunities   150
Data Generation   151
Evaluation of Cash Flow Information:
  The Payback Method   154
The Time Value of Money   156
Evaluation of Cash Flow Information:
  The Net Present Value (NPV) Method   161
  The Hurdle Rate   161
  NPV Calculations   163
Evaluation of Cash Flow Information: The Internal
  Rate of Return Method (IRR)   165
  Variable Cash Flow   166
Project Ranking   168
Summary   169
Key Concepts   169

CHAPTER THIRTEEN/LEASE OR BUY? A TAXING QUESTION 171

Accounting Issues 172
  Operating vs. Capital Leases 172
  Criteria for Capital Leases 173
Management Considerations for Leasing 174
Tax Considerations for Leasing 176
Key Concepts 179

CHAPTER FOURTEEN/COST ACCOUNTING 180

Cost vs. Expense: The Inventory Process 181
Period Costs vs. Product Costs 184
Manipulation of Product Costs 185
Cost Systems: Process, Job-Order, and
  Standard Costs 186
Activity Based Costing (ABC) 189
The Unit Cost Problem 191
Key Concepts 194

CHAPTER FIFTEEN/BUDGETING 196

Definition and Role of Budgets 196
The Master Budget 197
Budget Preparation 198
  Preliminaries 198
  Forecastng 199
  Departmental Budgets 200
Using Budgets for Control 201
  Static Budgets 201
  Flexible Budgeting 204
  Flexible Budget Variance and Volume Variance 204
  Price and Quantity Variances 205
Key Concepts 207

PART IV   *FINANCIAL STATEMENT ANALYSIS*

**CHAPTER SIXTEEN/A CLOSER LOOK AT FINANCIAL
STATEMENT**   211

The Balance Sheet   212
   Current Assets   214
   Long-Term Assets   215
   Liabilities   216
   Stockholders' Equity   216
The Income Statement   219
The Statement of Cash Flows   221
The Notes to the Financial Statements   225
Key Concepts   226

**CHAPTER SEVENTEEN/NOTES TO THE FINANCIAL
STATEMENTS**   227

Significant Accounting Policies   228
Other Notes   238
Other Information (Unaudited)—Price Level
   Information   241
Summary   241
Key Concepts   243

CHAPTER EIGHTEEN/RATIO ANALYSIS   244

Benchmarks for Comparison   246
Common Size Ratios   247
   The Balance Sheet: Assets   249
   The Balance Sheet: Equities   250
   The Income Statement   250
   Common Size Ratios: Additional Notes   251
Liquidity Ratios   252
Efficiency Ratios   254
   Receivables Ratios   254
   Inventory Ratios   256

Solvency Ratios   256
Profitability Ratios   259
   Margin Ratios   259
   Return on Investment (ROI) Ratios   260
Key Concepts   264

CHAPTER NINETEEN/SUMMARY AND CONCLUSION   **266**

REFERENCES   **269**

INDEX   **271**

NOTE: This book is not designed to make the reader a financial analyst, accountant, or tax expert. The purpose of the book is to allow you to better understand what such experts are doing, and to better communicate with them. One should not make any financial or tax decisions based on the contents of this book without first consulting an expert in the appropriate fields of accounting, finance, or tax.

Part I

INTRODUCTION

One

AN INTRODUCTION TO FINANCIAL MANAGEMENT

WHAT IS FINANCIAL MANAGEMENT?

The firm exists in order to increase the wealth of its owners. General management of the firm is concerned with knowing what products and services are needed and having an ability to produce and distribute those products and services. The area of financial management is concerned with the financial decisions that must be made in order to achieve a maximization of wealth for the owners of the firm.

This book focuses on the accounting and finance areas of financial management. *Accounting* is a system for providing financial information. It is generally broken down into two principal divisions: financial accounting and managerial accounting. *Finance* has traditionally been thought of as the area of financial management that supervises the acquisition and disposition of the firm's resources, especially cash.

The *financial accounting* aspect of accounting is a formalized system designed to record the financial history of the firm. The financial accountant is simply a historian who uses dollar signs. An integral part of the financial accountant's job is to report the firm's history from time to time to interested individuals, usually through the firm's annual and quarterly reports.

The managerial accountant looks forward whereas the financial accountant looks backward. Instead of reporting on what has happened, the *managerial accountant* provides financial information that might be used for making improved decisions regarding the future. Providing financial information for virtually any decision that could be improved by a forecast or by an analysis is the responsibility of the managerial accountant. In many firms the same individual is responsible for providing both financial and managerial accounting information.

Finance has expanded significantly from the function of borrowing funds and investing the excess cash resources of the firm. In its broader sense the finance function involves providing financial analyses to improve decisions that will impact on the wealth of the firm's owners. Whereas the managerial accountant will provide the information for use in the analyses, the finance officer often will perform the actual analyses.

THE GOALS OF FINANCIAL MANAGEMENT

At first thought, we might simply say that the goal of financial management is to aid in the maximization of owner wealth, or more simply, maximization of the firm's profits. Profits are, after all, the bottom line. That's true, but as all managers know, the corporate environment has many other goals—maximization of sales, maximization of market share, maximization of the growth rate of sales, and maximization of the market price of the firm's stock, for example.

On a more personal level, managers are concerned with maximization of salary and perks. Such maximization is often tied in with the maximization of return on investments (ROI), return on equity (ROE), return on assets (ROA), or return on net assets (RONA). (See Chapter 18 for a discussion of these terms.) The list of goals within the organization is relatively endless, and our intention is to narrow the range rather than broaden it.

From the perspective of financial management there are two overriding goals: profitability and viability. The firm wants to be profitable, and it wants to continue in business. It is possible to be profitable and yet fail to continue in business. Both goals require some clarification and additional discussion because they surface time and time again throughout this book.

Profitability

In maximizing profits there is always a tradeoff with risk. The greater the risk we must incur, the greater the anticipated profit we demand. Certainly, given two equally risky projects we would always choose to undertake the one with a greater anticipated return. More often than not, however, our situation revolves around whether the return on a specific investment is great enough to justify the risk involved.

Consider keeping funds in a passbook account insured by the Federal Depositors Insurance Corporation (FDIC). You will earn a profit or return (in nominal terms—we'll talk about inflation later) of about $5\frac{1}{2}\%$. The return is low, but so is the risk. Alternatively, you could put your money in a non-bank moneymarket fund where the return might be considerably higher. However, the investment would not be insured by the FDIC. The risk is clearly greater. Or you could put your money into the stock market. In general, do we expect our stocks to do better or worse than a moneymarket fund? Well, the risks inherent in the stock market are significantly higher than in a moneymarket fund. If the expected return weren't higher, would anyone invest in the stock market?

That doesn't mean that everyone will choose to accept the same level of risk. Some people keep all their money in bank accounts, and others choose the most speculative of stocks. Some firms will be more willing than others to accept a high risk in order to achieve a high potential profit. The key here is that in numerous business decisions the firm is faced with a tradeoff—risk vs. return. Throughout this book, when decisions are considered, the question that will arise is, "Are the extra profits worth the risk?" It is, I hope, a question that you will be somewhat more comfortable answering before you've reached the end of this book.

Viability

Firms have no desire to go bankrupt, so it is no surprise that one of the crucial goals of financial management is ensuring financial viability. This goal is often measured in terms of *liquidity* and *solvency*. Liquidity is simply a measure of the amount of resources a firm has that are cash or are convertible to cash in the *near-term*, to meet the obligations the firm has that are coming due in the near term. Accountants use the phrases "near-term," "short-term," and "current" interchangeably. Generally the near-term means one year or less. Thus a firm is liquid if it has enough near-term resources to meet its near-term obligations as they become due for payment.

Solvency is simply the same concept from a long-term perspective. *Long-term* simply means more than one year. Does the firm have enough cash generation potential over the next three, five, and ten years to meet the major cash needs that will occur over those periods? A firm must plan for adequate solvency well in advance because the potentially large amounts of cash involved may take a long period of planning to generate. The roots of liquidity crises that put firms out of business often are buried in inadequate long-term solvency planning in earlier years.

So a good strategy is maximization of your firm's liquidity and solvency, right? No, wrong. The treasurer has a complex problem with respect to liquidity. Every dollar kept in a liquid form (such as cash, treasury bills, or moneymarket funds) is a dollar that could have been invested by the firm in some longer-term, higher yielding project or investment. There is a tradeoff in the area of viability and profitability. The more profitable the treasurer attempts to make the firm by keeping it fully invested, the lower the liquidity and the greater the possibility of a liquidity crisis and even bankruptcy. The more liquid the firm is kept, the lower the profits. Essentially this is just a special case of the tradeoff between risk and profitability discussed earlier.

We mentioned that profitability and viability are not synonymous. A firm can be profitable every year of its existence, yet go bankrupt anyway. How can this happen? Frequently it is the result of rapid growth and poor financial planning. Consider a firm whose sales are so good that inventory is constantly being substantially expanded. Such expansion requires cash payments to suppliers well in advance of ultimate cash receipt from sales.

Consider the hypothetical firm, Growth Company, which starts the year with $40,000 in cash and receivables of $80,000. It also has 10,000 units of inventory. Its units are sold for $10 each and they have a cost of $8, yielding a profit of $2 on each unit sold. During January it collects all of its outstanding receivables (no bad debts!), thus increasing available cash to $120,000. January sales are 10,000 units, up 2,000 from the 8,000 units sold last December.

Due to increased sales, Growth decides to expand inventory to 12,000 units. Of the $120,000 available, it spends $96,000 on replacement and expansion of inventory (12,000 units acquired @ $8). This leaves a January month-end cash balance of $24,000.

During February all $100,000 of January's sales (10,000 units @ $10) are collected, increasing the available cash to $124,000. In February the entire 12,000 units on hand are sold and are replaced in stock with an expanded total inventory of 15,000 units. Everyone at Growth is overjoyed. They are making $2 on each unit sold. They are collecting 100% of their sales on a timely basis. There appears to be unlimited growth potential for increasing sales and profits. The reader may suspect that we are going to pull the rug out from under Growth by having sales drop or customers stop paying. Not at all.

In March, Growth collects $120,000 from its February sales. This is added to the $4,000 cash balance from the end of February (the beginning balance in February was $24,000, they collected $100,000 during February, but they spent $120,000 to buy 15,000 more units, leaving a cash balance of only $4,000). They have an available cash balance of $124,000 in March. During March, all 15,000 units in inventory are sold and inventory is replaced and expanded to 20,000 units. Times have never been better. Except for one problem. Growth only has $124,000, but the bill for their March purchases is $160,000 (i.e., 20,000 units @ $8). They are $36,000 short in terms of cash needed to meet current needs. Depending on the attitude of their supplier and their banker, Growth may be bankrupt.

Two key factors make this kind of scenario common. The first is that growth implies outlay of substantial amounts of cash for the increased inventory levels needed to handle a growing sales volume.

The second is that growth is often accompanied by an expansion of plant and equipment, again well in advance of the ultimate receipt of cash from customers.

Do growing companies have to go bankrupt? Obviously not. But they do need to plan their solvency along with their growth. The key is to focus on the long-term plans for cash. It is often said that banks prefer to lend to those who don't need the money. Certainly banks don't like to lend to firms like Growth, who are desperate for the money. A more sensible approach for Growth than going to a bank in March would be to lay out a long-term plan for how much they expect to grow and what the cash needs are for that amount of growth. The money can then be obtained from the issuing of bonds and additional shares of stock. Or, orderly bank financing can be anticipated and approved well in advance.

Apparently, even in a profitable environment the finance officer's constant demand for cash flow projections are a real concern. Liquidity and solvency are crucial to the firm's viability. Throughout the book, therefore, we will constantly return to this issue as well as that of profitability. In fact, the reader will become aware that a substantial amount of emphasis in financial accounting is placed on providing the user of financial information with indications of the firm's liquidity and solvency.

Part II of this book provides a framework for accounting. It assumes that the reader has relatively little formal financial background. Many readers will find most of it to be new information. Others may find it a good review of material with which they are already generally familiar. Some readers may even find it rather elementary. For those more advanced readers, it might be appropriate to skip Part II and proceed directly to Parts III and IV.

Part III discusses specific areas of interest for financial decision making. It gets into the various choices for inventory and depreciation methods, including a discussion of tax implications. It also discusses leasing, leverage (both operating and financial), cost accounting, and long-term investment decision making. These topics should be of interest to all readers.

Part IV of the book concentrates on the financial statement as the key to financial analysis. Emphasis is placed on the use of ratio analysis and on understanding the notes to the financial statements. The impact of inflation on accounting data and the accountant's response to the problem of inflation are also discussed in that section.

KEY CONCEPTS

Financial management—management of the finances of the firm in order to maximize the wealth of the firm's owners.

Accounting—the provision of financial information.

  a. Financial accounting—provision of retrospective information regarding the financial position of the firm and the results of its operations.
  b. Managerial accounting—provision of prospective information for making improved managerial decisions.

Finance—provision of analyses concerning the acquisition and disposition of the firm's resources.

Goals of Financial Management

  a. Profitability—a tradeoff always exists between maximization of expected profits and the acceptable level of risk. Undertaking greater risk requires greater anticipated returns.
  b. Viability—a tradeoff always exists between viability and profitability. Greater liquidity results in more safety, but lower profits.

Part II

THE FRAMEWORK OF ACCOUNTING

Two

ACCOUNTING CONCEPTS

In most MBA programs, accounting is required in the first semester of study. Accounting has frequently been referred to as the language of business. The buzz words you encounter in accounting are used as a normal part of the everyday language of finance, marketing, and other areas of financial management. Receivables, payables, journal entries, ledgers, depreciation, equity, LIFO, and MACRS are a smattering of the terms that you encounter if you have any dealings with the financial officers of your firm. All these terms have their roots in accounting.

Therefore Part II of this book focuses on introducing the reader to accounting and to many of the terms used by accountants. Specifically Part II emphasizes the financial accounting system, that is, reporting the financial history and current financial status of the firm.

BASICS

Accounting centers on the business entity. An entity is simply the unit for which we wish to account. Entities frequently exist within a larger entity. An entity can be a department or a project or a firm. For example, Joe's Chilidog Stand is a firm that is an entity. However, if it is not a corporation and it is owned solely by Joe, the Internal Revenue Service considers it to be part of the larger entity, Joe. That larger entity includes Joe's salary, other investments, and various other sources of income in addition to the chilidog stand.

From an accounting point of view there are two crucial aspects of the entity concept. First, once we have defined the entity we are interested in, we shouldn't commingle the resources and obligations of that entity with those of other entities. If we are interested in Joe's Chilidog Stand as an accounting entity, we mustn't confuse the cash that belongs to Joe's Chilidog Stand with the cash that Joe has.

Second, we should view all financial events from the entity's point of view. For example, consider that the Chilidog Stand buys chilidog rolls "on account." A transaction on account gives rise to an obligation or account payable on the part of the buyer and an account receivable on the part of the seller. In order for both the buyer and seller to keep their financial records, or "books," straight, each must record the event from their own viewpoint. They must determine whether they have a payable or a receivable.

We assume throughout this book that the firm you work for is the entity. Once we establish the entity we want to account for, we can begin to keep track of its financial events as they happen. There is a restriction, however, on the way in which we keep track of these events. We must use a monetary denominator for recording all financial events that affect the firm. Even if no cash is involved, we describe an event in terms of amounts of currency. In the United States, accounting revolves around dollars; elsewhere the local currency is used.

This restriction is an important one for purposes of communication. The financial accountant not only wants to keep track of what has happened to the firm but also wants to be able to communicate the firm's history to others after it has happened. Conveying information about the financial position of the firm and the results of its operations would be cumbersome at best without this monetary restriction. Imagine trying to list and describe each building, machine, parcel of land, desk, chair, and so on owned by the firm. The financial statement would be hundreds if not thousands of pages long.

Yet, don't be too comfortable with the monetary restriction either, because currencies are not stable vis-à-vis one another, nor are they internally consistent over time. In the face of continuing inflation, the assignment of a dollar value creates its own problems. For example, the value of inventory, buildings, and equipment constantly changes as a result of inflation.

ASSETS

The general group of resources owned by the firm represents the firm's assets. An asset is anything with economic value that can somehow help the firm provide its goods and services to its customers, either directly or indirectly. The machine that makes the firm's product is clearly an asset. The desk in the chief executive's office is also an asset, however indirect it may be in generating sales.

Assets may be either tangible or intangible. Tangible assets have physical form and substance and are generally valued and shown on the financial statements. Intangible assets don't have any physical form. They consist of such items as a good credit standing, skilled employees, and patents developed by the firm. It is difficult to precisely measure the value of intangible assets. As a result, accountants usually do not allow these assets to be recorded on the financial statements.

An exception to this rule occurs if the intangible asset has a clearly measurable value. For example, if we purchase that intangible from someone outside of the firm, then the price we pay puts a reasonable minimum value on the asset. It may be worth more, but it can't be worth less or we, as rational individuals, wouldn't have paid as much as we did. Therefore the accountant is willing to allow the intangible to be shown on the financial statement for the amount we paid for it.

If you see a financial statement that includes an asset called *goodwill*, it is an indication that a merger has occurred at some time in the past. The firm paid more for the company it acquired than could be justified based on the market value of the specific tangible assets of the acquired firm. The only reason a firm would pay more than the tangible assets themselves are worth is because the firm being acquired has valuable intangible assets. Otherwise the firm would have simply gone out and duplicated all of the specific tangible assets instead of buying the firm.

After the merger, the amount paid in excess of the market value of the specific tangible assets is called goodwill. It includes the good credit standing the firm has with suppliers, the reputation for quality and reliability with its customers, the skilled set of employees already working for the firm, and any other intangible benefits gained by buying an ongoing firm rather than buying the physical assets and attempting to enter the industry from scratch.

The implication of goodwill is that a firm may be worth substantially more than it is allowed to indicate on its own financial statements. Only if the firm is sold will the value of all of its intangibles be shown on a financial statement. Thus we should exercise care in evaluating how good financial statements are as an indication of the true value of the firm.

LIABILITIES

Liabilities, from the word *liable,* represent the obligations that a firm has to outside creditors. Although there generally is no specific one-on-one matching of specific assets with specific liabilities, the assets taken as a whole represent a pool of resources available to pay the firm's liabilities. The most common liabilities are money owed to suppliers, employees, financial institutions, bondholders, and the government (taxes).

OWNERS' EQUITY

Equity represents the value of the firm to its owners. For a firm owned by an individual proprietor we refer to this value as owner's equity. For a partnership we speak of this value as partners' equity. For a corporation we talk of this value as shareholders' or stockholders' equity. This book commonly uses the term *stockholders' equity* whenever the equity of the owners is meant. Except in the rare cases where a topic is relevant only to corporations, the reader from a proprietorship or partnership can simply convert the term in his or her mind to the appropriate one cited.

The stockholders' equity of a firm is often referred to as the "net worth" of the firm or its "total book value." Book value per share is simply the total book value divided by the number of shares of stock outstanding.

The equity of the owners of the firm is quite similar to the equity commonly referred to with respect to home ownership. If you were to buy a house for $200,000 by putting down $40,000 of your own money and borrowing $160,000 from a bank, you would say that your equity in the $200,000 house was $40,000.

If the house were a factory building owned by a firm, the $200,000 purchase price could be viewed as the value of the factory building asset, the $160,000 loan as the firm's liability to an outside creditor, and the $40,000 difference as the stockholders' equity, or the portion of the value of the building belonging to the owners.

THE ACCOUNTING EQUATION

The relationship among the assets, liabilities, and stockholders' equity is shown in the following equation and provides a framework for all of financial accounting.

$$\text{Assets} = \text{Liabilities} + \text{Stockholders' Equity}$$

The left side of this equation represents the firm's resources. The right side of the equation gives the sources of the resources. Another way to view this equation is to let the right side represent the claims on the resources. The liabilities represent the legal claims of the firm's creditors. The stockholders' equity is the owners' claim on any resources not needed to meet the firm's liabilities.

The right side of the equation is frequently referred to as the equity side of the equation because the liabilities and stockholders' equity both represent legal claims on the firm's assets. Therefore, both can be thought of in an equity sense. Frequently the entire equation is referred to as the firm's assets and equities.

By definition, this equation is true for any entity. Once the firm's assets and liabilities have been defined, the value of ownership or stockholders' equity is merely a residual value. The owners own all of the value of the assets not needed to pay off obligations to creditors. Therefore, the equation need not ever be imbalanced because there is effectively one term in the equation, *stockholders' equity*, which changes automatically to keep the equation in balance. We refer back to this basic equation of accounting throughout this book.

KEY CONCEPTS

Entity—the unit for which we wish to account. This unit can be a person, department, project, division, or firm. Avoid commingling the resources of different entities.

Monetary denominator—all resources are assigned values in a currency such as dollars in order to simplify communication of information regarding the firm's resources and obligations.

Assets—the resources owned by the firm.
   a. Tangible assets—assets having physical substance or form.
   b. Intangible assets—assets having no physical substance or form. Results in substantial valuation difficulties.

Liabilities—obligations of the firm to outside creditors.

Owners' equity—the value of the firm to its owners, as determined by the accounting system. This is the residual amount left over when liabilities are subtracted from assets.

Fundamental equation of accounting—

$$\text{Assets} = \text{Liabilities} + \text{Owners' Equity}$$

Three

AN INTRODUCTION TO THE KEY FINANCIAL STATEMENTS

This chapter is a brief introduction to the key financial statements contained in annual reports. We will discuss the balance sheet (or statement of financial position), the income statement, and the statement of cash flows. These statements are crucial to understanding the finances of a firm and we will focus on them in several later chapters.

THE BALANCE SHEET

The statement of financial position, more commonly referred to as the balance sheet, indicates the financial position of a firm at a particular point in time. Basically, it illustrates the basic accounting equation (Assets = Liabilities + Stockholders' Equity) on a specific date; that date being the end of the accounting period. The accounting period ends at the end of the firm's year. Most firms also have interim accounting periods, often monthly for internal information purposes, and quarterly for external reports.

By default, a firm ends its year at the end of the calendar year. Alternatively a firm may pick a fiscal year-end different from that of the calendar year. This choice often depends on making things easier and less expensive. One factor in this decision is the firm's inventory cycle. At year-end, most firms that have inventory have to physically count every unit. If you make shipments on a seasonal basis, the low point in the inventory cycle makes a good year-end, because it takes less time and cost to count the inventory than it would at other times during the year.

Another factor in the selection of a fiscal year is how busy your accounting and bookkeeping staff is. At the end of the fiscal year, many things have to be taken care of by both your internal accountants and your external auditor. An audit must take place, with time-consuming questions and information demands by the CPA. Tax returns must be prepared. Reports to the Securities and Exchange Commission are required for publicly held companies.

Thus, if you can find a time that the accounting functions within the firm are at a slow point, it makes for a good fiscal year-end. For example, many universities end their fiscal year on June 30 because this date gives them all of July and August to get things done before the students start returning to campus.

The basic components of a balance sheet are shown in Exhibit 3–1, which uses the hypothetical Coffin Corporation as an example. The first asset subgroup is current assets, and the first liability subgroup is current liabilities. As mentioned earlier, the terms *short-term, near-term* and *current* are used interchangeably by accountants and usually refer to a period of time less than or equal to one year. Current assets generally are cash or will become cash within a year. Current liabilities are obligations that must be paid within a year. These items get prominent attention by being at the top of the balance sheet. Locating the current assets and current liabilities in this way ensures that the reader can quickly get some assessment of the liquidity of the firm.

The long-term (greater than a year) assets are broken into several groupings. Fixed assets represent the firm's property, plant, and equipment. Investments are primarily securities purchased with the intent to hold onto them as a long-term investment.

EXHIBIT 3-1.

Coffin Corporation
Balance Sheet
December 31, 1992

ASSETS		LIABILITIES & STOCKHOLDERS' EQUITY	
		Liabilities	
Current Assets	$ 5,000	Current liabilities	$ 3,000
		Long-term liabilities	4,000
Fixed Assets	10,000	Total Liabilities	$ 7,000
		Stockholders' Equity	
Investments	3,000	Contributed Capital	$ 5,000
		Retained Earnings	7,000
Intangibles	1,000	Total Stockholders' Equity	$12,000
		TOTAL LIABILITIES &	
TOTAL ASSETS	$19,000	STOCKHOLDERS' EQUITY	$19,000

Securities purchased for short-term interest or appreciation are included in the current asset category. Intangibles, although frequently not included on the balance sheet, are shown with the assets when accounting rules allow their presentation on the financial statements.

In addition to current liabilities, the firm also typically has obligations that are due more than a year from the balance sheet date. Such liabilities are termed *long-term* liabilities.

The stockholders' equity consists of contributed capital and retained earnings. Contributed capital (sometimes referred to as "paid-in capital") represents the amounts that individuals have paid directly to the firm in exchange for shares of ownership such as common or preferred stock. Retained earnings represent the portion of the income that the firm has earned over the years that has not been distributed to the owners in the form of dividends.

Retained earnings, like all items on the equity side of the balance sheet, represent a claim on a portion of the assets and are not an asset themselves. Retained earnings of $100,000,000 does not imply that somewhere the firm has $100,000,000 of cash readily available that could be used for a dividend. It is far more likely that as the firm earned profits over the years, the portion of those profits that was not distributed to the owners was invested in plant and equipment in order to generate larger profits in the future. Retained earnings represents the stockholders' ownership of the plant and equipment rather than a secret stash of cash.

THE INCOME STATEMENT

The income statement compares the firm's revenues to its expenses. Revenues are the monies a firm has received or is entitled to receive in exchange for the goods and services it has provided. Expenses are the costs incurred in order to generate revenues. Net income is simply the difference between revenues and expenses. The simplest form of an income statement appears in Exhibit 3–2.

Unlike the balance sheet, which is a photograph of the firm's financial position at a point in time, the income statement tells what happened to the firm over a period of time, such as a month or a year.

The income statement is frequently used as a vehicle for the presentation of changes in retained earnings from year to year. Since maximizing the wealth of the stockholders of the firm is a key goal of the firm, it is important to convey to stockholders the changes in the amount of the firm's income that is being retained for use by the firm. As noted earlier, this use may consist of purchasing buildings and equipment to increase the firm's future profits.

EXHIBIT 3-2.

Coffin Corporation
Income Statement
For the Year Ending December 31, 1992

Revenues	$20,000
Less Expenses	12,000
NET INCOME	$ 8,000

EXHIBIT 3-3.

Coffin Corporation
Statement of Income and Retained Earnings
For the Year Ending December 31, 1992

Revenues	$20,000
Less Expenses	12,000
Net Income	$ 8,000
Retained Earnings, January 1, 1992	4,000
Total	$12,000
Less Dividends Declared	5,000
Retained Earnings, December 31, 1992	$ 7,000

A combined statement of income and retained earnings might appear as in Exhibit 3-3. The year's net income is added to the beginning retained earnings. This combined amount is the total accumulated earnings of the firm that have not been distributed to its owners. Dividends declared during the year are then subtracted because they are a distribution to the owners of a portion of the accumulated earnings of the firm. The resulting balance represents the firm's retained earnings as of the end of the year. Alternatively, changes in retained earnings for the year may be presented in a separate statement of retained earnings, such as the one in Exhibit 3-4. Note that

EXHIBIT 3-4.

Coffin Corporation
Statement of Retained Earnings
For the Year Ending December 31, 1992

Retained Earnings, January 1, 1992	$ 4,000
Net Income for the Year Ending December 31, 1992	8,000
Total	$12,000
Less Dividends Declared	5,000
Retained Earnings, December 31, 1992	$ 7,000

in both Exhibit 3-3 and 3-4, the retained earnings as of December 31, 1992, is the same number as that which appears on the Balance Sheet (Exhibit 3-1) as of December 31, 1992.

THE STATEMENT OF CASH FLOWS

The balance sheet and income statement are the traditional financial statements that have been required in annual reports for many years. In contrast, the statement of cash flows has only been required since the late 1980s. It replaced the statement of changes in financial position, which provided information about changes in the firm's *working capital*. Working capital refers to the current assets and current liabilities of the organization.

This relatively new statement has been added to the annual report in response to demands for better information about the firm's cash inflows and outflows. The current assets section of the balance sheet of the firm shows how much cash the firm has at the end of each accounting period. This can be compared from year to year to see how much the cash balance has changed, but that gives little information about how or why it has changed.

This can result in erroneous interpretations of financial statement information. For example, a firm experiencing a liquidity crisis (inadequate cash to meet its currently due obligations) may sell off a profitable part of its business. The immediate cash injection from the sale may result in a substantial cash balance at year-end. On the balance sheet this may make the firm appear to be quite liquid and stable. However, selling off the profitable portion of the business may have pushed the firm even closer to bankruptcy. There is a need to explicitly show how the firm obtained that cash.

The statement of cash flows details where cash resources come from and how they are used. It provides more valuable information about liquidity than can be obtained from the balance sheet and income statements. Exhibit 3-5 presents a simplified example of what a statement of cash flows would look like.

EXHIBIT 3-5.

Coffin Corporation
Statement of Cash Flows
For the Year Ending December 31, 1992

Cash Flows from Operating Activities		
Collections from Customers	$19,000	
Payments to Suppliers	(8,000)	
Payments to Employees	(3,000)	
Net Cash from Operating Activities		$8,000
Cash Flows from Investing Activities		
Purchase of New Equipment	$ (6,000)	
Net Cash Used for Investing Activities		(6,000)
Cash Flows from Financing Activities		
Borrowing from Creditors	$ 2,000	
Issuance of Stock	1,000	
Payment of Dividends	(2,000)	
Net Cash from Financing Activities		1,000
NET INCREASE/(DECREASE) IN CASH		$3,000
CASH, BEGINNING OF YEAR		1,000
CASH, END OF YEAR		$4,000

NOTES TO FINANCIAL STATEMENTS

As you continue to read this book, you will find that the accounting numbers don't always tell the entire story. For a variety of reasons, these three financial statements tend to be inadequate to fully convey the results of operations and the financial position of the firm.

As a result, accountants require that notes be provided to supplement the financial statements that we have discussed. These notes provide detailed explanations and are included in annual reports as an integral part of the overall financial statements. Notes to financial statements are discussed somewhat further in Chapter

4. Also, a detailed presentation on notes to financial statements is made in Chapter 17.

KEY CONCEPTS

Fiscal year-end—the firm's year-end should occur at a slow point in the firm's normal activity to reduce disruption caused in determining the firm's results of operations and year-end financial position.

The balance sheet—tells the financial position of the firm at a point in time.

> *Asset classification*—assets are commonly classified on the balance sheet as current, fixed, investments, and intangibles.

> *Liability classification*—liabilities are generally divided into current and long-term categories.

> *Stockholders' equity* is divided into contributed capital and retained earnings.

> a. *Contributed or paid-in capital* is the amount the firm has received in exchange for the issuance of its stock.

> b. *Retained earnings* are the profits earned by the firm over its lifetime that have not been distributed to its owners in the form of dividends.

The income statement—a summary of the firm's revenues and expenses for the accounting period (month, quarter, year).

Statement of cash flows—shows the sources and uses of the firm's cash.

Notes to the financial statements—vital information supplementing the key financial statements.

Four

THE ROLE OF THE OUTSIDE AUDITOR

The stock market crash of 1929 brought to light substantial inadequacies in financial reporting. Investigations of bankrupt companies showed numerous arithmetic errors and cases of undetected fraud. These investigations also disclosed the common use of a widely varying set of accounting practices. A principal outcome of these investigations was that the newly formed Securities and Exchange Commission (SEC) required that publicly held companies must annually issue a report to stockholders. The report must contain financial statements prepared by the firm's management and audited by a certified public accountant (CPA).

Annual reports are frequently referred to as certified reports or certified statements, although in fact it is the outside auditor who has been certified, not the statements themselves. Each state licenses CPAs and in granting the license certifies them as experts in accounting and auditing. The CPA merely gives an expert opinion regarding the financial statements of a company. There is no certification of correctness of the financial statements.

What exactly is the CPA's role in performing an audit? Well, some people consider the CPA to be the individual who walks out onto the field of battle after the fighting has died down and the smoke has cleared and then proceeds to shoot the wounded. CPAs have always been respected individuals, but in their role as auditors they tend to be seen in a rather unpleasant light, as the foregoing analogy indicates. This is largely due to a lack of understanding of what the CPA's role really is. The SEC, in requiring audited statements, was particularly concerned with arithmetic accuracy and the use of a clear, consistent set of accounting practices.

Ultimately the SEC's desire is that a reliable set of financial statements, one that presents a "fair representation," of what has occurred, is given to the users of financial statement information. Those users include stockholders, bankers, suppliers, and other individuals. The CPA's focus is on the financial statements rather than on individual employees in the firm. Errors will occur as long as humans are involved in the accounting process. The CPA has no interest in discrediting individuals. The CPA merely wants to assure that the most significant of the errors are discovered and corrected.

GENERALLY ACCEPTED ACCOUNTING PRINCIPLES (GAAP)

Achieving a result that everyone would consider to be a fair representation is quite difficult. This end result is especially troublesome because accounting represents more of an art than a science. In many instances, strong arguments can be posed for alternative accounting treatments. Selection of one uniform set of rules for all firms is not a simple exercise.

For example, consider a firm drilling for oil. The firm buys a tract of land intending to drill 100 exploratory wells. Suppose that statistically for every 100 wells drilled, the industry average is one well with commercially produceable quantities. (That statistic and all of the other numbers in this example are hypothetical and do not reflect true oil industry information.)

The firm expects to spend $100,000 on each well they drill and expects to recover $20,000,000 worth of oil from the successful well.

After one year, 50 wells have been drilled at a cost of $5,000,000 and no oil has been discovered. Consider how the firm might attempt to present this on its financial statements. Exhibit 4–1 provides income statements under three alternative accounting methods. Parentheses around a number is an accountant's indication of a subtraction or a negative number.

In all three methods, the net income will be the same for the two-year period. If the firm finds oil, it will receive $20,000,000 in return for a two-year cost of $10,000,000, leaving a profit of $10,000,000. If the firm doesn't find oil, then the combined two years must indicate an expenditure of $10,000,000 with no revenue, or a loss of $10,000,000.

Although the two-year totals are the same under all three methods, oil or no oil, the income reported in each year varies substantially depending on the method chosen. Method One takes things as they come. In year one no oil is found, so the $5,000,000

EXHIBIT 4-1.
Alternative Accounting Methods for Oil Exploration

	YEAR ONE	YEAR TWO	
	ACTUAL RESULT	IF OIL FOUND	IF NO OIL
Method One			
Revenue	$ 0	$20,000,000	$ 0
Less Expense	5,000,000	5,000,000	5,000,000
Net Income	$ (5,000,000)	$15,000,000	$ (5,000,000)
Method Two			
Revenue	$ 0	$20,000,000	$ 0
Less Expense	0	10,000,000	10,000,000
Net Income	$ 0	$10,000,000	$(10,000,000)
Method Three			
Revenue	$10,000,000	$10,000,000	$(10,000,000)
Less Expense	5,000,000	5,000,000	5,000,000
Net Income	$ 5,000,000	$ 5,000,000	$(15,000,000)

spent is down the drain, so to speak. The firm reports a loss of $5,000,000 for the year.

Method Two argues that the $5,000,000 was an investment in a two-year project rather than being a loss. On the basis of the hypothetical oil industry statistics, the firm will likely find oil next year, and it gives an unduly harsh picture of the firm's results to show it as a loss. Furthermore, if the firm does show a loss, then next year if it finds oil the firm will have to show a $15,000,000 gain, which is an unduly optimistic picture of the results of year two. The firm didn't lose money one year and then make a lot the next. The firm made a steady profit from their efforts over the two-year period. (Before being too critical of this argument consider a construction company. Should the construction company be required to show all money spent on construction as a loss if the total construction is not finished by year-end?)

Method Three argues that because statistically the firm expects to find oil, and because half of the work is completed by the end of year one, the firm should report half the profits by the end of year one. In this method $10,000,000 of revenue is recorded in Year 1, even though oil has not yet been found. If no oil is found in Year 2, the Year 1 revenue must be eliminated by showing negative revenue in Year 2. Comparing the three methods at the end of year one leaves the user of financial statements with the information that the firm either made a profit of $5,000,000, or broke even, or lost $5,000,000 during the year.

You may have a favorite among the three methods. Accountants will not allow use of Method Three. It is considered to be overly optimistic, because for a small number of holes drilled, such as 100, there may well (excuse the pun) be no oil at all. Methods One and Two, however, each have strong proponents and substantial theoretical support. Accountants frequently prefer a conservative approach and Method One provides it. On the other hand, accountants like to "match" expense with the revenue it causes to be generated. This preference would support Method Two.

This particular example has been a major controversy in accounting. It represents only one of a number of situations where the accounting profession has difficulty selecting one consistent rule and saying that it should be applied across the board to all firms in all situations. There is no true theory of accounting to resolve these dilemmas. The only way to achieve a logical order is by agreement on an arbitrary set of rules.

Comparison of different firms would be simplified if the set of rules selected permitted very little leeway for the firm. However, politically, accountants have never been able to accomplish this because selection of one method over another will usually help one set of firms and hurt another set. In most instances, firms have no choice but there are a substantial number of situations where alternative rules are allowed.

Then how does that make readers of financial statements any better off now than they were before 1929 and the subsequent establishment of the SEC? Today there are substantial tests of arithmetical accuracy that weren't previously required. This broad statement doesn't simply mean that the CPA checks every addition or subtraction. There are audit tests to make sure that payables and receivables have been correctly recorded and stated. Inventory is checked to see that the proper amounts have been recorded. These audit tests are conducted throughout all of the firm's resources and obligations.

However, of equal importance are the accountants' rules of disclosure. In 1929, a firm choosing from among alternative methods didn't necessarily disclose which method it had used. Today the firm can only choose from a relatively narrow set of alternative rules. Whenever the firm makes a choice, that choice must be explicitly stated somewhere in the financial statements.

Who makes the rules that firms must follow in their accounting practices? There is a rule-making body called the Financial Accounting Standards Board (FASB). The pronouncements of this board carry the weight of competent authority, according to the American Institute of Certified Public Accountants (AICPA). The AICPA is a body much like the physicians' AMA and has substantial influence with its membership. So much influence that all CPAs look to it to specify the rules their clients must follow. If the CPA chooses not to follow one of the rules, he or she is subject to strong sanctions.

The FASB's (pronounced faz-B) rules are called Generally Accepted Accounting Principles (GAAP). GAAP constitute a large number of pages of detailed technical rulings. Following are just a few of the most universally applicable rules. As we go through the book, additional rules relevant to the discussion will be noted.

Going concern.   In valuing a firm's assets, it is assumed that the firm will remain in business in the foreseeable future. If it appears that a firm may not remain a going concern, the auditor is required to indicate that in his or her report on the financial statements. The rationale is that if a firm does go bankrupt, its resources may be sold at forced auction. In that case, the resources may be sold for substantially less than their value as indicated on the firm's financial statements.

Conservatism.   The principle of conservatism requires that sufficient attention and consideration be given to the risks taken by the firm. In practice this results in asymmetrical accounting. There is a tendency to anticipate possible losses, but not to anticipate potential gains.

There has been considerable argument over whether this rule actually protects investors. There is the possibility that the firm's value will be understated as a result of the accountant's extreme efforts not to overstate its value. From an economic perspective, we could argue that one could lose as much by failing to invest in a good firm, as by investing in a bad one.

Matching.   In order to get a fair reflection of the results of operations for a specific period of time, we should attempt to put expenses into the same period as the revenues that caused them to be generated. This principle of matching provides the basis for depreciation. If we buy a machine with an expected ten-year life, can we charge the full amount paid for the machine as an expense in the year of purchase? No, because that would make the firm look like it had a bad first year followed by a number of very good years. The machine provides service for ten years; it allows us to make and sell a product in each of the years. Therefore its cost should be spread out into each of those years for which it has helped to generate revenue.

Sometimes these principles can conflict with each other. The conservatism principle lends support to using the first method in the earlier oil drilling example. However, the matching principle lends support to the second method. Some of the most difficult reporting problems faced by CPAs arise when several of the generally accepted accounting principles come into conflict with each other.

Cost. The cost of an item is what was paid for it, or the value of what was given up to get it. This relationship seems innocuous enough, but it will become the center of a controversy shortly.

Objective evidence. This rule requires accountants to ensure that financial reports are based on such evidence as reasonable individuals could all agree on within relatively narrow bounds.

For example, if we had bought a piece of property for $50,000 and we could produce a cancelled check and deed of conveyance showing that we paid $50,000 for the property, then reasonable people would probably agree that the property cost $50,000. Our cost information is based upon objective evidence. Twenty years after the property is purchased management calls in an appraiser who values the property at $500,000. The appraisal is considered to be subjective evidence. Different appraisers might vary substantially as to their estimate of the property's value. Three different appraisers might well offer three widely different estimates for the same property.

In such a case, the rules of objective evidence require the property to be valued on the financial statements based on the best available objective evidence. This is the cost—$50,000! Consider the implications of this for financial reporting. If you thought that financial statements give perfectly valid information about the firm, this should shake your confidence somewhat. Financial statements provide extremely limited representations of the firm. Without an understanding of GAAP the reader of a financial statement may well draw unwarranted conclusions.

Materiality. The principle of materiality requires the accountant to correct errors that are "material" in nature. Material means large or significant. Insignificant errors may be ignored. But how does one define significance? Is it $5, or $500, or $5,000,000?

Significance depends substantially on the size and particular circumstances of the individual firm.

Rather than set absolute standards, accountants define materiality in terms of effects on the users of financial statements. If there exists a misstatement so significant that reasonable, prudent users of the financial statements would make a different decision than they would if they had been given correct information, then the misstatement is material and requires correction.

Thus, if an investor can say, "Had I known that, I never would have bought the stock," or a banker can say, "I never would have lent the money to them if I had known the correct total assets of the firm," then we have a material misstatement. The implications of this are that accountants do not attempt to uncover and correct every single error that has occurred during the year. In fact, to do so would be prohibitively expensive. There is only an attempt to make sure errors that are material in nature are uncovered.

Consistency. In a world in which alternative accounting treatments frequently exist, users of financial statements can be seriously misled if a firm switches back and forth among alternative treatments. Therefore, if a firm has changed its accounting methods, the auditor must disclose the change in his or her report. A note must be included along with the statements to indicate the impact of the change.

Full disclosure. Accountants, being a cautious lot, feel that perhaps there may be some relevant item that users of financial statements should be aware of, but for which no rule exists that explicitly requires disclosure. So, to protect against unforeseen situations that may arise, there is a catchall generally accepted accounting principle called full disclosure. This rule requires that if there is any other information that would be required for a fair representation of the results and financial position of a firm, then that information must be disclosed in a note to the financial statement.

Full disclosure is a tremendously important rule and its use has grown to the point that the notes to the financial statements are often much more extensive in length, detail, and at times valuable content, than the financial statements themselves.

THE AUDIT

The Management Letter and Internal Control

In performing an audit, the CPA checks for arithmetic accuracy as previously mentioned. In performing this check, the external auditor focuses on the system rather than the individual.

Consider a system in which an individual is issuing invoices to customers based on a shipping document. The individual takes a copy of the shipping document from the in-box, records the amount, issues the invoice, and places the shipping document in the out-box. Again and again, over and over, this same mechanical process is repeated. Occasionally the clerk takes the shipping document, sips his coffee, and puts the document in the out-box without having issued an invoice. Errors do happen.

The auditor will not try to discover every such error. The cost of virtually re-examining every financial transaction would be prohibitive. Instead, by sampling some fraction of the documents processed, the auditor attempts to determine how often errors are occurring and how large they tend to be. The goal is to see if a material error may exist.

What if the accountant feels that the clerk is making too many errors and the potential for a material misstatement may exist? The clerk must be fired and replaced with a more conscientious individual, right? No, wrong. Humans will all make errors and the accountant wants the system to acknowledge that fact. The focus is on what accountants call the "internal control" of the accounting system. Basically, adequate internal control means that the system is designed in such a way as to catch and correct the majority of errors automatically, before the auditor arrives on the scene.

In our example with the clerk, the solution to the problem may be to have the clerk initial each shipping document immediately after he or she processes the invoice. A second individual would then review the shipping documents to see that all have been initialled. Those that haven't been initialled would be sent back for verification of whether an invoice was issued and for correction if need be. Errors can still occur—initialling the document after sipping the coffee, even though the invoice hasn't been processed—but they are less likely and should occur less often.

The auditor issues an internal control memo, often called a management letter, which points out the internal control weaknesses to management. Although there may be some expense involved for the firm to follow some of the recommendations, the inducement is that of reduced audit fees. Internal control weaknesses require an expanded audit so that the CPA can ascertain whether a material misstatement does exist. If the internal control is improved, the auditor will feel more comfortable relying on the client's system and less audit testing will be required. The management letter is given to the firm's top management and is not ordinarily disclosed to the public.

Fraud and Embezzlement

In a firm with good internal control, fraud and embezzlement are made difficult through a system of checks and balances. The auditor does not consider it to be a part of his job to detect all frauds. In fact, many cases of embezzlement are virtually impossible to uncover.

Although no statistics exist, it is likely that discovered embezzlements in this country amount to only the tip of the iceberg of what is really occurring. It is usually the greedy embezzlers that are caught. The modest embezzlers have an excellent chance of going undetected, especially if collusion among several employees exists.

A common misperception is that embezzlement leaves a hole in the bankbook. All of a sudden we go to withdraw money from our bank account and find that a million dollars is missing. This sort of open embezzlement is really the exception, not the rule.

Consider an individual whose job is to approve bills for payment. Suppose he were to print up stationery for Joe's Roofing Repair and send an invoice for $400 to his company. What happens? He will receive the invoice at work and will approve it for payment. Large payments may require a second approval. Therefore larger embezzlements may require a partner if they are to go undetected.

Who is likely to question a small repair bill in a large corporation? Or perhaps a series of small bills for office supplies? Our embezzler could be running ten phony companies. One can easily conceive of an employee upon retirement after 40 years of apparently faithful service, admit to having charged the firm $1,000 a year for the last 35 years for maintenance and supply for a water cooler in the southern plant, even though the southern plant never had a water cooler.

Doesn't this type of embezzlement cause a cash shortage? No! We record the roofing repair expense or water cooler expense and reduce the cash account by the amount of the payment. Can the auditor issue his report on the financial statements of this company without discovering the fraud? Certainly. But then, doesn't that result in a material misstatement in the financial statements? Probably not, for several reasons.

First, the modest thief, not choosing to draw unwanted attention, would be unlikely to steal a material amount of money. Second, the money is being correctly reported as an expense. From the auditor's viewpoint, there is a misclassification of expense. We are calling the expense a roofing repair expense when in fact it should be called miscellaneous embezzlement expense. There would be no impact on the balance sheet nor on the firm's net income if we were to correct this misclassification! The cash account isn't overstated because the account was appropriately reduced when we paid the expense. The income isn't overstated because we did record an expense, even if we didn't correctly identify its cause.

How can the fraud be detected? If we send a letter to Joe's Roofing Repair and ask if their invoice was a bona fide bill, we will likely get an affirmative response, albeit coming from the embezzler himself. If we directly ask the employee if he approved the bill for payment, he will say yes, because he did approve it for payment to himself. In order to really see if this type of embezzlement is going on, we would have to trace each bill back to the individual in the organization who originally ordered the work done or the goods purchased. Unfortunately, the cost of the audit work involved is likely to far exceed the amount likely to have been embezzled.

The result is that the auditor tests some documents in an effort to scare the timid, but it is possible for numerous small frauds to go undetected. The auditor is also likely to suggest in the management letter that large payments require two approvals. This would make embezzlement of large amounts less likely unless there is collusion among at least two employees.

The Auditor's Report

In addition to the management letter, the auditor issues a letter to the top management of the corporation and to its stockholders. This *opinion letter* generally has three standard paragraphs that are reproduced almost verbatim in most auditors' reports. You might compare the auditor's letter in your firm's financial statement to the sample letter on the following page.

These three paragraphs are the standard *clean* opinion report. The first paragraph is referred to as the *opening* or *introductory* paragraph. The second paragraph is the *scope* paragraph. The third paragraph is the *opinion* paragraph. If there are any additional paragraphs, they represent unusual circumstances which require further explanation.

The opening paragraph serves to inform the users of the financial statements that an audit was performed by the auditor. In some cases auditors perform consulting or other services aside from audits. Also, by specifying the items that were audited (the specific financial statements), the auditor is implying that certain parts of the annual report were not audited. For example, if the President of the company provides a letter reviewing the past year and the prospects for the coming year, any numbers contained in that letter are not audited. The opening paragraph also indicates explicitly that the company's management bears the ultimate responsibility for the contents of the financial statements.

The scope paragraph describes the breadth or scope of work undertaken as a basis for forming an opinion on the financial statements. This paragraph explains the type of procedures auditors follow in carrying out an audit. Note that just as firms must follow generally accepted accounting principles in preparing their statements, Certified Public Accountants must follow generally accepted auditing standards in auditing those statements.

The opinion paragraph describes whether the financial statements provide a fair representation of the financial position, results of operations, and cash flows of the company, in the opinion of

REPORT OF THE INDEPENDENT AUDITORS

To the Directors and Stockholders of Executive Corporation:

We have audited the accompanying balance sheets of Executive Corporation as of December 31, 1992 and 1991, and the related statements of income, retained earnings, and cash flow for the years then ended. These financial statements are the responsibility of the Company's management. Our responsibility is to express an opinion on these financial statements based on our audits.

We conducted our audits in accordance with generally accepted auditing standards. Those standards require that we plan and perform the audit to obtain reasonable assurance about whether the financial statements are free of material misstatement. An audit includes examining, on a test basis, evidence supporting the amounts and disclosures in the financial statements. An audit also includes assessing the accounting principles used and significant estimates made by management, as well as evaluating the overall financial statement presentation. We believe that our audits provide a reasonable basis for our opinion.

In our opinion, the financial statements referred to above present fairly, in all material respects, the financial position of Executive Corporation as of December 31, 1992 and 1991, and the results of its operations and its cash flows for the years then ended in conformity with generally accepted accounting principles.

Steven A. Finkler, CPA

date

the auditor. A clean opinion, such as this one, indicates that in the opinion of the auditor, exercising due professional care, there is sufficient evidence of conformity to generally accepted accounting principles (GAAP), and there is no condition requiring further clarification. This paragraph does not contend that the financial statements are completely correct. It does not even certify that there are no material misstatements. The CPA does not give a guarantee or certification. He merely gives an expert opinion.

Note that the opinion of the CPA evidenced above is that the financial statements are a fair representation of the firm's financial position. This is a somewhat audacious remark. Considering the intangible assets that are not recorded on the financial statements despite their potentially significant value, and considering that plant, property and equipment are recorded on the balance sheet at their cost, even though their value today may be far in excess of cost, you have to have a lot of chutzpah to say the statements are fair.

The key is that the accountant merely says the statements are a fair presentation in accordance with generally accepted accounting principles. In other words this *fairness* is not meant to imply fair in any absolute meaning of the word *fair.*

Certainly this creates a problem in that many users of the financial statements are unfamiliar with the implications of GAAP. Such individuals may interpret the word *fair* in a broader sense than is intended. This is why it is vital that in looking at an annual report an individual read the notes to the financial statements as well as the statements themselves. Later in the book we will discuss the notes to the financial statements in some detail.

The auditor may issue an *adverse, qualified,* or *disclaimer* opinion, if it is not possible to issue a clean opinion. An adverse opinion is a severe statement. It indicates that the auditor believes that the firm's financial statements are not presented fairly, in accordance with GAAP. A disclaimer indicates that the auditor was unable to compile enough evidence to form an opinion on whether or not the financial statements are a fair representation in accordance with GAAP. A qualified opinion indicates that the financial statements are a fair representation in conformity with GAAP, except as relates to a specific particular area.

In some cases the audit opinion letter will also contain additional paragraphs containing explanations. This is generally the case if there is a significant uncertainty, or a material change in the application of GAAP. Such paragraphs highlight special circumstances that might be of particular concern to the users of the financial statements. An example of a significant uncertainty would be a law suit of such magnitude that, if the case is lost, it might cause the firm to become insolvent. A material change in GAAP must be reported because it makes the current financial statement no longer completely comparable to the previous ones for the same company. The presence of more than the standard opening, scope, and opinion paragraphs should alert the user to exercise special care in interpreting the numbers reported in the financial statements.

The Management Report

In recent years it has become a common practice for the annual report of the firm to include not only the firm's financial statements and an auditor's report, but also a management report. In contrast with the management letter written by the CPA and given to the firm's management, the management report is written by the firm's management, and is addressed to readers of the annual report.

The management report explains that while the financial statements have been audited by an independent CPA, ultimately they are the responsibility of the firm's management. The report also discusses the organization's system of internal control, and the role of its audit committee. The audit committee, consisting of members of the Board of Directors, has the responsibility for supervising the accounting, auditing, and other financial reporting matters of the firm.

KEY CONCEPTS

Audited financial statements —a presentation of the firm's financial position and its results of operations, in accordance with generally accepted accounting principles.

Generally Accepted Accounting Principles (GAAP)—a set of rules used as a basis for financial reporting. A firm must comply with these rules to receive an unqualified letter of opinion from a CPA stating that the financial statements are a fair representation of the firm's financial position and results of operations. Some key GAAP:

   a. *going concern*—financial statements are prepared based upon the assumption that the firm will remain in business for the foreseeable future.

   b. *conservatism*—in reporting the financial position of the firm sufficient consideration should be given to the various risks the firm faces.

   c. *matching*—expenses should be recorded in the same accounting period as the revenues that they were responsible for generating.

   d. *cost*—the value of what was given up to acquire an item.

   e. *objective evidence*—financial reports should be based on such evidence as reasonable individuals could all agree upon within relatively narrow bounds.

   f. *materiality*—errors in financial reports only require correction if they are material in amount. An error is material if any individual makes a different decision based upon the incorrect information resulting from the error than if he or she possessed the correct information.

   g. *consistency*—to avoid misleading users of financial reports, firms should generally use the same accounting methods from period to period.

   h. *full disclosure*—financial reports should disclose any information needed to assure that the reports are a fair presentation.

The management letter—a report to top management that makes suggestions for the improvement of internal control to reduce the likelihood of errors and undetected frauds or embezzlements.

The auditor's report—a letter from the outside auditor giving an opinion on whether or not the firm's financial statements are a fair presentation of the firm's results of operations, cash flows, and financial position in accordance with GAAP.

The management report—a letter from the organization's management which is part of the annual report. This letter indicates management's responsibility for the financial statements.

Five

VALUATION
OF ASSETS
AND EQUITIES

One would not expect there to be much controversy over the valuation of balance sheet items. They are simply recorded at what they're worth. Unfortunately, it isn't as easy as that. Consider having bought a car three years ago for $20,000. Today it might cost you $24,000 to buy a similar car. Is your car worth $20,000 or $24,000?

Wait, it's more complicated than that. Your old car is no longer new and so its value has gone down with age. Because the old car is three years old, and generally cars are expected to have a five-year useful life, your car has lost 60% of its value, so it's only worth $8,000. However, due to inflation, you could sell the car for $14,000 and you'd have to pay $16,000 to buy it on a used car lot.

What is the value of your car? Obviously valuation is a complex issue. This chapter looks at how accountants value assets, liabilities and stockholders' equity for inclusion in financial statements. In addition, several other useful valuation methods that are not allowed for financial statement reporting will be discussed.

As a manager you at times have a need for financial information that differs from that provided by the financial statements. By now you may already be getting an idea of some of the problems with financial statements. Their information is the result of complying with a set of generally accepted accounting principles (GAAP). These rules may not always result in the provision of information relevant to a particular decision at hand. After looking at the different methods, examples of how financial statements might be useful for managerial decisions will be discussed.

ASSET VALUATION

Historical Cost or Acquisition Cost

Financial statements value assets based on their historical or acquisition cost. This is done in order to achieve a valuation based on the GAAP of objective evidence. If the firm values all of its assets based on what is paid for them at the time it acquired them, there can be no question as to the objectivity of the valuation.

For example, let's suppose that some number of years ago a railroad company bought land at a cost of $10 an acre. Suppose that 1,000 acres of that land runs through the downtown of a major city. Today, many years after the acquisition, the firm has to determine the value at which it wishes to show that land on its current financial statements. The historical cost of the land is $10,000 ($10 per acre multiplied by 1,000 acres). By historical cost, we mean the historical cost to the firm as an entity. The firm may have bought the land from previous owners who paid $1 per acre. Their historical cost was $1 per acre, but to our entity the historical or acquisition cost is $10 per acre.

Accountants are comfortable with their objective evidence. If the land cost $10,000 and the firm says it cost $10,000, then everyone gets a fair picture of what the land cost. However, accountants don't clearly state that the $10,000 figure appearing on the balance sheet represents the cost rather than the current value of the land. One might well get the impression from the balance sheet that the property is currently worth only $10,000.

In fact, today that land might be worth $10,000,000 (or even $100,000,000). The strength of using the historical cost approach is that the information is objective and verifiable. However, the historical cost method also has the weakness of providing outdated information. It doesn't give a clear impression of what assets are currently worth. Despite this serious weakness, historical or acquisition cost is the method that must be used on audited financial statements.

Price-Level Adjusted Historical Cost

Accountants are ready to admit that the ravages of inflation have played a pretty important part in causing the value of assets to change substantially from their historical cost. The longer the time between the purchase of the asset and the current time, the more likely it is that a distortion exists between the current value of an item and its historical cost. One proposed solution to the problem is price-level adjusted historical cost or PLAHC (pronounced plack). This method is frequently referred to as *constant dollar valuation.*

The idea behind constant dollar valuation is that most of the change in the value of assets over time has been induced by price-level inflation. Thus, if we adjust the value of all assets based on the general rate of inflation, we would report each asset at about its current worth. While this approach may sound good, it has some serious flaws. In order to use the method, we must agree on the use of a particular price index. Accountants like that because once everyone agrees to use a specific index, anyone can take historical cost information, adjust it based on the index, and come out with the same new PLAHC value for each asset. In other words, the results of this method are objective and verifiable.

Before the weakness of this method can be examined, a short introduction to price indices is in order for those whose only contact with them has been the inevitable television report of the increase in the Consumer Price Index (CPI). The federal government has established a wide variety of indices such as the CPI and the Wholesale Price Index. The government creates the indices by defining a typical package of goods that would be purchased by an average buyer during the year. The total cost for that package of goods in the *base*

year is determined. The base year is the year that the index is first
established, or is recalibrated.

The total cost for the typical package of goods in the base year
is referred to as 100% of the base year cost, or simply 100. At a later
point in time, if the same package of goods costs twice as much to
buy, then prices have doubled. The index value would be 200 to represent that goods cost 200% as much as they did in the base year. The
government recalibrates each index from time to time, creating a
new base year and resetting the index value at 100.

Indexing leads to a number of interesting problems. For example, consider the railroad land discussed previously. Suppose that
when the land was bought the price level was 25 and that today it is
275. This difference represents quite an increase in general price
levels. It means that prices have leaped to 1100% of their earlier
level over the period the land was held (275 divided by 25 times
100%). Using that increase to adjust the cost of the land, it would
have a value of $110,000 (11 times the historical cost). What hap-
pened to the $10,000,000 figure cited previously as the current mar-
ket value?

Unfortunately, not everything increases at the same rate of
inflation. During the Persian Gulf Crisis, in 1990, the price of gasoline increased much faster than the average inflation rate. Therefore, other items must have increased at a slower rate. The land in
the railroad example apparently rose in value much faster than the
general inflation rate. The CPI is too general an index to accurately
determine price changes in specific items.

To some extent, the problem could be cured by using a more
specific index. For example, we could get a national index for land
prices. Of course, land prices in Sunbelt cities rose much more in
recent years than land in the Northeast. We could remedy that with
a state index, but for most states metropolitan land prices rose at a
substantially different rate than the more rural areas. We could use
an index for land prices in a specific city, but even within a city we
find old deteriorating neighborhoods and vibrant, growing neighborhoods. The problem is not easily solved.

Where does that leave us? Well, PLAHC gives an objective
measurement of assets. Some individuals view this measurement as
superior to historical cost because it has made some effort to recog-
nize the realities of what assets are currently worth. On the other

hand, others are uncomfortable with a method that represents itself as having adjusted the cost of an item for inflation, yet can allow an asset worth $10,000,000 to be shown on the balance sheet at only $110,000. Perhaps it is better to leave the item at its cost and inform everyone that it is the cost and is not adjusted for inflation, rather than to say that it has been adjusted for inflation when the adjustment may be a poor one. Price-level adjustment may leave the user of financial information with an uncalled for confidence in the valuation used.

Net Realizable Value

A third alternative for the valuation of assets is to measure them at what you could get if you were to sell them. This concept of valuation makes a fair amount of sense. If you were a potential creditor, be it banker, supplier, etc., you might well wonder, "If this firm were to sell off all of its assets, would it be able to raise enough cash to pay off all of its creditors?"

The term *net* is used in front of *realizable value* to indicate that we wish to find out how much we could realize net of any additional costs that would have to be incurred to sell it. Thus, commissions, packing costs, and the like would be a reduction in the amount we could expect to obtain.

This method doesn't seek to find the potential profit. We aren't interested in the comparison of what it cost to what we're selling it for. We simply want to know what we could get for it. In the case of the railroad land, its net realizable value is $10,000,000 less any legal fees and commissions the railroad would have to pay to sell it.

Is this a useful method? Certainly. Does it give a current value for our assets? Definitely. Then why not use it on financial statements instead of historical cost? The big handicap of the net realizable value method is that it is based on someone's subjective estimate of what the asset could be sold for. There is no way to determine the actual value of each of the firm's assets unless they are sold. This always poses a problem from an accountant's point of view. Another problem occurs if an asset which is quite useful to the firm does not have a ready buyer. In that case, the future profits method that follows provides a more reasonable valuation.

Future Profits

The main reason a firm acquires most of its assets is to use them to produce the firm's goods and services. Therefore, a useful measure of their worth is the profits they will contribute to the firm in the future. This is especially important in the case where the assets are so specialized that there is no ready buyer. If the firm owns the patent on a particular process, the specialized machinery for that process may have no realizable value other than for scrap.

Does that mean that the specialized machinery is worthless? Perhaps yes, from the standpoint of a creditor who wonders how much cash the firm could generate if needed to meet its obligations. From the standpoint of evaluating the firm as a going concern, a creditor may well be more interested in the ability the firm has to generate profits. Will the firm be more profitable because it has the machine than it would be without it?

Under this relatively sensible approach, an asset's value is set by the future profits the firm can expect to generate because it has the asset. However, once again the problem of dealing with subjective estimates arises. Here we are even worse off than with the previous valuation approach. At least we can get outside independent appraisers to evaluate the realizable value of buildings and equipment. However, under this method estimates of future profit streams require the expertise of the firm's own management. Even with that expertise, the estimates often turn out to be off by quite a bit.

Replacement Cost

This approach is essentially the reverse of the net realizable value method. Rather than considering how much we could get for an asset, were we to sell it, we consider how much it would cost us to replace that asset. While this might seem to be a difference that splits hairs, it really is not.

Suppose that last year you could buy a unit of merchandise for $5 and resell it for $7. This year you can buy the unit for $6 and sell it for $8. You have one unit remaining that you bought last year. Today its historical cost is $5, the amount you paid for it; its net realizable value is $8, the amount you can sell it for; and its replacement cost is $6, the amount you would have to pay to replace it in your inventory. Three different methods result in three different valuations.

Replacement cost (often referred to as current cost) is another example of a subjective valuation approach. Unless you actually go out and attempt to replace an asset, you cannot be absolutely sure what it would cost to do so. Therefore, this method is not considered by accountants to provide objective evidence. It cannot be used to determine the numbers reported on the balance sheet and income statement.

Which Valuation Is Right?

Unfortunately, none of these methods (see Exhibit 5–1) is totally satisfactory for all information needs. Different problems require

EXHIBIT 5-1.

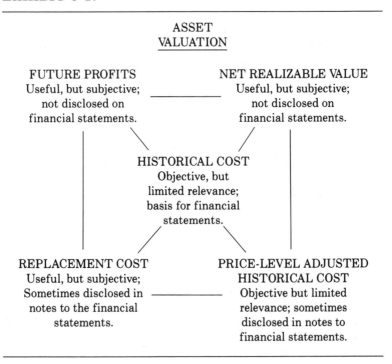

ASSET
VALUATION

FUTURE PROFITS
Useful, but subjective;
not disclosed on
financial statements.

NET REALIZABLE VALUE
Useful, but subjective;
not disclosed on
financial statements.

HISTORICAL COST
Objective, but
limited relevance;
basis for financial
statements.

REPLACEMENT COST
Useful, but subjective;
Sometimes disclosed in
notes to the financial
statements.

PRICE-LEVEL ADJUSTED
HISTORICAL COST
Objective but limited
relevance; sometimes
disclosed in notes to
financial statements.

different valuations. The idea that there is a different appropriate valuation depending on the question being asked may not seem to be quite right. Why not simply say what it's worth and be consistent?

From the standpoint of financial statements, we have little choice. GAAP requires the use of historical cost information and that restricts options substantially in providing financial statements. You might say, "Okay, the financial statements must follow a certain set of rules, but just among us managers what is the asset's real value?" Still we respond, "Why do you want to know?" We really are not avoiding the question. Let's consider a variety of possible examples.

First, assume that one of your duties is to make sure the firm has adequate fire insurance coverage. The policy is currently up for renewal and you have obtained a copy of your firm's annual report. According to the balance sheet, your firm has $40,000,000 of plant and equipment. You don't want to be caught in the cold, so you decide to insure it for the full $40 million. Nevertheless, you may well have inadequate insurance. The $40 million merely measures the historical cost of your plant and equipment.

Which valuation method is the most appropriate? In this case, the answer is replacement cost. If one of the buildings were to burn down, then our desire would be to have enough money to replace it. Other measures, such as net realizable value, are not relevant to this decision.

Suppose we are considering the acquisition of a new machine. What measure of valuation is the most appropriate? We could value the machine at its historical cost—that is, the price we are about to pay for it. This method cannot possibly help us to decide if we should buy the asset. Looking at an asset's value from the point of view of its cost would lead us to believe that every possible asset should be bought, because by definition it would be worth the price we pay for it.

How about using the net realizable value? What would the net realizable value of the machine be the day after we purchase it? Probably less than the price we paid because it is now used equipment. In that case, we wouldn't ever buy the machine. How about using replacement cost? On the day we buy a machine, the replacement cost will simply be the same as its historical cost.

Logically, why do we wish to buy the machine? Because we want to use it to make profits. The key factor in the decision to buy the machine is whether or not the future profits from the machine will be enough to more than cover its cost. So the appropriate valuation for the acquisition of an asset is the future profits it will generate.

Finally, consider the divestiture of a wholly-owned subsidiary that has been sustaining losses and is projected to sustain losses into the foreseeable future. What is the least amount that we would accept in exchange for the subsidiary? Historical cost information is hopelessly outdated and cannot possibly provide an adequate answer to that question. Replacement cost information can't help us. The last thing in the world we want to do is go out and duplicate all of the assets of a losing venture. If we base our decision on future profits, we may wind up paying someone to take the division because we anticipate future losses, not profits.

The appropriate valuation in this case would be net realizable value. Certainly we don't want to sell the entire subsidiary for less than we could get by auctioning off each individual asset. If we did, we might well find that the buyer would simply turn around and break up the subsidiary for the underlying realizable value of the assets.

As you can see, it is essential that you be flexible in the valuation of assets. As a manager, you must do more than simply refer to the financial statements. In order to determine the value of assets, you must first assess why the information is needed. Based on that assessment, you can determine which of the five methods discussed here provides the most useful information for the specific decision to be made.

VALUATION OF LIABILITIES

Valuation of liabilities does not cause nearly as many problems as valuation of assets. With assets, we have the continuous problem of how to value a machine, or piece of equipment, or piece of land—perhaps a unique piece of land. On the other hand, with liabilities, if you owe Charlie 50 bucks, it's not all that hard to determine exactly what your liability is, it's 50 bucks.

In general, our liability is simply the amount we expect to pay in the future. Suppose we purchase raw materials for our production process at a price of $580 on open account with the net payment due in 30 days. We have to pay $580 when the account is due. Therefore, our liability is $580. The crucial aspects are that our obligation is to be paid in cash and it is to be paid within one year. Problems arise if either of these aspects does not hold.

For instance, what if we borrow $7,000 from a bank today and have an obligation to pay $10,000 to the bank three years from today. Is our liability $10,000? No, it isn't. Banks charge interest for the use of their money. The interest accumulates as time passes. If we are to pay $10,000 in three years, that implies that $3,000 of interest will be accumulating over that three-year period. We don't owe the interest today, because we haven't yet had the use of the bank's money for the three years. As time passes, each day we will owe the bank a little more of the $3,000 of interest. Today, however, we owe only $7,000, from both a legal and accounting point of view.

You might argue that legally we owe the bank $10,000. That really isn't so, although the bank might like you to believe that it is. Let's suppose that you borrowed the money in the morning. That very same day, unfortunately, your rich aunt passes away. The state you live in happens to have rather fast processing of estates and around one o'clock in the afternoon you receive a large inheritance in cash. You run down to the bank and say that you don't need the money after all. Do you have to pay the bank $10,000?

If you did, your interest for one day would be $3,000 on a loan of $7,000. That is a rate of about 43% per day, or over 15,000% per year. Perhaps there would be an early payment penalty, but it would be much less than $3,000. Generally, accountants ignore possible prepayment penalties and record the liability at $7,000.

Another problem occurs if the liability is not going to be paid in cash. For example, perhaps we have received an advance payment for an order of widgets that we intend to fill over the coming year. What we owe is widgets, but we have to make some attempt to value that liability. Take the example one step further. We have received $18,000 for the widgets, but they will only cost us $9,000 to make. Is our liability $18,000 or $9,000?

In cases where the obligation is nonmonetary in nature, we record the obligation as the amount received, not the cost of providing the nonmonetary item. What if for some reason we cannot provide the widgets? Will the customer be satisfied to receive $9,000 because that's all it would have cost us to make the widgets? No, the customer needs to get the full $18,000 back, so we must show that amount as the liability. If, over time, we make partial shipments, we can reduce the liability in a pro rata fashion.

VALUATION OF STOCKHOLDERS' EQUITY

The valuation of stockholders' equity is relatively easy. Recall that assets are equal to liabilities plus stockholders' equity. Once the value of assets and liabilities has been determined, the stockholders' equity is whatever it must take to make the equation balance. Remember that the stockholders' equity is, by definition, a residual of whatever is left after enough assets are set aside to cover liabilities. Thus, given the rigid financial statement valuation requirements for assets and liabilities, there is little room left for interpreting the value of stockholders' equity.

On the other hand, might there not be another way to determine the value of the firm to its owners? For a publicly held firm the answer is clearly yes. The market value of the firm's stock is a measure of what the stock market and the owners of the firm think it's worth. If we aggregate the market value of the firm's stock, we have a measure of the total value of the owners' equity.

Is the market value of the firm likely to equal the value assigned by the financial statements? Probably not. The financial statements tend to substantially undervalue a wide variety of assets. Intangible assets that may be quite valuable are not always included in financial statements. Further, historical cost asset valuation causes the tangible assets to be understated in many cases. Thus, the assets of the firm may be worth substantially more than the financial statements indicate. If the public can determine that to be the case (usually with the aid of the large number of financial analysts in the country), the market value of the stock will probably exceed the value of stockholders' equity indicated on the financial statements.

This discussion of valuation of assets and equities has left us in a position to better interpret the numbers that appear in financial statements. Financial statements are the end product of the collection of information regarding a large number of financial transactions. Each transaction is recorded individually into the financial history of the firm using the valuation principles of this chapter. Chapter 6 discusses the process of recording the individual transactions—how and why it's done. Chapter 7 demonstrates how all of the transactions, perhaps millions or even billions during the year, can be consolidated into three one-page financial statements.

KEY CONCEPTS

Asset valuation—there are a variety of asset valuation methods. The appropriate value for an asset depends on the intended use of the asset valuation information.

    a. *Historical cost*—the amount an entity paid to acquire an asset. This amount is the value used as a basis for tax returns and financial statements.

    b. *Price-level adjusted historical cost*—a valuation method that adjusts the asset's historical cost, based on the general rate of inflation.

    c. *Net realizable value*—a valuation of assets based on the amount we would receive if we sold it, net of any costs related to the sale.

    d. *Future profits*—this valuation method requires each asset to be valued on the basis of the amount of additional profits that can be generated because we have the asset.

    e. *Replacement cost*—under this method each asset is valued at the amount it would cost to replace that asset.

Liability valuation—the value of liabilities depends on whether they are short-term or long-term and whether or not they are to be paid in cash.

    a. *Short-term cash obligations*—amounts to be paid in cash within a year are valued at the amount of the cash to be paid.

    b. *Long-term cash obligations*—amounts to be paid in cash more than a year in the future are valued at the amount to be paid, less the implicit interest included in that amount.

c. *Nonmonetary obligations*—an obligation to provide goods or services rather than cash, where the liability is generally valued at the amount received, rather than the cost of providing that item.

Stockholders' equity valuation—given a value for each of the assets and liabilities, stockholders' equity is the residual amount that makes the fundamental equation of accounting balance.

Six

RECORDING FINANCIAL INFORMATION

DOUBLE ENTRY AND THE ACCOUNTING EQUATION

Financial accounting consists largely of keeping the financial history of the firm. In performing financial accounting, the accountant attempts to keep close track of each event occurring that has a financial impact on the firm. This is done in order to facilitate financial statement preparation. By keeping track of things as they happen, the accountant can periodically summarize the firm's financial position and the results of its operations.

In order to keep track of the firm's financial history, the accountant has chosen a very common historical device. In the navy one keeps a chronological history of a voyage by daily entries into a log. For a personal history, individuals make entries in their diary. Explorers frequently record the events of their trip in a journal. Accountants follow in the tradition of the explorers, each day recording the day's events in a journal, often referred to as a *general journal.* The entries the accountant makes in the journal are simply called *journal entries,* a term that most readers of this book have heard many times. The general journal is often called the *book of original entry.* This term is derived because an event is first entered into the firm's official history via a journal entry.

In recording a journal entry, we need adequate information to describe an entire event. To be sure that all elements of a financial event (more commonly referred to as a transaction) are recorded, accountants use a system called *double-entry bookkeeping.* In order to understand double-entry, we should think in terms of the basic equation of accounting, that is:

$$ASSETS(A) = LIABILITIES(L) \\ + STOCKHOLDERS' \ EQUITY(SE)$$

Any event having a financial impact on the firm affects this equation because the equation summarizes the entire financial position of the firm. Furthermore, by definition this equation must always remain in balance. Absolutely nothing possibly can happen (barring a mathematical miscalculation) that would cause this equation not to be in balance because stockholders' equity has been defined in such a way that it is a residual value that brings the equation into balance.

If the equation must remain in balance, then a change of any one number in the equation must change at least one other number. We have great latitude in which other number changes. For example, we might begin with the equation looking like:

$$\begin{array}{ccccc}
A & = & L & + & SE \\
\$150,000 & = & \$100,000 & + & \$50,000
\end{array}$$

If we were to borrow \$20,000 from the bank, we would have more cash, so assets would increase by \$20,000 and we would owe money to the bank. Our liabilities would increase by \$20,000. Now the equation would be:

$$\begin{array}{ccccc}
A & = & L & + & SE \\
\$170,000 & = & \$120,000 & + & \$50,000
\end{array}$$

The equation is in balance. Compare this equation to the previous one. Two numbers in the equation have changed. The term *double-entry* merely signifies that it is not possible to change one number in an equation without changing at least one other number.

However, the two numbers changed need not be on different sides of the equation. For example, what if we bought some raw materials inventory for $15,000 and paid cash for it. Our asset cash has decreased while our asset inventory has increased. The equation now is:

$$A \quad = \quad L \quad + \quad SE$$
$$\$170,000 = \$120,000 + \$50,000$$

The equation appears as if it hasn't changed at all. That's not quite true. The left side of the equation has both increased and decreased by $15,000. Although the totals on either side are the same, our journal entry would have recorded the specific parts of the double entry change that took place on the left side of the equation.

DEBITS AND CREDITS: THE ACCOUNTANT'S SECRET

It wouldn't be much fun to be an accountant if you didn't have a few tricks and secrets. Part III of this book discusses a few of the more interesting tricks; for now you'll just have to settle for a secret, the meaning of debit and credit.

Earlier an accountant's journal was compared to a navy log book. That's not the only similarity. Sailors use the terms *port* and *starboard*. Many a time you've watched an old seafaring movie, and in the middle of a fierce storm, with the skies clouded and the winds blowing, the seas heaving and the rains pouring, someone yells out, "Hard to the port!" The sailor at the large oaken wheel, barely able to stand erect in the gusts of wind and torrential downpour, struggles hard to turn the ship in the direction ordered. Perhaps you thought they were heading for the nearest port—ergo, "Hard to the port." Not at all. The shouted command was to make a left turn.

It seems that port simply stated means left and starboard really means right. Of course, it's more sophisticated than that, port means the left-hand side as you face toward the front of the boat or ship and starboard means the right-hand side as you face the front. Really what port means is debit, and starboard means credit. Certainly we can drape the terms *debit* and *credit* in vague definitions and esoteric uses, but essentially debit means left (as you face the accounting document in front of you) and credit means right.

Perhaps you had figured that out on your own, perhaps not. If you had, then you are potentially threatening to take away the jobs of your accountants and bookkeepers. To prevent that, some rather interesting abbreviations have been introduced to common accounting usage. Rarely will the accountant write out the words *debit* or *credit*. Instead, abbreviations are used. The word *credit* is abbreviated Cr. Got it? Then you can guess the abbreviation for debit: Dr! If you didn't guess it's not too surprising, given the absence of the letter "r" from the word debit. How did this abbreviation come about? Accounting as we know it today has its roots from in Italy during the 1400s. Italy is the home of Latin, and were we to trace the word debit back to its Latin roots, the "r" would turn up.

The terms *debit* and *credit* deserve a little more clarification. Prior to actually using the terms *debit* and *credit,* accountants perform a modification to the accounting equation, (that is, Assets (A) equal Liabilities (L) plus Stockholders' Equity (SE)). Essentially, this modification requires examination of what causes stockholders' equity to change. Chapter 3 said that stockholders' equity (SE) equaled contributed capital (CC) plus retained earnings (RE). So we could think of our basic equation as assets equal liabilities plus contributed capital plus retained earnings, or:

$$A = L + CC + RE$$

In order to find out where we are at the end of a year, we would need to know where we started and what changes occurred during the year. The changes in assets are equal to the change in liabilities plus the change in contributed capital plus the change in retained earnings, or:

$$\Delta A = \Delta L + \Delta CC + \Delta RE$$

where the symbol "Δ" indicates a change in some number. For example, ΔA represents the change in assets.

Moving a step further, retained earnings increase as a result of net income and decrease when dividends are paid. Net income consists of revenues (R) less expenses (E). Revenues make owners better off and expenses make owners worse off. Dividends (D) are a distribution of some of the firm's profits to its owners. Therefore, our basic equation of accounting now indicates that the change in assets is equal to the change in liabilities plus the change in contributed capital plus the revenues, less the expenses and dividends, or in equation form,

$$\Delta A = \Delta L + \Delta CC + \Delta R - \Delta E - \Delta D$$

The only problem with this equation as it now stands is that accountants are very fond of addition, but only tolerate subtraction when absolutely necessary. The above equation can be manipulated using algebra. We can add the change in expenses and the change in dividends to both sides of the equation. Doing so produces the following equation.

$$\Delta A + \Delta E + \Delta D = \Delta L + \Delta CC + \Delta R$$

Having made these changes in the basic equation, we can return to our discussion of debits and credits. When we say that debit means left, we are saying that debits are increases in anything on the left side of this equation. When we say that credit means right, we are saying that credits increase anything on the right side of this equation. Of course, that leaves us with a slight problem. What do we do if something on either side decreases? We will have to reverse our terminology. An account on the left is decreased by a credit and an account on the right is decreased by a debit.

Debits and credits are mechanical tools that aid bookkeepers. Debits and credits have no underlying theoretical or intuitive basis. In fact, the use of debits and credits as explained here may seem counterintuitive. Cash, which is an asset, is increased by a debit. Cash is decreased by a credit.

If you think about this, it may not quite tie in with the way you've been thinking about debits and credits until now. In fact, what we've said here may seem to be downright wrong. Most individuals who are not financial officers have relatively little need to use the terms *debit* and *credit* in a business setting. We come upon the terms much more often in their common lay usage. Unfortunately, whoever first said, "He's a credit to . . . ," didn't really understand the discipline from which the word was being taken.

Most of us have come into contact with the terms *debit* and *credit* primarily from such events as the receipt of a debit memo from the bank. Perhaps we have a checking account where we are charged 30¢ for each check we write. If we write twenty checks one month, we will receive a notice from the bank that they are debiting our account by $6. Something here doesn't tie with the earlier discussion of debits and credits.

If a debit increases items on the left, and assets are on the left, our assets should increase with a debit. But when the bank debits our account, it takes money away from our account. When we make a deposit, the bank credits, or increases our account. The discrepancy results from the entity concept of accounting discussed in Chapter 2. Under the entity concept each entity must view financial transactions from its own point of view. In other words, the firm shouldn't worry about the impact on its owners or managers or customers, it should only consider the impact of a transaction on itself.

When the bank debits your account, it is not considering your cash balance at all! The bank is considering its own set of books. To the bank, you are considered a liability. You gave the bank some money and it owes it to you. When the bank debits your account, it is saying that it can reduce an item on the right. The bank is reducing a liability. To you as an entity, there is a mirror image. While the bank is reducing its liability, on your records you must reduce your cash. Such a reduction is a credit. Therefore, receipt of a debit memo should cause you to record a credit on your books or financial records.

Consider returning merchandise to a store. The store issues you a credit memo. From the store's point of view, it now owes you money for the returned item. The store's liability has risen so it has a credit. From your point of view, you have a receivable from that store and receivables are assets. Thus you have an increase in an asset, or a debit.

In other words, about the best way to insult your accountant is to call him a credit (that is, liability) to the firm! You'll have to reflect on this new way of thinking about debits and credits for awhile if you're not accustomed to it, and you wish to become fluent in the use of debits and credits. Unfortunately, because the items on one side of the equation increase with debits and the items on the other side decrease with debits, and vice versa for credits, it can take a while before it becomes second nature. Imagine a product manager trying to explain to an accountant that a new product is going to generate extra cash of $100,000. The accountant says, "Okay, debit cash $100,000," and the product manager says, "No, no, I said it *will generate* $100,000, not use it!" Of course the accountant replies, "That's what I said, debit cash a hundred grand!!"

If you still find debits and credits to be somewhat confusing, don't be overly concerned. Trying to look at things from a mirror image of what you've been used to all your life isn't easy. Fortunately, debits and credits are simply bookkeeping tools, and you don't need to use them extensively to understand the concepts of accounting and finance.

RECORDING THE FINANCIAL EVENTS

Now we are going to work through an example in which we will actually record a series of transactions for a hypothetical firm, Executive Corporation, for 1992. The purpose of this example is to give you a feel for the way that financial information is recorded, and to show the process by which millions of transactions occurring during a year can be summarized into several pages of financial statements. At the same time, we will use the specific transactions in the example to highlight a number of accounting conventions, principles, and methods.

Exhibit 6–1 presents the balance sheet for Executive Corporation as of December 31, 1991. From this balance sheet, we can obtain information for assets, liabilities, and stockholders' equity for the beginning of 1992. Year-end closing balances will be identical to opening balances for the following year. Our basic equation at the start of 1992 is as follows.

$$A \quad = \quad L \quad + \quad SE$$
$$\$150,000 \; = \; \$67,000 \; + \; \$83,000$$

EXHIBIT 6-1.

Executive Corporation
Balance Sheet
As of December 31, 1991

ASSETS

Current Assets:		
Cash	$52,000	
Accounts Receivable	18,000	
Inventory	20,000	
Total Current Assets		$ 90,000
Fixed Assets:		
Plant and Equipment		60,000
TOTAL ASSETS		$150,000

EQUITIES

LIABILITIES		
Current Liabilities:		
Accounts Payable	$17,000	
Wages Payable	10,000	
Total Current Liabilities		$ 27,000
Long-Term Liabilities:		
Mortgage Payable		40,000
TOTAL LIABILITIES		$ 67,000
STOCKHOLDERS' EQUITY		
Common Stock		$ 10,000
Retained Earnings		73,000
TOTAL STOCKHOLDERS' EQUITY		$ 83,000
TOTAL LIABILITIES & STOCKHOLDERS' EQUITY		$150,000

In order to examine financial events during the year, we are interested in the change in this equation. As previously explained, the change in the equation may be stated as follows:

$$\Delta A + \Delta E + \Delta D = \Delta L + \Delta CC + \Delta R$$

Every financial event is a transaction that affects the basic equation of accounting. We will keep track of whether or not each transaction complies with the rules of double entry by examining its effect on this equation. After a journal entry is recorded, placing an event into the financial history of the firm, this equation must be in balance or some error has been made.

Therefore, the equation for each journal entry must balance in order for the overall equation to remain in balance. This doesn't necessarily require a change to both sides of the equation. For instance, we could add $5 to an account on one side of the equation and subtract $5 from a different account on the same side of the equation. We would still be in balance even though we haven't changed anything on the other side.

EXECUTIVE CORPORATION
1992 FINANCIAL EVENTS

1. January 2. Purchased a three-year fire insurance policy for $3000. A check was mailed. The starting point for making a journal entry is to determine what has happened. In this case, we have $3,000 less cash than we used to and we have paid in advance for three years worth of insurance. Any item that we would like to keep track of is called an *account*, because we want to account for the amount of that item. Here, the balance in our cash account (an asset) has gone down, and our prepaid insurance (P/I) account (also an asset) has increased. This results in offsetting changes on the left side of the equation, so there is no net effect or change to the equation.

$$\Delta A \qquad + \Delta E + \Delta D = \Delta L + \Delta CC + \Delta R$$

Cash – 3,000   = No change on right side
P/I + 3,000

2. January 18. The firm mails a check to its supplier for $15,000 of the $17,000 it owed them at the end of last year (Refer to Exhibit 6–1 for the account payable liability balance at the end of the previous year). This requires a journal entry showing a decrease in the cash balance and a reduction in the accounts payable (A/P) liability to our supplier.

$$\Delta A \qquad + \Delta E + \Delta D \ = \qquad \Delta L \qquad + \Delta CC + \Delta R$$
$$\text{Cash} - 15{,}000 \qquad\qquad = \text{A/P} - 15{,}000$$

3. February 15. The firm places an order with an equipment manufacturer for a new piece of machinery. The new machine will cost $10,000, and delivery is expected early next year. A contract is signed by both Executive Corporation and the equipment manufacturer. In this case there is no journal entry, even though there is a legally binding contract.

   In order for there to be a journal entry, three requirements must be fulfilled. The first is that we know how much money is involved. In this case, we do know the exact amount of the contract. Second, we must know when the transaction is to be fulfilled. Here, we know that delivery will take place early the following year. Finally, the accountant requires that there must have been some exchange, and that the transaction be recorded only to the extent that there has been an exchange. From an accounting point of view, Executive has not yet paid anything, nor has it received anything. There is no need to record this into the financial history of the firm via the formal process of a journal entry.

   This doesn't mean that the item must be totally ignored. If an unfilled contract involves an amount that is material, then the principle of full disclosure would require that a note to our financial statements disclose this future commitment. However, the balance sheet itself may not show the machine as an asset, nor a liability to pay for it.

4. March 3. Executive purchases inventory on account for $15,000. They will be able to sell the inventory for $30,000. The effect of this transaction is to increase the amount of inventory (Inv.) asset that we have and to increase a liability, accounts payable (A/P). Do we record the newly purchased

inventory at $15,000 or the amount for which we can sell it? According to the cost principle, we must value inventory at what it cost, even though we might be able to sell it for more than that amount.

$$\Delta A \qquad + \Delta E + \Delta D \;=\; \Delta L \qquad + \Delta CC + \Delta R$$

$$\text{Inv} + 15{,}000 \qquad\qquad = \text{A/P} + 15{,}000$$

5. April 16. Cash of $14,000 is received from customers for purchases from last year. This increases one asset, cash, while reducing another asset, accounts receivable (A/R).

$$\Delta A \qquad + \Delta E + \Delta D = \Delta L + \Delta CC + \Delta R$$

$$\begin{aligned}\text{Cash} + 14{,}000 & \qquad = \text{No change on right side}\\ \text{A/R} - 14{,}000 &\end{aligned}$$

6. May 3. Executive sells inventory that had cost $28,000 for a price of $56,000. The customers have not yet paid for the goods although they have received them. This is an income generating activity. Executive has revenues of $56,000 from the sale. It also has an expense of $28,000, the cost of resources used to generate the sale. We can treat this as two transactions. The first transaction relates to the revenue and the second to the expense.

First, we have had a sale of $56,000, so we have to record revenue of $56,000 (Sales). We haven't been paid yet, so we have an account receivable of $56,000. This leaves the accounting equation in balance.

The second transaction concerns inventory and expense. In order to make the sale, we shipped some of our inventory. Thus, we have less inventory on hand. This reduction in inventory represents the cost of the sale, so in addition to reducing the inventory account, we record a cost of goods sold expense (CGS) equal to the decrease in inventory. Once again, this transaction leaves the accounting equation in balance.

$$\Delta A \quad + \quad \Delta E \quad + \Delta D = \Delta L + \Delta CC + \quad \Delta R$$

$$\begin{aligned}\text{A/R} + 56{,}000 & \qquad\qquad\qquad = \qquad \text{Sales} + 56{,}000\\ \text{Inv} - 28{,}000 & \quad \text{CGS} + 28{,}000 \end{aligned}$$

7. June 27. Executive places a $9,000 order to resupply its inventory. The goods have not yet been received. In this case there will be no formal journal entry. Our purchasing department undoubtedly keeps track of open purchase orders. However, as in the case of the equipment contract previously discussed, there is no journal entry until there is an exchange by at least one party to the transaction. We haven't paid for the goods and the supplier has not yet supplied them.

8. November 14. Workers were paid $18,000. This payment included all balances outstanding from the previous year. Because we are paying $18,000, cash will decrease by $18,000. Is this all an expense of the current year? No. We owed workers $10,000 from work done during the previous year. Thus, only $8,000 is an expense of the current year. Our journal entry will show that labor expense (Lab) rises by $8,000 and that wages payable (W/P) decline by $10,000. Note that three accounts have changed. Double-entry accounting requires that at least two accounts change. The equation would not be in balance if only one account changed. However, it is perfectly possible that more than two accounts will change. Here we can see that although three accounts have changed, in net, the equation is in balance.

$$\Delta A \quad + \quad \Delta E \quad + \Delta D = \quad \Delta L \quad + \Delta CC + \Delta R$$

Cash − 18,000   Lab + 8,000   = W/P − 10,000

9. December 31. At year-end, Executive makes its annual mortgage payment of $10,000. The payment reduces the mortgage balance by $4,000. It doesn't quite seem correct to pay $10,000 on a liability but only reduce the obligation by $4,000. Actually, mortgage payments are not merely repayment of a debt. They also include interest that is owed on the debt. If Executive is making mortgage payments on their plant and equipment just once a year, then this payment includes interest on the $40,000 balance outstanding at the end of last year.

    If the mortgage is at a 15 percent annual interest rate, then we owe $6,000 of interest for the use of the $40,000 over the last year. Thus the transaction lowers cash by $10,000, but increases interest expense (IE) (also on the left side of the equation) by $6,000. The reduction of $4,000 on the right side to reduce the mortgage payable (M/P) balance exactly leaves the equation in balance.

$$\Delta A \quad + \quad \Delta E \quad + \Delta D = \quad \Delta L \quad + \Delta CC + \Delta R$$

$$\text{Cash} - 10{,}000 \quad \text{IE} + 6{,}000 \quad = \text{M/P} - 4{,}000$$

10. December 31. A dividend of $3,000 is declared and paid to Executive's stockholders. This creates two changes on the left side of the equation. Cash decreases and dividends (Div) increase. Recall that a dividend is not an expense, but rather is a distribution of some of the firm's profits to its owners.

$$\Delta A \quad + \Delta E + \quad \Delta D \quad = \Delta L + \Delta CC + \Delta R$$

$$\text{Cash} - 3{,}000 \quad \text{Div} + 3{,}000 \quad = \text{No change on right side}$$

11. December 31. At year-end, Executive makes an adjustment to their books to indicate that one year's worth of prepaid insurance has been used up. Many financial events happen at a specific moment in time. In those cases, we simply record the event when it happens. Some events, however, happen over a period of time. Technically one could argue that a little insurance coverage was used up each and every day, so the accountant should have recorded the expiration of part of the policy each day, or for that matter, each minute.

There is no need for that degree of accuracy. The accountant merely wants to make sure that the books are up to date prior to issuing any financial reports based on them. Therefore, a number of adjusting entries are made at the end of the accounting period.

One might ask why the accountant bothers to make such an entry even then. Why not wait until the insurance is completely expired? The matching principle would not allow that. In each case of an adjusting entry, the overriding goal is to place expenses into the correct period; the period in which revenues were generated as a result of those expenses.

In the case of the insurance, we have used up one-third of the $3,000, three-year policy, so we must reduce our asset, prepaid insurance (P/I) by $1,000, and increase our insurance expense (Ins) account by $1,000.

$$\Delta A \quad + \quad \Delta E \quad + \Delta D = \Delta L + \Delta CC + \Delta R$$

$$\text{P/I} - 1,000 \quad \text{Ins} + 1,000 \qquad = \text{No change on right side}$$

12. December 31. Executive also finds that it owes office employees $3,000 at the end of the year. These wages will not be paid until the following year. This requires an adjusting entry in order to accrue this year's labor expenses. The entry increases labor expense and at the same time increases the wages payable liability account.

$$\Delta A \quad + \quad \Delta E \quad + \Delta D = \quad \Delta L \quad + \Delta CC + \Delta R$$

$$\text{Lab} + 3,000 \qquad = \text{W/P} + 3,000$$

13. December 31. The plant and equipment that the firm owns are now one year older. In order to get a proper matching of revenues for each period and the expenses incurred to generate those revenues, the cost of this plant and equipment was not charged to expense when it was acquired. Instead we allocate some of the cost to each year in which the plant and equipment helps the firm to provide its goods and services. The journal entry increases an expense account called depreciation expense (Depr) to show that some of the cost of the asset is becoming an expense in this period. In this year the expense amounts to $6,000. The calculation of annual depreciation expense is discussed in Chapter 9.

The other impact (recall that the double-entry system requires at least two changes) is on the value of the plant and equipment (P&E). Because the plant and equipment is getting older, we wish to adjust its value downward by the amount of the depreciation.

$$\Delta A \quad + \quad \Delta E \quad + \Delta D = \Delta L + \Delta CC + \Delta R$$

$$\text{P\&E} - 6,000 \quad \text{Depr} + 6,000 \qquad = \text{No change on right side}$$

These transactions for Executive Corporation give a highly consolidated view of the thousands, millions, or quite possibly billions of transactions that are recorded annually by a firm. These few transactions cannot hope to have captured every individual transaction or type of transaction that occurs in your particular firm. However, in this brief glance you can begin to understand that there is a systematic approach for gathering the raw bits of data that make up the financial history of the firm.

There may be an enormous number of individual journal entries for a firm during the year. Chapter 7 examines how we can consolidate and summarize these numerous individual journal entries to provide useful summarized information to interested users of financial statements.

KEY CONCEPTS

Double-entry accounting—each financial event affects the basic equation of accounting. In order for the equation to remain in balance, the event must affect at least two items in the equation, therefore the "double" entry.

Journal—a book (or computer memory file) in which all financial events are recorded in chronological sequence.

Debits—increases in assets, expenses, and dividends declared accounts; decreases in liability, revenue, and contributed capital accounts.

Credits—increases in liability, revenue, and contributed capital accounts, and decreases in asset, expense, and dividends declared accounts.

Timing for recording transactions—journal entries can only be made if we know with reasonable certainty the amount of money involved, the timing of the event, and if there has been exchange by at least one party to the transaction.

Adjusting entries—most financial events occur at one specific point in time and are recorded as they occur. Some financial events occur continuously over time, such as the expiration of insurance or the accumulation of interest. Adjusting entries are made immediately prior to financial statement preparation to bring these accounts up to date.

Seven

REPORTING FINANCIAL INFORMATION

Chapter 6 discussed the way that each of the numerous financial transactions affecting the firm can be recorded into the firm's financial history through the use of a journal and journal entries. When we get to the end of an accounting period (typically month, quarter, or year), we want to report what has occurred. We need some method of summarizing the massive quantity of information we've recorded into a format concise enough to be useful to those who desire financial information about the firm.

Financial statements are used to present the firm's financial position and results of operations to interested users of financial information. As in Chapter 3, the financial statements themselves are only several pages long. How can we process our journal entry information in such a way as to allow for such a substantial summarization? We do it via use of a ledger.

LEDGERS

A ledger is a book of accounts. An account is simply any item that we would like to keep track of. Every account that might be affected by a journal entry is individually accounted for in a ledger.

Although today many firms have computerized their book-keeping systems so that they no longer have a ledger book, you can think of a ledger as if it were simply a book. Each page in the ledger book represents one account. For instance, there is a page for the cash account and one for the inventory account and one for retained earnings. Every time we make a journal entry, we are changing the amount that we have in at least two accounts in order to keep the basic equation of accounting in balance.

An immediate benefit of the ledger system is that it allows us to determine how much we have of any item at any point in time. For example, suppose that someone asked us on May 4th how much cash we currently have. One way to provide that information would be to review each and every journal entry that we made since the beginning of the year, determine which ones affected cash, and calculate by how much the cash total has changed. That presents an enormous amount of work.

Using a ledger approach, immediately after making a journal entry, we update our ledger for each account that has changed as a result of that entry. For example, in Chapter 6, the first thing that happened to Executive Corporation in 1992 was a purchase of insurance for $3,000, which was paid in cash. This expenditure requires us to go to the ledger account for cash and show a decrease of $3,000, as well as go to the ledger account for prepaid insurance and show an increase of $3,000. At the same time, we could update the balance in each account.

The ledger is, in some respects, a more complete picture of the firm than the journal is. Each year the journal indicates what happened or changed during that year. The ledger contains not only this year's events, but also tells us where we were when we started out at the beginning of the year. For instance, Executive Corporation had $52,000 in cash at the end of 1991, according to Exhibit 6-1. Our cash account in the ledger would show $52,000 as the opening balance at the beginning of 1992. Thus, when we purchased our insurance on January 2, 1992, we would be able to determine that our initial balance of $52,000 was decreased by $3,000, and that there is a remaining cash balance of $49,000. This gives a better overall picture of the firm than the $3,000 change alone does.

Essentially, the ledger combines account balances from the beginning of the year with the journal entries that were recorded during the year. All of the beginning balances for this year can be found by looking at last year's ending balance sheet. The balance sheet is the statement of financial position. The firm's financial position at the beginning of the year will be identical to its financial position at the end of the previous year. Therefore, the ledger accounts start the year with balances from the year-end balance sheet of the previous year. During the year the changes that occur and are recorded as journal entries, are used to update the ledger accounts. The year-end balance in each account is simply the sum of the opening balance plus the changes recorded in that account during the year.

EXECUTIVE CORPORATION'S FINANCIAL STATEMENTS

Exhibit 7-1 presents the information from which we can prepare a set of financial statements for Executive Corporation. This exhibit represents a highly abbreviated ledger for the entire corporation for the whole year. All of the journal entries for the year have been recorded. Each horizontal line represents one ledger account. The opening balance is recorded for each account, based on information from Exhibit 6-1, Executive Corporation's December 31, 1991, Balance Sheet. The vertical columns represent the individual numbered journal entries from Chapter 6. A running balance in each account has not been provided in this example.

A number of the ledger accounts in Exhibit 7-1 start with a zero balance. This occurs for one of two reasons. The first reason is simply that there was no balance at the end of last year, so there is no balance at the beginning of this year. Such is the case with prepaid insurance. The second reason is that some items are kept track of year by year rather than cumulatively. The income statement accounts relate specifically to the accounting period. We kept track of our income for 1991. Once 1991 was over and its results

EXHIBIT 7-1.

Executive Corporation Ledger for 1992 (000's omitted)

LEDGER ACCOUNT	BEGINNING BALANCE	1	2	3	4	5	6	7	8	9	10	11	12	13	ENDING BALANCE
Assets															
Cash	$52	-3	-15			+14			-18	-10	-3				$17
Prepaid Insurance	0	+3										-1			2
Accounts Receivable	18					-14	+56								60
Inventory	20				+15		-28								7
Plant & Equipment	60													-6	54
Expenses															
Cost of Goods Sold	0						+28								28
Labor	0								+8				+3		11
Interest	0									+6					6
Insurance	0											+1			1
Depreciation	0													+6	6
Dividends	0										+3				3
Liabilities															
Accounts Payable	17		-15		+15										17
Wages Payable	10								-10				+3		3
Mortgage Payable	40									-4					36
Stockholders' Equity															
Common Stock	10														10
Retained Earning	73														73
Revenue	0						+56								56

75

reported in our financial statements, we wish to keep track of
1992's income separately from 1991's. Therefore, all of the revenue
and expense accounts start 1992 with a zero balance. When we get
to the end of this year and say, "What was our revenue this year,"
we want to know the revenue of this year separate and apart from
any revenue we made in earlier years.

The revenue and expense accounts are called *temporary accounts* because we will start them over each year with a zero balance. The dividends declared account is also a temporary account.
It keeps track of how much dividends we declared during the entire
year. There is a separate permanent account, dividends payable,
which would keep track of any dividends we've declared but not yet
paid.

The key to conveying financial information is the ending balance of each ledger account. As long as we are using a system where
each journal entry is *posted,* or recorded in the individual ledger
accounts involved, we are able to determine the ending balance in
each ledger account. Those ending balances provide the information needed for a complete set of financial statements.

The Income Statement

Exhibit 7-2 presents the 1992 Income Statement for Executive Corporation. The income statement for any firm consists merely of a
comparison of its revenues and expenses. In order to prepare this
statement, we would have to look at the ending balance in each
revenue and expense ledger account. The revenue account at the
bottom of Exhibit 7-1 shows revenue of $56,000, which is exactly
the same as the revenue in the income statement in Exhibit 7-2. You
can compare each of the expenses between Exhibits 7-1 and 7-2 as
well, and will find them to be the same. This must be so, because
the way that the income statement was prepared was to simply take
the ending balances from each of the revenue and expense ledger
accounts.

The Balance Sheet

The retained earnings ledger account in Exhibit 7-1 has the same
balance at the end of the year as it had at the beginning of the year.

EXHIBIT 7-2.

Executive Corporation
Income Statement
For the Year Ending December 31, 1992

Revenue		$56,000
Less Expenses:		
Cost of Goods Sold	$28,000	
Labor	11,000	
Interest	6,000	
Insurance	1,000	
Depreciation	6,000	
Total Expenses		52,000
Net Income		$ 4,000

The retained earnings of a firm increase when it has income, and decrease when dividends are declared. In fact, every revenue will increase retained earnings, while expenses and dividends will decrease it. We have had all of these items, but the retained earnings account hasn't changed. The reason for this is that we have been keeping track of the specific changes in revenues, expenses, and dividends, instead of simply showing their impact on the retained earnings account.

By keeping track of revenues and expenses in detail rather than directly indicating their impact on retained earnings, we have generated additional information. This information has been used to derive an income statement. If we simply changed retained earnings directly whenever we had a revenue or expense, we would not have had the information needed to produce an income statement.

Nevertheless, we cannot produce a balance sheet without updating the information in our retained earnings account. Exhibit 7-3 provides a statement that updates both of the stockholders' equity accounts.

In Exhibit 7-3, we can see that the common stock balance did not change this year. Possible changes would include additional issuance of common stock through a private offering or a general offering to the public, issuance of stock as part of employee incentive plans, or retirement of stock. Retained earnings, as noted above, increase as a result of a positive net income (they decrease as a result of losses), and decrease when dividends are declared. (The parentheses around the $3,000 of dividends indicate that the $3,000 is being subtracted.)

All of the information used in Exhibit 7-3 comes either directly or indirectly from the ledger accounts in Exhibit 7-1. The common stock balance did not change during the year. Had there been changes to the common stock account, we could have determined what they were from the ledger account. Entries into ledger accounts are dated, allowing easy reference to the journal to review any transaction in its entirety. The dividend figure in Exhibit 7-3 is the ending balance in the dividends ledger account from Exhibit 7-1. The net income figure in Exhibit 7-3 does not appear anywhere in Exhibit 7-1. It is, however, merely a summary of the year-end revenue and expense items from the income statement, Exhibit 7-2. All of the Exhibit 7-2 items came directly from Exhibit 7-1. We now have all of the information we need to produce a balance sheet.

The balance sheet for Executive Corporation for 1992 appears in Exhibit 7-4. The asset and liability balances came directly from Exhibit 7-1 and the stockholders' equity balances came from our derivation in Exhibit 7-3. The preparation of this financial statement is really quite simple, given the ledger account balances. The

EXHIBIT 7-3.

Executive Corporation
Analysis of Changes in Stockholders' Equity
For the Year Ending December 31, 1992

	COMMON STOCK	RETAINED EARNINGS
Beginning Balance 1/1/92	$10,000	$73,000
Capital Contributions during 1992	0	
Net Income for 1992		4,000
Dividends Declared 1992		(3,000)
Ending Balance 12/31/92	$10,000	$74,000

EXHIBIT 7-4.

Executive Corporation
Balance Sheet
As of December 31, 1992

ASSETS

Current Assets:		
Cash	$17,000	
Prepaid Insurance	2,000	
Accounts Receivable	60,000	
Inventory	7,000	
Total Current Assets		$ 86,000
Fixed Assets:		
Plant and Equipment, net		54,000
TOTAL ASSETS		$140,000

EQUITIES

LIABILITIES		
Current Liabilities:		
Accounts Payable	$17,000	
Wages Payable	3,000	
Total Current Liabilities		$ 20,000
Long-Term Liabilities		
Mortgage Payable		36,000
TOTAL LIABILITIES		$ 56,000
STOCKHOLDERS' EQUITY		
Common Stock		$ 10,000
Retained Earnings		74,000
TOTAL STOCKHOLDERS' EQUITY		$ 84,000
TOTAL LIABILITIES & STOCKHOLDERS' EQUITY		$140,000

balances are simply transferred to the financial statement, with the main work involved being the determination of which accounts are short-term and which accounts are long-term.

The Statement of Cash Flows

The one remaining financial statement that is widely used to report the results of operations is the statement of cash flows. As discussed in Chapter 3, this statement focuses on the firm's sources and uses of cash. This statement also provides insight about the firm's liquidity, or its ability to meet its current obligations as they come due for payment.

The statement of cash flows shows where the firm got its cash and how it used it over the entire period covered by the financial statement. This feature is similar to the income statement, which shows revenues and expenses for the entire accounting period, and is different from the balance sheet which shows the firm's financial position at a single point in time. The statement of cash flows is divided into three major sections: cash from operating activities; cash from investing activities; and cash from financing activities.

The operating activities are those that relate to the ordinary revenue and expense producing activities of the firm. Firms tend to be particularly interested in how their day-to-day revenues and expenses impact on cash balances. These activities include items such as payments to employees and suppliers and collections of cash from customers. A controversial element is interest and dividends. Many people believe that interest and dividends are more closely associated with investing and financing activities. However, interest and dividends *received,* and interest paid must be included with operating activities because of their impact on revenues and expenses.

The investing activities of the firm relate to the purchase and sale of fixed assets and securities. It is clear that the purchase of stocks and bonds represents an investing activity. The accounting rule-making body determined that the purchase of property, plant, and equipment also represented an investment, and should be accounted for in this category. Lending money (and receiving repayments) also represents an investing activity.

The financing activities of the firm are concerned with borrowing money (or repaying it), issuance of stock, and the payment of dividends. Note that when a firm lends money it is investing. However borrowing money relates to getting the financial resources the firm needs to operate. Thus, borrowing is included in the financing category, along with issuance of stock. Dividends paid are considered to be a financing activity because they are a return of financial resources to the firm's owners. They are not included in operating activities because dividends paid are not classified as an expense, but rather as a distribution to the firm's owners of income earned.

There are two different approaches to calculating and presenting the statement of cash flows. These are the direct and the indirect methods. Exhibit 7-5 presents an example of the Statement of Cash Flows, prepared using the direct method. The direct method lists each individual type of account that resulted in a change in cash.

Looking at Exhibit 7-1, we can see that cash was affected by transactions 1, 2, 5, 8, 9, and 10. Review of each of those journal entries provides the information needed to prepare Exhibit 7-5. For example, transaction 1 consisted of a $3,000 payment for insurance. Therefore, the decrease in cash was for an operating activity, specifically payment for insurance.

This may be a cumbersome task when there are a large number of individual transactions. For example, how much cash was collected from customers during 1992? By looking at transaction 5 from Exhibit 7-1, we know that the answer is $14,000. We can see the increase in cash and the reduction in accounts receivable. Typically, however, there would be an extremely large number of individual journal entries related to receipts from customers.

Accountants usually prepare the cash flows statement by making general inferences from the changes in the balances of various accounts. Note that the accounts receivable at the beginning of the year were $18,000, and revenues from sales to customers during the year were $56,000. Combining what was owed to us at the beginning of the year with the amount customers purchased this year indicates that there was a total of $74,000 which we would hope to eventually collect from customers. At the end of the year the accounts receivable balance was $60,000. Therefore we can infer

EXHIBIT 7-5.

Executive Corporation
Statement of Cash Flows
For the Year Ending December 31, 1992

Cash Flows from Operating Activities		
Collections from Customers	$14,000	
Payments to Employees	(18,000)	
Payments to Suppliers	(15,000)	
Payments for Insurance	(3,000)	
Payments for Interest	(6,000)	
Net Cash Used for Operating Activities		$(28,000)
Cash Flows from Investing Activities		
None		
Net Cash Used for Investing Activities		0
Cash Flows from Financing Activities		
Payment of Mortgage Principal	$ (4,000)	
Payment of Dividends	(3,000)	
Net Used for Financing Activities		(7,000)
NET INCREASE/(DECREASE) IN CASH		$(35,000)
CASH, DECEMBER 31, 1991		52,000
CASH DECEMBER 31, 1992		$ 17,000

that $14,000 must have been collected (the $74,000 total due us, less the $60,000 still due at the end of the year).

Let's consider another example. The mortgage payable account started with a balance of $40,000 and ended with a balance of $36,000 (Exhibit 7-1). Rather than reviewing all of the journal entries related to mortgage payments, accountants would infer that $4,000 was spent on the financing activity of repaying debt. However, this inference process requires care. It is possible, for instance that $20,000 was paid on the mortgage principal, but a new mortgage of $16,000 was taken on a new piece of equipment. The statement of cash flows must show both the source of cash from the new mortgage, as well as the payment of cash on the old mortgage. Therefore preparation of the statement requires at least some in-depth knowledge about changes in the accounts of the firm.

An alternative approach for developing and presenting the statement of cash flows is referred to as the indirect method. The indirect method starts with net income as a measure of cash from operations. It then makes adjustments to the extent that net income is not a true measure of cash flow. Exhibit 7-6 was prepared using the indirect method.

One of the most common adjustments to income is for depreciation. When buildings and equipment are purchased, there is a cash outflow. Each year, a portion of the cost of the buildings or equipment is charged as a depreciation expense. That expense does lower net income, but it does not require a cash outflow. Therefore, the amount of the depreciation expense is added back to net income to make net income more reflective of true cash flows. In Exhibit 7-6 we see that the $6,000 depreciation expense is added to net income.

There are a variety of other items that cause net income to over or understate the true cash flow. For example, if customers buy our product or service, but don't pay for it before the end of the year, then income will overstate cash inflow. Therefore, in Exhibit 7-6, there is a negative adjustment for the increase in accounts receivable.

Many of the adjustments to net income, which are needed to determine cash flow from operating activities, are quite confusing. Therefore many people prefer use of the direct method. However, because net income is considered essential to the process of generating cash, the net income reconciliation is required. If the direct method is used, the Cash Flows from Operating Activities portion of the indirect method (Exhibit 7-6), must be included as a supporting schedule.

The information contained in the statement of cash flows is quite dramatic in this example. Although Exhibit 7-2 indicated that there was a positive net income of $4,000, the firm is using substantially more cash than it is receiving. In some cases this might reflect recent spending on buildings and equipment. A decline in cash is not necessarily bad. However, in this case, we note from the statement of cash flows (Exhibit 7-5 or 7-6) that no money was used for

EXHIBIT 7-6.

Executive Corporation
Statement of Cash Flows
For the Year Ending December 31, 1992

Cash Flows from Operating Activities		
Net Income		$ 4,000
Adjustments		
Depreciation Expense	$ 6,000	
Decrease in Inventory	13,000	
Increase in Accounts Receivable	(42,000)	
Increase in Prepaid Insurance	(2,000)	
Decrease in Wages Payable	(7,000)	
Total Adjustments to Net Income		(32,000)
Net Cash Used for Operating Activities		$(28,000)
Cash Flows from Investing Activities		
None		
Net Cash Used for Investing Activities		0
Cash Flows from Financing Activities		
Payment of Mortgage Principal	$(4,000)	
Payment of Dividends	(3,000)	
Net Used for Financing Activities		(7,000)
NET INCREASE/(DECREASE) IN CASH		$(35,000)
CASH, DECEMBER 31, 1991		52,000
CASH, DECEMBER 31, 1992		$17,000

investing activities. The largest decline in cash came from operations. What was the single largest cause of the decline? Exhibit 7-5 would seem to indicate that payments to employees was the largest item. It was the largest cash outflow.

However, this is an example where the net income reconciliation provides particularly useful information. Looking at the cash flows from operating activities section of Exhibit 7-6, the most striking number is the $42,000 increase in receivables. A growing company is likely to have growing receivables. In this case, however, the growth in receivables seems to be unusually large. What does this mean? It could mean that the firm needs to make a stronger effort to collect payment from its customers on a timely basis. Or it could mean that sales were made to buyers who can't pay. The statement of cash flows highlights the receivables problem for the user of the statement. If receivables continue to grow at this rate, the firm will run out of cash, probably before the end of the next year. Although there is no crisis yet, there may be unless we take this situation into account in managing the firm and in planning for cash inflows and outflows for the coming year.

LOOKING AHEAD

Part II has presented an introduction to accounting, a vital framework for financial management. We have spent a considerable amount of time defining financial statements, their components, how we value items that appear on financial statements, and the mechanics of recording financial information and putting together a firm's set of financial statements. In Part IV we reverse gears and start to tear apart financial statements to learn how to interpret the information they contain. Now that we know where they come from, we will be better able to glean all the information possible out of them, and to use that information to better manage our firm.

However, before we begin the financial statement analysis of Part IV, we will be examining a variety of financial decisions in Part III. The financial managers of the firm are often faced with decisions that have relatively little impact on the underlying productivity of the firm, but which can have a tremendous impact on its profitability. Nonfinancial managers frequently observe de facto decisions made by financial officers. In Part III we examine the reasons why many of these decisions are made.

For example, why accelerate the depreciation on our equipment? Why did we recently shift to a LIFO method of inventory, and what is LIFO anyway? Why do we lease equipment, when you would think it would be cheaper to own it? These are just a few of the questions addressed by Part III of this book.

KEY CONCEPTS

Ledger—a book (or computer memory file) in which we keep track of the impact of financial events on each account. The ledger can provide us with the balance in any account at any point in time.

Income statement preparation—the income statement is directly prepared from the year-end ledger balances of the revenue and expense accounts.

Balance sheet preparation—ledger account balances can be used to provide an analysis of changes in stockholders' equity accounts. This analysis, together with other ledger account balances, is used to prepare the balance sheet.

Statement of cash flows—this statement shows the sources and uses of the firm's cash. It specifically shows cash from operating, investing, and financing activities. It can be prepared under two alternative methods:

a. *the direct method*—lists the change in cash caused by each account.

b. *the indirect method*—starts with net income as an estimate of cash flow, and makes a series of adjustments to net income to determine cash flow from operating activities.

Part III

FINANCIAL DECISIONS

Eight

LEVERAGE

Part III of this book is concerned with financial decisions. Which inventory or depreciation method is best for our firm? Is a project going to yield an acceptable rate of return? Will a merger be profitable? One of the most important of the various financial decisions is how much leverage a firm should employ.

A fundamental decision made by any business is the degree to which it incurs fixed costs. A fixed cost is one that remains the same regardless of the level of operations. As sales increase, fixed costs don't increase. As a result, profits can rise rapidly during good times. On the other hand, during bad times fixed costs don't decline, so profits fall rapidly.

The degree to which a firm locks itself into fixed costs is referred to as its *leverage position*. The more highly leveraged a firm, the riskier it is because of the obligations related to fixed costs that must be met whether the firm is having a good year or not. At the same time, the more highly leveraged, the greater the profits during good times. This presents a classic problem of making a decision where there is a tradeoff between risk and return.

There are two major types of leverage, financial and operating. Financial leverage is specifically the extent to which a firm gets its cash resources from borrowing (debt) as opposed to issuance of additional shares of capital stock (equity). The greater the debt compared to equity, the more highly leveraged the firm because debt legally obligates the firm to annual interest payments. These interest payments represent a fixed cost.

Operating leverage is concerned with the extent to which a firm commits itself to high levels of fixed costs other than interest payments. A firm that rents property using cancellable leases has less leverage than a firm that commits itself to a long-term noncancellable lease. A firm that has substantial vertical integration has created a highly leveraged situation. Consider what happens if Executive Corporation vertically integrates by acquiring its raw materials supplier, Embiay, Inc. Raw materials will now cost the company less, because it doesn't have to buy them from an outside firm. But when times are bad, the firm will have to bear the fixed costs associated with the Embiay subsidiary. Had there still been two separate companies, Executive could have simply slowed its purchases of raw materials from Embiay without having to bear Embiay's fixed costs.

In the cases of both financial and operating leverage, the crucial question is how much leverage is appropriate. We can't answer that question in absolute terms, but this chapter can provide you with an understanding of the topic. This understanding should make it simpler to make appropriate choices or to understand what went into making the choices your firm has already made.

FINANCIAL LEVERAGE

Let's start our discussion of financial leverage with a relatively easy example. Assume you were to buy a small building as a piece of investment property. You buy the building for $100,000 and pay the full amount in cash.

Suppose that a year later you sell the building for $130,000. Your pretax profit is $30,000. This is a 30 percent pretax return on your original investment of $100,000.

As an alternative to paying the full $100,000 cash for the investment, you might have to put $10,000 cash down and borrow $90,000 from the bank at 15 percent interest. This time when you sell the property for $130,000 you repay the $90,000 to the bank, along with $13,500 interest. After deducting your original $10,000 investment, $16,500 is left as a pretax profit. This is a pretax return of 165 percent on your $10,000 investment. Compare the 30 percent we calculated earlier to this rate of return of 165 percent. That's leverage!

Note that we had a net profit of $30,000 without leverage, but only $16,500 in the leveraged case. Although we earned a higher return, we had less profits. That's because in the unleveraged case we had invested $100,000 of our money, but in the leveraged case we had invested only $10,000. If we have additional investment opportunities available to us, we could have invested our full $100,000, borrowed $900,000, and had a pretax profit of $165,000 on the same investment that yields $30,000 in the unleveraged situation. Financial leverage can not only increase your yield from investments, but can also allow you to consider projects that are much larger than would be feasible without borrowing.

Suppose, however, that the property were sold after one year for $70,000 rather than $130,000. On a $100,000 unleveraged investment, the loss would be $30,000 before taxes. This would be a 30 percent loss on our original $100,000 investment.

In the leveraged case, the loss will be magnified. We would have to repay the bank the $90,000 loan plus $13,500 of interest. These payments total to $103,500, which is $33,500 greater than the $70,000 proceeds from the sale. Further, we've lost our initial $10,000 investment. The total loss is $43,500 before taxes. On our initial investment of $10,000, this constitutes a loss of 435 percent. That's leverage too!

Clearly the firm must decide if the 165 percent possible gain is worth the risk of a 435 percent loss. Whether it is or not depends on the likelihood of the increase in value versus the probability of a decline. If the project really were a sure thing, leverage would certainly make sense. Rarely are projects sure things. Yet, managers should try to decide how confident they are of the success of a project, and weigh that confidence against the implications for the firm if the project does indeed fail.

Not all managers rate the same project as being equally likely to succeed. Some managers feel a particular project is great, while others may not think as highly of it. Further, even if all managers agreed on how likely a project were to succeed, they would not all make the same decision about financial leverage. Some managers and firms tend to be more averse to risk than others. There are gamblers and conservatives. Usually stockholders align themselves with a firm that they feel does things the way they want them done. A person dependent on a steady level of income from stock dividends might prefer to buy the stock of a firm that shuns leverage and prefers a steady, if lesser income. A person looking for large potential appreciation in stock price might prefer the stock of a firm that is highly leveraged.

How Much Financial Leverage Is Enough?

In practice, the leverage decision is based on firm policy. Some firms raise almost all of their funds from issuing stock to stockholders and from earnings retained in the firm. Other firms borrow as much as they possibly can and raise additional money from stockholders only when they can no longer raise any additional money by borrowing. Most firms are somewhere in the middle. In our example, you didn't have to borrow $90,000 or nothing; you could have chosen to borrow some inbetween amount. Likewise, some firms maintain one-fourth as much debt as equity, some firms equal amounts of debt and equity, and some firms more debt than equity.

This decision is made by the firm's top corporate officers and the board of directors. Generally, the decision of issuing stock or borrowing money is not made by project managers evaluating the potential of individual projects.

The Rule of OPM

In making a decision regarding whether additional funds should be raised by debt or equity, there are several factors to be considered. The first rule of financial leverage is that it only pays to borrow if the interest rate is less than the rate of return on the money borrowed. We can refer to this as the "rule of OPM"—other people's money. If your firm can borrow money and invest it at a high enough rate so that the loan can be repaid with interest and still leave some after-tax profit for your stockholders, then your stockholders have profited on OPM. They have made extra profit with no extra investment. This greatly magnifies the rate of return on the amount they invested.

Why are lenders so generously allowing you to benefit at their expense? How can there be a system where a firm can increase profits to its stockholders without extra investment? The key is risk. The stockholders of your company don't increase their investment, but they do increase their risk. The lender may not reap all of the possible profits from the use of his money. But the lender does earn a contractually guaranteed rate of return. The lender gets back his money plus a set amount of interest, whether we make a fortune or lose our shirts.

The Collateral Factor

The amount that lenders let you borrow depends largely on your available collateral. Merely desiring to be highly leveraged doesn't guarantee that you can borrow enough to be highly leveraged. Because the lender isn't a partner if you strike it rich, he doesn't want to be a partner if you go bankrupt.

Stability of Earnings

Assuming that you have enough collateral to borrow as much as you might want, what factors should you consider in trying to arrive at a reasonable level of leverage? To a great degree, your desired leverage position depends on the degree to which your sales and profits fluctuate. The greater the fluctuation in sales and profits, the less leverage you can afford. If your firm is a stable, noncyclical firm that makes money in good times and bad, then use of OPM will help improve the rate of return earned by your shareholders. If cyclical factors in your industry or the economy at large tend to cause your business to have both good and bad years, then debt entails a greater risk.

For example, the airline industry, with its huge capital requirements (the new generation of jets cost over $100 million each) has traditionally been highly leveraged. The results have been very large profits during the good years, but substantial losses during periods when air traffic falls off, or competition is particularly intense. During the air traffic controller mass firing of 1981, the first impact was the grounding of 25 percent of all aircraft. Nevertheless, interest payments on those jets continued to be paid.

Cyclical factors shouldn't scare companies away from having any debt at all. The key is to accumulate no more interest and principal repayment obligations than can reasonably be met in bad times as well as good. Ultimately, considering the variability of your profit stream, a decision must be made regarding the level of extra risk you are willing to take to achieve a higher potential rate of return on stockholder investments.

OPERATING LEVERAGE

While financial leverage is a problem that is almost strictly the domain of the firm's highest levels of management together with its financial officers, operating leverage is an issue that directly affects the line managers of the firm. The level of operating leverage a firm selects should not be made without input from the managers directly involved in the production process. For example, one of the most significant operating leverage issues is the choice of technology levels. Selection of the highest level of technology available is not always in the best interests of the business.

Suppose that we are opening a chain of copy centers. Each center will provide a full service operation. Customers can drop work off in the morning and pick it up later in the day or the week. The employees will do the actual photocopying. We are faced with the choice of renting a relatively slow copy machine, or the newest technology machine, which is considerably faster. The faster machine is also considerably more expensive to lease.

It will generally be the case that newer technology has a higher fixed cost and lower variable cost than the older technology. Variable costs are those that vary directly with volume. If we double the number of copies made, we double the amount of paper, printing ink toner, and labor time needed for making the copies. One of the principle functions of new technology is to reduce the variable costs of production.

It may turn out that a machine that can reduce the variable costs is more expensive to make, and thus has a higher purchase or lease price than the older generation machine. However, even if it doesn't cost more to make, its manufacturer will charge more for the new machine than for the older machine. Intuitively, if the new machine is in some respect better than the old machine (that is, it lowers the variable cost without reducing quality), and doesn't cost more to buy, then no one will buy the older machine. Thus, anytime we see two technologies being sold side by side, such as slow and fast copy machines, we can expect the faster machine to have a higher rental fee or purchase price, and therefore a higher fixed cost.

Let's assume that we could lease the slower, older technology copy machine for $10,000 per year, or a faster, newer technology copy machine for $25,000 per year. Both produce photocopies of equal quality. Both use the same quantities of paper and ink toner, but the faster machine requires less operator time. Therefore, the labor cost is much lower for the faster machine. As a result, the variable cost of copies on the slow machine is 6 cents each, while the variable cost of copies from the fast machine is only 3 cents each. Is the faster machine the better bet?

That depends. Suppose we sell each copy we make for 10 cents. Then, for each copy we sell we receive 10 cents and spend an extra 6 cents or 3 cents (depending on our choice of machine) for the variable costs. The difference between the price and the variable costs is referred to as the *contribution margin*. This margin represents the amount of money available to be used to pay fixed costs and provide the firm with a profit.

If we use the slower machine, we receive 10 cents and spend 6 cents, leaving 4 cents to be used toward paying the rent on the copy machine. If we sell enough copies, there will be enough individual contributions of 4 cents apiece to pay the full $10,000 rent and leave some receipts for a profit.

Break-Even Analysis

How many copies must we make before we "break-even?" Break-even analysis requires dividing the fixed costs by the contribution margin per unit. This is equivalent to saying, "How many times do we have to get a contribution of 4 cents before we have covered our fixed cost of $10,000?" For the slower machine, $10,000 divided by 4 cents equals 250,000. We need to make and sell a quarter of a million copies to break-even. For the faster machine, the contribution margin is 7 cents per unit, because the price is 10 cents and the variable costs are only 3 cents. The $25,000 rental fee for the fast machine, divided by a 7 cent contribution margin per unit, results in a break-even point of 357,143 copies. Apparently, we can make a profit on the slower machine at a lower output level than we can with the faster machine.

If we sell more copies than the break-even point for the machine we have, we make a profit. If we sell fewer copies than the break-even point, we lose money. Consider sales of 300,000 copies per year. Our revenue would be $30,000 at 10 cents per copy. For the slow machine, our costs would be $10,000 fixed rental cost, plus $18,000 of variable cost (300,000 copies at 6 cents). The total cost would be $28,000 and we would have a pretax profit of $2,000. For the fast machine, the fixed rental cost is $25,000. The variable cost would be $9,000 (300,000 copies at 3 cents). The total cost would be $34,000 and we would have a loss of $4,000. This ties in with our earlier calculation, because we are above the break-even point for the slow machine, but below the break-even point for the faster machine.

If we sell 400,000 copies, we might expect the faster machine to come out better than the slower machine. After all, both are operating at a level above their break-even point. The faster machine is earning a profit of 7 cents for every extra copy above the break-even point, while the slower machine is only earning a profit of 4 cents a copy. While there is some truth to this reasoning, we must be careful. The slower machine has been earning profits, albeit not much per copy, ever since the 250,000 copy point was passed. The faster machine has been earning profits, albeit a larger amount per copy, only since passing 357,143 copies. You can't assume that the faster machine is better for us as long as our volume exceeds its break-even point. In this case, our revenue is $40,000 (400,000 copies at 10 cents). The slow machine has costs of $10,000 rental plus $24,000 variable (400,000 copies at 6 cents), leaving a pretax profit of $6,000, while the fast machine has a $25,000 rental plus $12,000 of variable cost (400,000 copies at 3 cents). The faster machine is making a profit of $3,000 now, but that's only half as much the slow machine.

At 500,000 copies, the two machines produce an equal pretax profit of $10,000. Above that point, the faster machine generates a higher profit because every extra copy yields a 7 cent profit as compared to the 4 cent profit from the slower machine. On the other hand, for each copy less than 500,000, the slower machine has a higher profit, because its profits go down only 4 cents per copy, while the faster machine's profits fall off at a rate of 7 cents per copy.

Which machine should we lease? That depends on our expected volume and how sure we are of our projections. If we expect to always make more than 500,000 copies, the fast machine is preferred. If we will always make less than 500,000 copies, the slow machine is preferred. If we expect to make less than 250,000 copies, we should get out of the business.

The problem of operating leverage that faces us is what to do if we expect to make more than 500,000 copies in general, but sometimes it may be less than that. We can play it safe with the slower machine and be sure of a profit, or at least not a huge loss. We have a lower fixed cost (rent of $10,000) and therefore a lower operating leverage. On the other hand, we can get the faster machine that produces a much higher profit if sales are good. In that case we take a chance. We have a higher fixed cost (rent of $25,000) and therefore a higher operating leverage. If sales fall off, profits will decline much faster, and any loss will be much larger than it would have been.

Again, as in the case of financial leverage, we are trading off risk and return. The less the variability in our production volume, the lower the risk associated with incurring the larger fixed costs in order to achieve a higher profit.

Technology is only one example. Should we buy our buildings and equipment or rent them? If we buy them, we incur fixed charges even if volume falls off. If we rent with relatively short leases, the annual cost is likely to be greater, but it is easier to terminate the fixed costs in the face of business downturns. Another operating leverage decision is whether to acquire plant and facilities and manufacture all components of our product or to subcontract the manufacturing and merely do assembly. With subcontracting, we can terminate contracts when demand declines. If we buy the plant and equipment, the fixed costs remain even when demand falls off.

Ultimately, this decision falls into management's lap. Once managers consider the likelihood of sales variability, a decision has to be made as to whether the risks associated with the fixed costs of financial and operating leverage are worth the higher potential return. However, in the case of operating leverage, the decision has much greater ramifications for the way in which the firm's production takes place. Financial leverage is concerned with where the money comes from—lenders or owners, but not with what we do with the money. On the other hand, issues of vertical integration, buying versus renting, and choice of technology, can impact more broadly on the normal functioning of the firm. Such decisions can have vital competitive implications. Therefore, a greater number of line managers should participate in decisions regarding the degree and nature of operating leverage. Further, the potential impact of both financial and operating leverage on risk and return make it clear that the firm shouldn't simply allow these decisions to happen, but should be making explicit decisions on what is in the best interests of the firm and its owners.

Both of these financial decisions, how much financial leverage and how much operating leverage the firm should have, are fundamental to the firm. We can simply let things develop, handling items on a crisis basis, or we can make such decisions on a rational planned basis. In Part IV, one of the topics examined is the solvency of the firm. Is the firm able to meet its interest costs and other fixed obligations? More often than not, the firms that have solvency problems are the ones that didn't formally address the leverage issues head on.

KEY CONCEPTS

Leverage—represents locking in a set level of fixed cost. As revenues rise, these costs don't rise, so profits rise rapidly. As revenues decline, these costs remain, so profits fall rapidly.

Financial leverage—the degree to which the firm chooses to finance its operations by borrowing money, thus locking in fixed interest charges.

The rule of OPM—if the return from invested capital exceeds the current interest rate on borrowed funds, then the firm's owners benefit if the firm borrows, thus allowing the owners to profit from the use of other people's money.

Operating leverage—the degree to which the firm chooses to lock in fixed costs other than interest in order to leverage profits during good times. Examples of high operating leverage are vertical integration and the use of high technology.

Stability of earnings—the less variable the firm's earnings, the lower the risks and greater the advantages of being highly leveraged.

Nine

DEPRECIATION: HAVING YOUR CAKE AND EATING IT TOO!

The matching principle of accounting requires that firms use depreciation. Suppose we buy a machine with a ten-year useful life. This machine will produce products over its entire ten-year lifetime. Therefore, it will be generating revenues in each of those ten years. The matching principle holds that we would be distorting the results of operations in all ten years if we considered the entire cost of the machine to be an expense in the year in which it was acquired. We would be understating income in the first year and overstating it in subsequent years.

Instead of expensing the equipment, we consider it to be a long-term asset when it is acquired. As time passes, and the equipment becomes used up, we allocate a portion of the original cost as an expense in each year. Thus the revenue received each year from the sale of the machine's output is matched with some of the machine's cost.

Okay, if we have to do it that way, there is some intuitive rationale. But where is the financial decision? It seems as if there is little choice left for the financial manager. In fact that is not true. There are several complicating factors. First we must determine the valuation to be used as a basis for determining each year's depreciation. Next we must consider whether the asset really does get used up proportionately throughout its life. Perhaps it gets used up to a greater extent in some years than in others. Finally, what are some of the tax implications of the depreciation methods we decide to use? These questions make up the topic of this chapter.

AMORTIZATION

Amortization simply means the spreading out of a cost over a period of time. It is a generic term used for any type of item that is being prorated over time. The term *depreciation* is a specialized subset of amortization. Depreciation technically should be used with respect to the using up of plant and equipment. The term *depreciation* comes from the word *deprecate*—indicating a breaking down or physical depreciation and wearing out. Because plant and equipment become physically used up over time, this term is appropriate.

Some items don't wear out or break down per se, and we don't refer to them as depreciating over time. For example, natural resources such as oil, gas, and coal are said to deplete. Deplete means to empty out and this is essentially what happens to a coal mine or oil well. Finally, some items neither deplete nor depreciate. For example, a patent loses its value over time. It doesn't break down, wear out, or empty out—it simply expires with the passage of time. When neither of the terms *depreciation* nor *depletion* is applicable, we refer to the item as amortizing. Therefore, for a patent, instead of depreciation expense or depletion expense, the annual reduction in value is referred to as amortization expense.

The terminology is discussed here so that you will understand what people are referring to when they use these terms. From an accounting point of view there is no substantive difference if we refer to an item as being depreciated, depleted, or amortized. In each case, the key question is, "by how much?" After all, it is the amount that we record as an expense that impacts on the firm's income, not the name by which we call it. William Shakespeare undoubtedly had depreciation on his mind when he wrote about roses.

This chapter speaks exclusively of depreciation, even though the principles generally apply in a similar fashion for assets to be depleted or amortized. The discussion initially focuses primarily on depreciation for financial statement purposes. Later this chapter discusses important tax laws concerning depreciation.

ASSET VALUATION FOR DEPRECIATION

Asset valuation for depreciation basically follows the rules of historical cost. Chapter 5 stated that the historical or acquisition cost of an asset is simply what we paid for the item when we acquired it. However, for depreciation purposes determination of asset cost is somewhat more complex.

The first problem that arises is the issue of what to do with the costs of putting an asset into productive service. For example, suppose that we purchase a machine for $20,000, and the machine cannot be used by us without modification of our electrical system. If we pay an electrician $1,000 to run a heavy-duty power line to the spot where the machine will be located, is that a current period expense? No, according to generally accepted accounting principles (GAAP), the cost of the electrical work provides us with benefits over the entire useful life of the machine. Therefore, matching requires that we spread the cost of the electrical work over the same period as the life of the machine. The way that is handled is by adding the cost of the electrical work to the cost of the equipment. Instead of our equipment showing a cost of $20,000, it will have a cost of $21,000 and we will depreciate that amount over its lifetime.

In fact, all costs to put an item into service will be added to the cost of that item so that they can be matched with the revenues over the useful life of the asset. This would include freight on the purchase, insurance while in transit to our factory, new fixtures, plant modifications, etc.

Is this treatment desirable from your perspective? Probably not. You have paid the electrician $1,000 in cash this year, but will show only part of that as an expense. If you could show it all as an expense, you would have a larger tax deduction this year. Over the life of the machine, the total taxes paid will be the same, because either way we are going to have a total $1,000 deduction for the cost of the electrical work. But by taking it sooner, we would essentially get an interest-free loan from the government. This basic approach of trying to take deductions sooner represents the deferral of tax payments to the future.

In the case described here, such a deferral is not an option available to us. If the money was spent to put an asset into service, it must be added to the cost of the asset and depreciated over the asset's life. That sounds very cut and clear. It turns out, however, that this is one of the many areas in accounting where things are anything but cut and clear. For instance, suppose we have a full-time electrician on our staff, whose main function is repair and maintenance of our equipment and factory. He is the person who runs the heavy duty cable for the new machine. How much of his salary and benefits should be allocated to the cost of the new machine? That is a matter of judgment, especially if the electrician isn't required by your firm to keep a log of how much time is spent on each job.

To resolve this problem you will make an estimate. The Internal Revenue Service (IRS) can contest the reasonableness of the estimate. However, that will only occur if they happen to audit you and if they happen to look at that specific item within their audit.

Perhaps this discussion has made you realize that the amount put into the equipment account is subject to some judgment. Consider this as well—while repairs and maintenance are current period expenses, replacements and improvements to an asset must be added to the cost and depreciated over the life remaining at the time of the replacement or improvement. Replacements and improvements are simply expenditures that extend the useful life of the asset, or improve its speed or quality, or reduce its operating costs.

If a motor burns out, is its replacement a routine repair or a capitalizable (capitalize means to add to the cost of a long-term item shown on the balance sheet) event? That depends on the circumstances. Do motors burn out quite regularly, or is it a rare event? Regular replacement may well be a repair, but infrequent major overhauls lead to treatment as a replacement. However, there is no clear right or wrong answer in many instances.

The Depreciable Base

Our problems are not yet over. How much of the asset's cost do we depreciate? Your first reaction may well be the entire cost, including the various additions to the purchase price that we have just discussed. This is basically true, except that there is still a matching problem. We wish to depreciate property that wears out in the productive process in order to get a portion of its cost assigned to each period in which it helped generate revenues. However, we only want to match against revenues those resources that actually have been used up. We don't necessarily consume 100 percent of most assets.

What if we bought a machine with a ten-year expected life at a cost of $20,000, including all of the costs to put it into service. Suppose further that after ten years we expect to be able to sell the machine for $2,000. Then we really have not used up $20,000 of resources over the ten years. We have only used up $18,000 and we still have a $2,000 asset left over. This $2,000 value is referred to as the machine's salvage value. Therefore, from an accounting perspective, we depreciate a machine by an amount equal to its cost less its anticipated salvage value. That difference is referred to as its depreciable base.

The salvage value will have to be estimated—at best, it will be an educated guess. Your accountant reviews the reasonableness of your salvage value estimates for financial statement preparation.

Asset Life

How long will a machine last? We attempt to depreciate an asset over its useful life. If we depreciate it over a period longer or shorter than its useful life, we won't obtain an accurate matching between revenues and the expenses incurred in order to generate those revenues. However, we can only guess an asset's true useful life. Often we see equipment that lasts well after the estimated useful life. This is not surprising considering the GAAP of conservatism. Better to write-off an asset too quickly and understate its true value, than to write it off too slowly (anticipating a longer life than ultimately results) and overstate its value.

What happens if we are still using the asset after its estimated useful life is over? We stop taking further depreciation. The role of depreciation is to allocate some of the cost of the asset into each of a number of periods. Once we have allocated all of the cost (less the salvage value), we simply continue to use the asset with no further depreciation. That means we will have revenues without depreciation expense matched against them. That is simply a result of a matching based on estimates instead of perfect foreknowledge.

What if we sell the asset for more than its salvage value? That presents no problem—we can record a gain for the difference between the selling price and the asset's *book value*. The book value of an asset is the amount paid for it, less the amount of depreciation already taken. Thus, if we bought our machine for $20,000, and sold it after ten years during which we had taken $18,000 of depreciation, the book value would be $2,000. According to our financial records, or books, its value is $2,000. If we sold it for $5,000, there would be a gain of $3,000.

What if the asset becomes obsolete after three years due to technological change and it is sold at that time for $500? Assuming we were depreciating it at a rate of $1,800 a year (to arrive at $18,000 of depreciation over ten years), then we would have taken $5,400 of depreciation (3 years at $1,800 per year) during those first three years. The book value ($20,000 cost less $5,400 of accumulated depreciation) is $14,600, and at a sale price of $500, we would record a loss of $14,100.

STRAIGHT-LINE VS. ACCELERATED DEPRECIATION

In the previous example we noted that $5,400 of depreciation had been taken over three years, if we assumed depreciation of $1,800 per year. The $1,800 figure is based on straight-line depreciation. It assumes that we take an equal share of the total depreciation each year during the asset's life.

In fact we have choices for how we calculate the depreciation. The straight-line approach is just one of several methods available to us. Not all equipment declines in productive value equally in each year of its useful life. Consider a machine that has a capacity of one million units of output over its lifetime. If it is run three shifts a day, it will be used up substantially quicker than if it is run only one shift a day. The *production units* method of depreciation bases each year's depreciation on the proportion of the machine's total productive capacity that has been used in that year. For instance, if the machine produces 130,000 units in a year, and its estimated total lifetime capacity is one million, we would take 13 percent (130,000 divided by 1,000,000) of the cost less salvage value as the depreciation for that year. Of course, this method entails substantial extra bookkeeping to keep track of annual production. The method is not commonly used in this country.

Two other methods exist that are commonly used—the declining balance method (really this is a group of similar methods as discussed below) and the sum-of-the-years digits method. These are called accelerated methods. The basic philosophy behind these methods is that some assets are likely to decline in value more rapidly in the early years of their life than in the later years. A car is an excellent example. If we consider the decline in value for a car, it is largest in its first year, not quite as large in the following year, and eventually tails off to a point where there is relatively little decline per year in the latter part of its life.

COMPARISON OF THE DEPRECIATION METHODS

We will use an example to demonstrate the principal depreciation methods and to allow us to compare the results using each method. Assume that we buy a machine for $20,000 and we have $4,000 of costs to put the machine into service. We expect the machine to have a useful life of six years and a salvage value of $3,000.

The straight-line method first calculates the depreciable base, which is the cost less salvage. In this case, the cost is the $20,000 price plus the $4,000 to put the machine into service. The salvage value is $3,000 so the depreciable base is $21,000 ($20,000 + $4,000 − $3,000). The base is then allocated equally among the years of the asset's life. For a six-year life, the depreciation would be 1/6 of the $21,000 each year, or $3,500 per year. The straight-line method is rather straightforward.

The declining balance method accelerates the amount of depreciation taken in the early years and reduces the amount taken in the later years. When someone refers to accelerated depreciation he or she is not referring to a shortening of the asset life for depreciation purposes. The life remains six years under the accelerated methods. Declining balance represents a group of methods. We will start with double declining balance (DDB), also referred to as 200 percent declining balance. We will discuss the other declining balance methods later.

The double declining balance approach starts out with a depreciable base equal to the asset cost ignoring salvage value. The cost is multiplied, not by $1/6$ as in the straight-line method, but by a rate that is double the straight-line rate. In this case we would multiply the depreciable base by 2 times $1/6$, or by $2/6$. Hence the word *double* in the name of this method. If we take $2/6$ of $24,000 (remember that cost includes the various costs to get the machine into service, and that this method ignores salvage value), we get $8,000 of depreciation for the first year. At that rate, the asset will be fully depreciated in just three years, and we've said that accelerated methods generally do not shorten the asset life!

Therefore, we need some device to prevent the depreciation from remaining at that high level of $8,000 per year. This device is the *declining balance*. Each year we subtract the previous year's depreciation from the existing depreciable base to get a new depreciable base. In this problem, we start with a base of $24,000 and take $8,000 of depreciation in the first year. This means that in the second year there will be a new depreciable base of $16,000 ($24,000 − $8,000). In the second year, our depreciation would be 2/6 of $16,000 or $5,333. For year three, we will determine a new base equal to $16,000 less year two's depreciation of $5,333. Thus we have a new base of $10,667 and so on.

However, there is one caveat to this process. We cannot take more depreciation during the asset's life than the asset's cost less its salvage value. In this problem, we can take no more than $21,000 of depreciation, regardless of the method chosen. We have achieved our goal of having higher depreciation in the early years and less in each succeeding year. The method, which simply doubles the straight-line rate, does have some intuitive appeal as an approach for getting the desired accelerated effect.

The declining balance family also includes 150 percent declining balance and 175 percent declining balance. In each of these methods, the only difference from the 200 percent, or double declining balance, is that the straight-line rate is multiplied by 150 percent or 175 percent instead of 200 percent to find the annual rate.

Sum-of-the-years digits (SYD) is a similar accelerated method. SYD takes the cost less salvage, that is, $21,000, the same as straight-line, and multiplies it by a fraction that consists of the life of the asset divided by the sum of the digits in the years of the life of the asset. That sum simply consists of adding from 1 to the last year of the asset's life, inclusive. In our example, we would add $1 + 2 + 3 + 4 + 5 + 6$, because the asset has a six-year life. The sum of these digits is 21. Therefore, we would multiply $21,000 by $6/21$ (the life of the asset divided by the sum). This gives us first-year depreciation of $6,000.

In each succeeding year, we would lower the numerator of the fraction by 1. That is, for year two the fraction becomes $5/21$ and the depreciation would be $5,000 ($21,000 × $5/21$). For year three the fraction becomes $4/21$ and the depreciation $4,000, and so on. Unlike the declining balance method, it is hard to find any intuitive appeal to this manipulation. All we can say is that it does achieve the desired result of greater depreciation in the early years, and it does account for the proper amount of total depreciation.

Exhibit 9-1 compares the three methods for this piece of equipment for its entire six-year life. It is especially important to note that all three methods produce exactly the same total depreciation over the life of the asset.

Ideally, in choosing a depreciation method for your firm, you would select from among straight-line, declining balance, and sum of the years digits based on the method that most closely approximates the manner in which your particular resources are used up and become less productive. You need not use the same method for all of your depreciable property.

Many firms simply choose the straight-line approach for reporting depreciation on their financial statements to be issued to their stockholders. The apparent reason for this is that it tends to cause net income to be higher in the early years than it would be using the accelerated methods and their high charges to depreciation expense.

Up until now, we have been speaking strictly in terms of recording information for financial statements. It is now time to consider the special tax treatment of depreciation.

EXHIBIT 9-1.

Comparison of Depreciation Methods

YEAR	STRAIGHT-LINE (ST. L)	DOUBLE DECLINING BALANCE (DDB)	SUM OF THE YEARS DIGITS (SYD)
1	$ 3,500	$ 8,000	$ 6,000
2	3,500	5,333	5,000
3	3,500	3,556	4,000
4	3,500	2,370	3,000
5	3,500	1,607	2,000
6	3,500	134	1,000
Total	$21,000	$21,000	$21,000

MODIFIED ACCELERATED COST RECOVERY SYSTEM (MACRS)

The Accelerated Cost Recovery System (ACRS) was enacted as part of the Economic Recovery Tax Act of 1981 and was revised by the Tax Equity and Fiscal Responsibility Act of 1982. Tax law revisions in 1986 replaced ACRS with the Modified Accelerated Cost Recovery System (MACRS). We will attempt to highlight some of the ACRS and MACRS tax rules and their implications, but will make no attempt to explain why a particular feature of the tax law was written as it was. Tax law is often based more on political compromise than accounting logic.

The first, and most important point that the reader should be aware of is that this is one place where you can actually have your cake and eat it too! It is not required that a firm use the same basis of depreciation for reporting to the Internal Revenue Service (IRS) as they use for reporting to their stockholders. The implications of that are enormous. We can use straight-line depreciation on our financial statements, thus keeping our depreciation expense relatively low, and be able to tell our stockholders that we had a very fine year. Then we can use accelerated depreciation, which is allowable under ACRS and MACRS, resulting in high depreciation expense. In the latter case, we tell the government that we had a bad year, and unfortunately can pay relatively little in taxes.

The changes in the tax law resulting from the 1981, 1982, and 1986 Acts are quite detailed. We will highlight many of the important issues here. However, we can't stress strongly enough the benefits of consulting a tax expert. Taxes are an area that requires up-to-date expertise. The tax law changes constantly not only because of congressional action, but also as a result of IRS rulings and interpretations, and the results of court cases. No tax decisions should be made based solely on the information contained in this book which provides only an overview of accounting and finance. A tax expert can review the circumstances concerning your particular firm and ensure that you both minimize your legal tax payments, and stay fully within the law in doing so.

ACRS and MACRS are both depreciation methods for tax purposes. The ACRS system governs depreciation for capital assets purchased after December 31, 1980, and before December 31, 1986. Assets purchased after December 31, 1986 fall under the provisions of MACRS. Therefore, we will focus most of our attention on the MACRS system. The most important aspect of ACRS and MACRS that represents a change from prior tax law is that they assign shorter lives to assets. Generally these shorter lives are not used in preparation of financial statements for reports to stockholders.

Under the MACRS and ACRS systems, the government assigns a life to your depreciable property. Not all assets are depreciable—for example, land supposedly lasts forever, so it cannot be depreciated, per se. Chapter 13 looks for a loophole with respect to the depreciation of land. The government also specifies your depreciation method.

The law does give some leeway in extending the life of the asset or choosing a less accelerated approach, but most firms find that the basic MACRS approach provides the quickest allowable deductions and therefore is beneficial in most cases. Remember that by accelerating a deduction, a profitable firm can push its tax payments off to the future, thus effectively getting an interest-free loan from the government.

Under MACRS asset lives are substantially shorter than their useful life estimates, and salvage value is ignored until we actually dispose of the asset. The government imposed lifetimes for depreciation under MACRS for different types of assets are three, five, seven, ten, fifteen, twenty, twenty-seven and a half, and thirty-one and a half years.

The three, five, seven, and ten year classes are depreciated under the 200% or double-declining balance system which substantially accelerates depreciation. The fifteen and twenty year classes are depreciated using a 150% declining balance method. The 27.5 and 31.5 year classes are depreciated on a straight-line basis.

The MACRS three-year category includes items that under prior rules were considered to have a life of four years or less. Specifically included in this class are some types of tractors, some equipment used for research and development, some machine tools, and racehorses more than two years old when placed into service. Leave it to Congress!

The MACRS five-year category includes property with a life of more than four, but less than 10 years. This class specifically includes computers, cars and light trucks, office machinery, and general purpose heavy duty trucks.

The MACRS seven-year class includes property that has a life of ten to fifteen years. This generally includes office furniture and fixtures.

The MACRS ten-year class is for property with a life of sixteen to nineteen years. Included are vessels, barges, and tugs. Note that special rules apply for depreciation of trees and vines bearing fruit or nuts that are placed in service after 1988. Such trees and vines are depreciated on a straight-line basis.

The MACRS fifteen-year class includes property with a life of twenty to twenty-four years. It also specifically includes certain types of public utility property.

The MACRS twenty-year class is for property with a useful life of 25 years or more, such as farm buildings.

Residential rental property falls into a 27.5 year class, and most non-residential real property has a class period of 31.5 years.

Although all of this may make your head swim, the government has kindly provided tables giving the percentage of the asset's cost to be taken as depreciation for tax purposes in each year of the asset's life. Exhibit 9-2 provides a table showing the portion of the asset to be depreciated each year under MACRS, for the 3 through 20 year classes. Note that the table contains 21 years because it is generally assumed that each asset (except real property) is put into service halfway into the year. The first and last years each contain only a half year of depreciation. (It should be noted as an aside, that there is a less favorable mid-quarter convention which applies if a substantial portion of a year's assets are placed into service in the last three months of the tax year.)

EXHIBIT 9-2.
MACRS Schedule for Property
Placed in Service after 1986

YEAR	APPROPRIATE PERCENTAGE					
	3-YEAR CLASS	5-YEAR CLASS	7-YEAR CLASS	10-YEAR CLASS	15-YEAR CLASS	20-YEAR CLASS
1	33.33	20.00	14.29	10.00	5.00	3.750
2	44.45	32.00	24.49	18.00	9.50	7.219
3	14.81	19.20	17.49	14.40	8.55	6.677
4	7.41	11.52	12.49	11.52	7.70	6.177
5		11.52	8.93	9.22	6.93	5.713
6		5.76	8.92	7.37	6.23	5.285
7			8.93	6.55	5.90	4.888
8			4.46	6.55	5.90	4.522
9				6.56	5.91	4.462
10				6.55	5.90	4.461
11				3.28	5.91	4.462
12					5.90	4.461
13					5.91	4.462
14					5.90	4.461
15					5.91	4.462
16					2.95	4.461
17						4.462
18						4.461
19						4.462
20						4.461
21						2.231

In some instances, it is possible to deduct in one tax year up to $10,000 of assets, rather than depreciating them under MACRS. This is an option available to the taxpayer for some types of property used in a trade or business. The available deduction is phased out if more than $200,000 worth of qualified property is placed into service during the tax year. To the extent that you can avail yourself of this rule, it can provide an even faster tax write-off of the asset than MACRS would generate.

What's the bottom line to all this? Essentially, you can base the income you report to your stockholders on straight-line depreciation extended over the asset's useful life and using a salvage value, and at the same time, use the ACRS/MACRS shortened life and in some cases accelerated depreciation methods for reporting to the IRS. Thus, you will tell your stockholders a net income that is higher than you tell the IRS. You therefore report relatively high income to the owners (your bosses), and yet pay relatively low taxes because of the higher depreciation reported to the government. Have you actually reduced your tax payments, or just shifted them off to the future? That is a very interesting question and one that is the basis for the discussion of deferred taxes in the next chapter.

KEY CONCEPTS

Matching—depreciation is an attempt to match the cost of resources used up over a period longer than one year with the revenues those resources generate over their useful lifetime.

Amortization—a generic term for the spreading out of costs over a period of time. Depreciation is a special case of amortization.

Amounts to be depreciated—the cost of an asset, less its salvage value, is depreciated over the asset's useful life. The cost is the fair market value at the time of acquisition, plus costs to put the asset into service, plus the costs of improvements made to the asset.

Depreciation methods—the asset may be depreciated on a straight-line basis, taking equal amounts in each year, or by an accelerated basis, which results in greater depreciation in the earlier years of the asset's life. Two common accelerated depreciation methods are double declining balance and sum-of-the-years digits.

Accelerated Cost Recovery System (ACRS) —the Economic Recovery Tax Act of 1981 created the ACRS method of depreciation. Under this law, depreciation for tax purposes is based on asset lifetimes significantly shorter than the useful life of the asset. In addition, it specifies allowable accelerated depreciation methods.

Modified Accelerated Cost Recovery System (MACRS) —a modification to ACRS effective for assets placed into service after 1986.

Ten

DEPRECIATION AND DEFERRED TAXES: ACCOUNTING MAGIC

Chapter 9 explained the use of straight-line depreciation for financial statements, and the use of the Modified Accelerated Cost Recovery System (MACRS) depreciation for the tax return. The fact that we can legally tell different depreciation stories to our stockholders and the Internal Revenue Service (IRS) has interesting ramifications upon the firm and its financial statements.

If we tell our stockholders that we had a good year, then they expect the firm to pay a lot of taxes on the profits we are currently making. And, even if we don't pay those taxes now, but instead defer payment to the future, the matching principle would seem to require that we record the expense for the taxes today, rather than later when they are paid. In fact, that is exactly the case. However, the implications of this *deferred tax* are quite unusual—almost magical.

A ONE-ASSET FIRM

The best way to see the full impact of deferred taxes is to look at an example. Let's assume that we have a firm with only one asset, and that the firm chooses to use straight-line depreciation for reporting to stockholders. Thus it uses straight-line on its *books* (the records for preparing financial statements for our stockholders). The firm uses the Modified Accelerated Cost Recovery System (MACRS) for its tax calculations.

For our example, we use a machine tool purchased and placed into service in 1991 with a cost of $9,000 including all costs to put it into service, and a salvage value of $1,000. It has a four-year useful life, but a three-year life under the MACRS depreciation system.

Assume that the firm has an annual income of $10,000 before calculating depreciation or taxes, and that the firm is in a 34 percent tax bracket. (At the time of the writing of this book, most corporations were subject to a tax rate of 34 percent. A firm with income of only $10,000 would be in a lower tax bracket. We are using 34 percent in this example for illustrative purposes, and because it is a rate paid by many corporations.) Further, assume that the asset is sold at the end of four years for exactly its $1,000 expected salvage value. Let's calculate first the depreciation and then the net income for each of the four years of the asset's life.

Exhibit 10-1 indicates that the straight-line depreciation would be $2,000 per year. This is based on a depreciable base of $8,000 (the $9,000 cost less the $1,000 salvage), divided by the four-year useful life. MACRS depreciation for the four-year useful life is $3,000 in the first year, $4,000 in the second year, $1,333 in the third year, and $667 in the fourth year. The MACRS depreciation is based on the percentages in Exhibit 9-3 for three-year MACRS property. The depreciation under MACRS is lower in the first year than the second year because of the half-year convention MACRS uses for first-year depreciation. All assets are generally assumed to be purchased at midyear under the MACRS system. Therefore, there is also a half-year of depreciation in the fourth year, 1994.

In Exhibit 10-1 the depreciation totals over the four-year period are not the same. This differs from the result observed in Chapter 9 in Exhibit 9-1. This is because the MACRS method ignores salvage value until we actually dispose of the asset. Not only does

EXHIBIT 10-1.
Annual Depreciation

YEAR	BOOKS (STRAIGHT-LINE)	TAX-RETURN (MACRS)
1991	$2,000	$3,000
1992	2,000	4,000
1993	2,000	1,333
1994	2,000	667
Total	$8,000	$9,000

MACRS depreciate the asset faster (that is, more depreciation in the early years), but it actually charges a greater total amount of depreciation (in this case $9,000 instead of $8,000).

What are the implications of the two depreciation calculations in Exhibit 10-1? By looking at Exhibit 10-2, we can see tax calculations for all four years for both our books and our tax returns. The tax calculations per books provide the information that is reported to stockholders. Each year is identical because we have used the straight-line method of depreciation.

Our tax returns don't show quite the same picture as our financial reports. First, there is a gain on the sale of the equipment. This gain is called depreciation recapture. During the four years we took $9,000 of depreciation for taxes, ignoring the salvage value. By ignoring salvage value, we were estimating that there would be no value to the asset when we disposed of it. Therefore, when we sell the property at the end of its useful life to us, any proceeds must be reported as a gain for tax purposes.

Note that the extra $1,000 of depreciation we took on our tax return as compared to our books ($9,000 vs. $8,000) exactly equals the gain. The IRS is recapturing the extra depreciation that we had taken in earlier years. For our financial statements there is no gain, because we took only $8,000 of depreciation on the asset that had cost us $9,000. The asset had a remaining value on our books of $1,000; exactly the amount we sold it for. Although recapture of depreciation means that we wind up repaying the government the tax savings we had achieved by taking the extra thousand dollars of depreciation, we have had the benefit of deferring part of that payment for a period of time.

In years one and two of the asset's life, the combination of the shorter life, the extra $1,000 of depreciation, and the MACRS accelerated system provide a greater amount of depreciation each year on our tax return, than appears on our financial statements. That lowers our tax currently due. You can see that in each of the first two years our actual tax payment is less than the amount we report as taxes to our stockholders. But will the total tax paid be lower over the life of the asset? No. Notice that in either case the total tax for the four years combined is $10,880. The only difference is *when* we pay the taxes.

Time, literally, is money. If we can postpone payment of taxes, with no other change in the operation of our business in any respect, then we are better off doing so. This postponement assumes we are in a fairly stable tax bracket, or at least not in a sharply rising tax bracket, in which case having the deduction in the future might save more taxes than the value of having the money for the interim period. Time is money because if we promise to pay the government later, instead of now, we can take the money we would have paid the IRS and invest it in some profitable opportunity for the interim.

Exhibit 10-2 shows the deferred tax each year. This is simply the difference between the amount of tax expense reported to our stockholders and the amount of tax we actually pay each year. In the first two years, the deferral is a positive amount. In the next two, the tax that had been deferred is paid to the government. Thus the change in the deferred tax account balance is negative in those years.

If we don't actually pay $2,720 each year, then aren't our financial statements giving the stockholders incorrect information when they report our annual tax expense? The statements show more expense than we are paying in the first two years and less than we are paying in the last two! For example, Exhibit 10-2 shows that in 1991 our financial statements report taxes of $2,720 to our stockholders, but according to our tax calculation we only pay the IRS $2,380! This difference is the result of the application of the matching principle. From an operations point of view, each of our four years was identical. Every aspect of the business is unchanged except for taxes paid. If we generate equal revenues each year, and have equal other ex-

EXHIBIT 10-2.
Comparison of Taxes per Books and Tax Returns

PER BOOKS	YEAR 1991	1992	1993	1994	FOUR YEAR TOTAL
Income Before Depreciation & Taxes	$10,000	$10,000	$10,000	$10,000	$40,000
Less Depreciation (Exhibit 10-1)	2,000	2,000	2,000	2,000	8,000
Pretax Income	$ 8,000	$ 8,000	$ 8,000	$ 8,000	$32,000
Tax Expense at 34% (a)	$ 2,720	$ 2,720	$ 2,720	$ 2,720	$10,880

PER TAX RETURNS					
Income Before Gain on Sale of Tool	$10,000	$10,000	$10,000	$10,000	$40,000
Add Gain on Sale				1,000	1,000
Income Before Depreciation & Taxes	$10,000	$10,000	$10,000	$11,000	$41,000
Less Depreciation (Exhibit 10-1)	3,000	4,000	1,333	667	9,000
Pretax Income	$ 7,000	$ 6,000	$ 8,667	$10,333	$32,000
Tax Paid at 34% (b)	$ 2,380	$ 2,040	$ 2,947	$ 3,513	$10,880
Deferred Tax Each Year (a) − (b)	$ 340	$ 680	$ (227)	$ (793)	
Cumulative Deferred Tax Balance	$ 340	$ 1,020	$ 793	$ 0	$ 0

penses each year, then an appropriate matching would allocate the taxes equally each year. That's what happens in the "books" section of Exhibit 10-2.

Essentially Congress, through the tax law, has produced a "pay me later" result. We pay the same amount in total, but just shift part of the payments to the latter years of an asset's life.

The accountant's interpretation is that the financial statement shows our tax expense correctly, however we are simply paying part now and part later. This is like purchasing any resource and paying part of the price now and part later. If we fully use the resource this period it becomes an expense this period, even though we haven't yet fully paid for it. For example, a worker may work today and generate a sale. If at year-end we have not yet paid the worker, we still record a labor or wage expense. We also record a liability to pay the worker, called wages payable. The amount of taxes due in the future instead of currently due is referred to as a deferred tax liability. The entire tax expense related to this year's income is therefore recorded this period.

According to Exhibit 10-2, in 1991 our accountant tells our stockholders that our taxes are $2,720, but we only have to pay the government $2,380. We are deferring payment of $340 to some point in the future. In 1992, we tell our stockholders that we have taxes of $2,720, but we only pay $2,040. We are deferring an additional $680. At the end of 1992, we owe the government a cumulative total of $1,020 ($340 from 1991 plus $680 from 1992). Yet we are not changing our total taxes, but simply altering the timing of the payments.

In 1993, we tell our stockholders that our taxes are $2,720, but we pay $2,947. At the end of 1992, we owed $1,020 in deferred taxes. In 1993, we decrease that by $227 so that the deferred tax balance is $793. In 1994 we tell our stockholders that our current taxes are $2,720, but we pay $3,513. The extra $793 paid to the government in 1994 is exactly the deferred tax balance that we had at the end of 1993. The result is that after the asset's useful life is complete, we have paid exactly the same total amount to the government as we reported to our stockholders. In that case was there any benefit from deferred taxes? Yes, we had the use of the government's money interest-free for several years.

The deferred tax account is shown like a long-term liability on the balance sheet. For any one asset, the deferred tax loan will be repaid to the government. However, what is true for one asset is not necessarily true for the entire firm. For many companies the balance in the deferred tax account will not become zero, but rather will grow continuously into the future. We will now discuss how that can happen.

DEFERRED TAXES FOR THE MULTI-ASSET FIRM

By looking at the one tool example, we can see the advantage of having a free loan from the government. However, what happens if the firm is growing and buys a new machine tool each year? For this example we use tools just like the one previously described: $9,000 cost; $1,000 salvage; and a four-year useful life.

In Exhibit 10-1, we calculated the depreciation for this tool as being $2,000 per year using the straight-line method for our books, that is for reporting to stockholders. We also found that the MACRS depreciation for each of the four years of the useful life of this asset would be $3,000 for the first year, $4,000 for the second year, $1,333 for the third year, and $667 the fourth year. Now assume that income before depreciation and taxes is growing by $10,000 per year. We will need this information momentarily.

In 1991 we own one tool; in 1992 we have two tools; and so on. If the firm is to continue its growth, in the fifth year, 1995, it will have to buy two tools—one for continued expansion and another one to replace the tool purchased in 1991 and sold for its salvage value at the end of 1994.

What will happen to our deferred liability as time passes and we accumulate tools? Exhibit 10-3 shows what will happen through 1995. Note that the 1991 results are exactly the same as those obtained in Exhibit 10-2 for 1991. At this point, we have a deferred tax balance of $340. In 1992, we will have two tools, and their effect on deferred taxes is an increase of $1,020. This is the result of a $680 increase in the deferral caused by the tool purchased in 1991 (see Exhibit 10-2 for the impact on the deferral caused by one tool in the second year of its life), plus a $340 increase in the deferral caused by the new, 1992 tool (see Exhibit 10-2 for the impact on the deferral caused by one tool in the first year of its life).

After two years we have a combined cumulative deferral on the two tools that equals $1,360. In 1993 we buy another tool. During 1993, our first tool that was purchased in 1991 will be in its third year. According to Exhibit 10-2, in the third year of a tool's life, there is a reduction in the deferral balance of $227. The tool purchased in 1992 will be in its second year, and will be causing the deferral to increase by $680. The new tool, just purchased in 1993 will be in its first year and will result in an additional deferral of

$340. The total effect of the depreciation in 1993 for the three tools combined is to increase the deferral by $793. This means that at the end of 1993 the balance in the deferred tax account will be $2,153.

The year 1994 is a transitional year for the deferral account. We now have four tools—one in each of the four years of their useful life. In 1994, the newest two tools will result in increases in the deferral account of $340 and $680. Meanwhile, the older two will be at a stage in their depreciable life whereby they will cause a reduction in the deferral account of $1,020 (see Exhibit 10-2 for the impact each year of a 4 year life on the deferred tax balance). It turns out that there is no net effect on the deferral account in this year!

This rather amazing result is simply explained. If we had one tool over the full four years of its lifetime, we would first defer some tax and later repay it. We have already noted that for any one asset, we get a change in the timing of tax payments, but pay the same exact total amount of tax over the asset's lifetime. With four tools, one of which is one year old, one of which is two years old, one of which is three years old, and one of which is four years old, we get the same total effect in one year for the four tools combined, as we would get for one tool over its full four-year life. However, the magic of deferred taxes is not yet fully apparent.

Consider what happens in 1995 when we buy one tool to replace the 1991 tool that is already fully depreciated and sold, and we buy a second one to maintain our rate of growth. That way we will have five productive tools in the fifth year. In Exhibit 10-3 we see that in 1995 the deferred tax increases by $340!

The first tool was purchased in 1991 and was sold in 1994. Therefore it has no depreciation for 1995. Nevertheless, the cumulative tax deferral increased during 1995! In fact, for a growing company, it is generally true that the deferred tax liability will constantly be increasing, and will never be paid back. This is because the accelerated depreciation on the two new tools will more than keep pace with the lower depreciation and the taxable gain on the sale of the old ones. The startling result is that for growing companies deferred taxes represent a permanent interest-free loan! A touch of accounting magic.

What about a company in a steady-state, neither growing nor contracting in productive capacity. That is the case presented in

EXHIBIT 10-3.
Comparison of Taxes per Books and Tax Returns for a Growing Firm

PER BOOKS	YEAR 1991	1992	1993	1994	1995
Income Before Depreciation & Taxes	$10,000	$20,000	$30,000	$40,000	$50,000
Less Depreciation on Tool Purchased in:					
1991	$ 2,000	$ 2,000	$ 2,000	$ 2,000	
1992		2,000	2,000	2,000	$ 2,000
1993			2,000	2,000	2,000
1994				2,000	2,000
1995 (2 tools)					4,000
Total Depreciation	$ 2,000	$ 4,000	$ 6,000	$ 8,000	$10,000
Pretax Income	$ 8,000	$16,000	$24,000	$32,000	$40,000
Tax Expense at 34% (a)	$ 2,720	$ 5,440	$ 8,160	$10,880	$13,600

PER TAX RETURNS

	1991	1992	1993	1994	1995
Income Before Gain on Sale of Tool	$10,000	$20,000	$30,000	$40,000	$50,000
Add Gain on Sale				1,000	1,000
Income Before Depreciation & Taxes	$10,000	$20,000	$30,000	$41,000	$51,000
Less Depreciation on Tool Purchased in:					
1991	$ 3,000	$ 4,000	$ 1,333	$ 667	
1992		3,000	4,000	1,333	$ 667
1993			3,000	4,000	1,333
1994				3,000	4,000
1995 (2 tools)					6,000
Total Depreciation	$ 3,000	$ 7,000	$ 8,333	$ 9,000	$12,000
Pretax Income	$ 7,000	$13,000	$21,667	$32,000	$39,000
Tax Paid at 34% (b)	$ 2,380	$ 4,420	$ 7,367	$10,880	$13,260
Deferred Tax Each Year (a) – (b)	$ 340	$ 1,020	$ 793	$ 0	$ 340
Cumulative Deferred Tax Balance	$ 340	$ 1,360	$ 2,153	$ 2,153	$ 2,493

Exhibit 10-4. In this exhibit, it is assumed that the company levels off in 1994 at four tools, and an income each year of $40,000 before depreciation and taxes. Once the firm reaches a level of four productive tools, it enters a steady-state, each year replacing one tool as it wears out. The firm neither expands nor contracts its productive capacity. Note from Exhibit 10-4 that once the firm reaches a steady-state in 1994, the deferred liability isn't growing, but it isn't being repaid either! It will go on this way, neither increasing nor decreasing, indefinitely. Effectively, each year one tool wears out and is sold, and one tool is purchased. The impact of the four tools, one in each year of its life, will exactly balance out in total for books and taxes. The deferral remains a liability, never growing, nor being paid. It is a permanent interest-free loan from the government.

In fact, suppose that society were undergoing a period of inflation, not a totally unreasonable assumption. Then it is likely that we will be replacing assets as they wear out with more expensive units. The result of inflation would be that the MACRS depreciation on new assets would be greater than it had been on the older assets. Thus, for a steady-state firm during inflation, the deferral will actually be increasing gradually over time.

What if our firm is actually declining in size? When a tool wears out, we don't replace it. Thus it's assumed that the firm has grown until it has four tools. But in the fifth year, not only is the firm not buying a tool for expansion, but also it isn't buying one to replace the tool wearing out that year. Also, income before depreciation and taxes is assumed to decline in a pro-rata fashion with the number of working tools.

In that case, we may well be repaying the deferred liability to the government. But then again, maybe we won't. Exhibit 10-5 presents the basic effect of not replacing assets during the fifth year. As you can see, apparently $340 will have to be repaid to the government in 1995. We say apparently because we are concerned with why the firm hasn't been replacing its assets as they wear out.

One major reason that firms contract in productive capacity is that they are losing money. But that's Catch-22. If you're losing money, then the $340 will not be repaid because firms only pay taxes when they have profits. Instead of repaying the $340, the firm will simply report to the IRS a loss smaller than otherwise would have been the case. As long as you are losing money, the deferral

EXHIBIT 10-4.

Comparison of Taxes per Books and Tax Returns for a Steady-State Firm

	YEAR				
PER BOOKS	1991	1992	1993	1994	1995
Income Before Depreciation & Taxes	$10,000	$20,000	$30,000	$40,000	$40,000
Less Depreciation on Tool Purchased in:					
1991	$ 2,000	$ 2,000	$ 2,000	$ 2,000	
1992		2,000	2,000	2,000	$ 2,000
1993			2,000	2,000	2,000
1994				2,000	2,000
1995 (1 tool)					2,000
Total Depreciation	$ 2,000	$ 4,000	$ 6,000	$ 8,000	$ 8,000
Pretax Income	$ 8,000	$16,000	$24,000	$32,000	$32,000
Tax Expense at 34% (a)	$ 2,720	$ 5,440	$ 8,160	$10,880	$10,880

PER TAX RETURNS					
Income Before Gain on Sale of Tool	$10,000	$20,000	$30,000	$40,000	$40,000
Add Gain on Sale				1,000	1,000
Income Before Depreciation & Taxes	$10,000	$20,000	$30,000	$41,000	$41,000
Less Depreciation on Tool Purchased in:					
1991	$ 3,000	$ 4,000	$ 1,333	$ 667	
1992		3,000	4,000	1,333	$ 667
1993			3,000	4,000	1,333
1994				3,000	4,000
1995 (1 tool)					3,000
Total Depreciation	$ 3,000	$ 7,000	$ 8,333	$ 9,000	$ 9,000
Pretax Income	$ 7,000	$13,000	$21,667	$32,000	$32,000
Tax Paid at 34% (b)	$ 2,380	$ 4,420	$ 7,367	$10,880	$10,880
Deferred Tax Each Year (a) – (b)	$ 340	$ 1,020	$ 793	$ 0	$ 0
Cumulative Deferred Tax Balance	$ 340	$ 1,360	$ 2,153	$ 2,153	$ 2,153

EXHIBIT 10-5.

Comparison of Taxes per Books and Tax Returns for a Firm Contracting Starting in 1995

PER BOOKS	YEAR				
	1991	1992	1993	1994	1995
Income Before Depreciation & Taxes	$10,000	$20,000	$30,000	40,000	$30,000
Less Depreciation on Tool Purchased in:					
1991	$ 2,000	$ 2,000	$ 2,000	$ 2,000	
1992		2,000	2,000	2,000	$ 2,000
1993			2,000	2,000	2,000
1994				2,000	2,000
1995 (0 tools)					0
Total Depreciation	$ 2,000	$ 4,000	$ 6,000	$ 8,000	$ 6,000
Pretax Income	$ 8,000	$16,000	$24,000	$32,000	$24,000
Tax Expense at 34% (a)	$ 2,720	$ 5,440	$ 8,160	$10,880	$ 8,160

PER TAX RETURNS					
Income Before Gain on Sale of Tool	$10,000	$20,000	$30,000	$40,000	$30,000
Add Gain on Sale				1,000	1,000
Income Before Depreciation & Taxes	$10,000	$20,000	$30,000	$41,000	$31,000
Less Depreciation on Tool Purchased in:					
1991	$ 3,000	$ 4,000	$ 1,333	$ 667	
1992		3,000	4,000	1,333	$ 667
1993			3,000	4,000	1,333
1994				3,000	4,000
1995 (0 tools)					0
Total Depreciation	$ 3,000	$ 7,000	$ 8,333	$ 9,000	$ 6,000
Pretax Income	$ 7,000	$13,000	$21,667	$32,000	$25,000
Tax Paid at 34% (b)	$ 2,380	$ 4,420	$ 7,367	$10,880	$ 8,500
Deferred Tax Each Year (a) – (b)	$ 340	$ 1,020	$ 793	$ 0	$ (340)
Cumulative Deferred Tax Balance	$ 340	$ 1,360	$ 2,153	$ 2,153	$ 1,813

will not be repaid. And you thought only magicians were adept at sleight of hand!

What if you are in fact a profitable, although contracting firm. The demand for your product is declining, but the units sold are sold at a good profit. In that case, you'd better watch out on three accounts. The first is that you will be repaying the deferral, something you don't really want to do. The second is that your firm is eventually going to go out of business as demand continues to decline, unless you find a new product. If you do find a new product, you will probably start growing again, and thus avoid repayment of the tax. Finally, you are not likely to remain a single firm. A marriage is highly likely. A growing firm is apt to try to take you over, or perhaps you will try to take over a growing firm. Your profitability, combined with their growth will result in one combined firm that pays less taxes than the two firms acting as two separate companies. Further, your profits are generating cash that is not needed for reinvestment. Whenever such a situation exists, a merger or acquisition is quite attractive.

SUMMARY

Let's summarize the situation with respect to deferred taxes. Depreciation represents the major, although not the only, source of timing differences between taxes as reported on financial statements and actual tax payments. (Other timing differences are discussed later in the book.) Although for any one asset the effect of depreciation is first a deferral of taxes and then later a repayment of those taxes, this is not necessarily the case for the firm as a whole. Deferral of taxes, due to new equipment purchases, will offset amounts expected to be repaid to the government as equipment purchased earlier becomes older. This may not always be the case. For example, if we have significant periods of time when we do not have to purchase any equipment because the actual useful life of our equipment far exceeds the period of time over which we can depreciate it, then we may be repaying some of the deferral during that period. That should not cause a serious concern. Even if we have to repay some of the interest-free loan, we were better off having it as long as we did.

For most firms, however, capital expenditures continue at a fairly smooth level over time, either at a constant or growing rate. For those firms, significant portions of the deferral are never repaid, even if equipment is lasting far longer than its estimated useful life. Therefore, on most balance sheets we can expect that the liabilities are overstated because of their inclusion of deferred taxes.

If the firm is actually declining in productive capacity, then the deferral will be repaid if the firm is profitable. However, if the firm is making money and is repaying the deferral, then the existence of a large deferred tax liability presents an opportunity for a mutually beneficial merger. If the firm is losing money, then the deferral will not be repaid. A bit more of accounting magic.

KEY CONCEPTS

Deferred taxes—if the pretax income reported to stockholders is more than that reported to the Internal Revenue Service, then a tax deferral will arise; that is, some of our current tax expense remains as a liability to be paid at some unstated time in the future, rather than being paid currently.

One asset—for any one asset it is generally true that the deferred tax is eventually paid.

Multi-asset—for a firm constantly retiring some equipment and adding new equipment, it is possible that the deferred tax may never be paid.

Eleven

INVENTORY COSTING: THE ACCOUNTANT'S WORLD OF MAKE-BELIEVE

THE INVENTORY EQUATION

Inventories are merely a stock of goods held for use in production, or for sale or resale. Retailers and wholesalers have merchandise inventory. They buy a product basically in the same form as that in which it is sold. Manufacturers have several classes of inventory—raw materials that are used in the manufacturing process to make a final product; work in process that consists of goods on which production has begun that has not yet been finished; and finished goods that are complete and awaiting sale.

This chapter takes the view of a merchandising firm to simplify the discussion, although the principles apply equally as well to manufacturing firms. Just as there is a basic equation of accounting, there is a basic equation for keeping track of inventory and its cost.

$$\text{Beginning Inventory (BI)} + \text{Units Purchased (P)} - \text{Units Sold (S)} = \text{Ending Inventory (EI)}$$

This equation can be understood from a reasonably intuitive point of view. Consider a firm selling clay statuettes. At the start of the year, they have 1,000 statuettes. During the year, they buy 4,000 statuettes. If they sell 3,000 statuettes, how many will be left at the end of the year?

$$BI + P - S = EI$$
$$1,000 + 4,000 - 3,000 = 2,000$$

We can readily see that there should be 2,000 statuettes on hand at year-end.

PERIODIC VS. PERPETUAL INVENTORY METHODS

Firms must make a major decision about the fashion in which they intend to keep track of the four items in the inventory equation. Beginning inventory poses no problem because it is the year-end balance from the previous year. This year's beginning inventory is always last year's ending inventory. All accounting systems are designed so as to keep track of purchases. A problem centers around the cost of goods sold and ending inventory.

If we wish, we can keep track of specifically how much of each of our products is sold. However, this requires a fair amount of bookkeeping. Certainly we keep track of the total dollars of sales from each transaction, but that in itself does not tell which goods (if our firm has more than one product) or how many are sold. Consider a hardware store that stocks thousands of small items. To record which items and how many of each are being sold could more than double the time it takes to ring up each sale. This could mean paying for at least twice as many cash register clerks.

A far simpler approach is to simply wait until year-end and then count what is left. Once we know the ending inventory, we can use our inventory equation to determine how many units of each product were sold. For example, if we started with 1,000 statuettes and purchased 4,000, then a year-end count of 2,000 on hand would indicate that we had sold 3,000 during the year.

$$\text{If:} \quad BI + P - S = EI$$
$$1,000 + 4,000 - S = 2,000$$
$$\text{then} \quad S = 3,000.$$

This method is called the *periodic method of inventory*. It requires us to take a physical count to find out what we have on hand at any point in time. It gets this name because we keep track of inventory from time to time, or periodically.

A major weakness of the periodic system is that at any point in time we don't know how much inventory we've sold and how much we have left. Therefore, our control over our inventory is rather limited. If running out of an item creates a serious problem, this method is inadequate. For example, if we cannot supply a major customer with a minor spare part, we may lose a substantial amount of future business.

There are several easy solutions to that problem in some situations. If parts are kept in a bin or a barrel, we can paint a stripe two-thirds of the way down the bin or barrel. When we see the stripe, we know it's time to reorder. Bookstores often solve this problem by placing a reorder card in a book near the bottom of the pile. When that book is sold an order is made to replenish the stock.

The periodic method has other weaknesses as well. Although we calculate a figure for units sold based on the three other elements of the inventory equation, we don't know for sure that just because a unit of inventory isn't on hand, it was sold. It may have broken, spoiled, evaporated, or been stolen. However, proponents of periodic inventory contend that all of those situations are a normal cost of doing business. If we treat those units as if they had been sold, then their cost winds up as part of the cost of goods sold expense. This is a reasonable place for such costs to be included. On the other hand, this means you have very little idea of how much really is being broken, stolen, and so on, and that takes away an element of control over your operations.

An alternative to periodic inventory accounting is the *perpetual method* for keeping track of units of inventory. Just as the name implies, you always, or perpetually, know how much inventory you have, because you specifically record each item. This method has been considered appropriate for companies selling relatively few high-priced items. In such cases, it is relatively inexpensive to keep track of each sale relative to the dollar value of the sale. Furthermore, control of inventory tends to be a more important issue with high-priced items.

Which of the two methods is considered more useful? Clearly the perpetual method gives more information and better control.

However, it also adds substantial bookkeeping cost. Most firms would choose perpetual if they could get it for the same money as periodic, but typically they can't. The result is a management decision as to whether the extra benefits of perpetual are worth the extra cost.

Recently, computers have been making significant inroads in allowing firms to switch to perpetual inventory without incurring prohibitively high costs. For example, supermarkets have been a classic example of the type of firm that couldn't afford perpetual inventory. Imagine a checkout clerk in the supermarket manually writing down each item as it's sold. The clerk rings up one can of peas, and then turns and writes down "one can of 6 ounce Green Midget peas." Then the clerk rings up one can of corn, and turns and writes down, "one can of 4 ounce House Brand corn," and so on. At the end of the day, another clerk would tally up the manual logs of each check-out clerk. The cost of this would be enormous. In such a situation, a firm would just keep track of total dollars of sales, and would take periodic inventories to see what is still on hand. Yet supermarkets run on extremely tight margins, so they can ill afford to run out of goods, nor can they afford the carrying cost of excess inventory.

Today we see more and more retail stores making use of the thin and thick black lines you see on many products, called the Uniform Price Code (UPC) or bar codes. These computer sensitive markings allow the store to save the cost of stamping the price on goods. The computer that reads the lines knows how much the price of each item is so the clerk no longer needs to see a stamped price. It also allows the clerk to ring up the goods at a much faster pace. Finally, it automatically updates the inventory. In many of the supermarkets using this system, the cash register tape gives you more information than just the price. Not only does it tell you that you bought a 4 ounce container of yogurt, but also that it was blueberry yogurt. That detailed information is available to the consumer because the computer needs the information to tell the purchasing department specifically the size, brand, and flavor of yogurt to be restocked. The potential time saved in stamping prices on goods and in the check-out process can offset much of the cost of the computerized system. On the other hand, many consumers have objected successfully to not being able to see the price on the items they are purchasing. As a result, many stores using the UPC still stamp prices on goods. The potential savings must be weighed against losses in customer satisfaction in addition to the direct costs of the computer system.

It should be noted that even on a perpetual system there is a need to physically count inventory from time to time (typically at least once a year). The perpetual method keeps track of what was sold. If there is pilferage or breakage, our inventory records will not be correct. However, when we use a perpetual system, we know what we should have. When we count our inventory, we can determine the extent to which goods that have not been sold are missing.

THE PROBLEM OF INFLATION

The periodic and perpetual methods of inventory tracking help us to determine the quantity of goods on hand and the quantity sold. Inflation has resulted in a great deal of attention being paid to another inventory problem—the determination of which units were sold and which units are on hand. Consider the following situation.

	QUANTITY	COST
Beginning Inventory	10,000	$100 each
Purchase March 1	10,000	110 each
Purchase June 1	10,000	120 each
Purchase September 1	10,000	130 each
Sales during year	30,000	

How many units are left in stock? Clearly from our basic inventory equation the answer to that is 10,000. Beginning inventory of 10,000, plus the purchases of 30,000, less the sales of 30,000 leaves ending inventory of 10,000. What is the value of those 10,000 units? Here a problem arises. Which 10,000 units are left? Does it matter? From an accounting point of view it definitely does matter. In Chapter 4 we noted that generally accepted accounting principles require us to value items on the balance sheet at their cost. In order to know the cost of our remaining units, we must know which units we sold and which are still on hand.

What would be the significance of arbitrarily stating that the units on hand were ones that cost $130 each, when perhaps they really are units we bought for $120 each back in June? For one thing we would overstate the inventory (and therefore assets) on the balance sheet by $10 per unit for 10,000 units, or $100,000. At the same time, we would be saying that we sold units that cost us $120 each, when the units we really sold were the ones that cost $130. The result would be to understate the cost of goods sold by $100,000. Understatement of an expense results in overstatement of net income. Thus both the balance sheet and income statement will be out of whack.

If we were content to merely report the quantity of units sold and the quantity of units on hand, we would have no need to know which were sold. However, the monetary restriction made in Chapter 2 requires that we assign dollar values to such financial statement items as inventory. If there had been no inflation, all of the units probably would have cost us the same $100 each. Once again, it really wouldn't matter which units had been sold if they all cost the same amount. It is the combination of the monetary restriction, plus inflation, plus the generally accepted accounting principles that require the valuation of assets at what they cost, which results in our need to know not only how many, but also which units are still on hand and which units have been sold.

COST-FLOW ASSUMPTIONS

The methods for determining which units were sold and which are on hand are referred to as *cost-flow assumptions*. There are four major alternative cost-flow assumptions.

Specific Identification. This is the accountant's ideal. It entails physically tagging each unit in some way so that we can specifically identify the units on hand with their cost. Then, when a periodic inventory is taken, we can determine the cost of all the units on hand and therefore deduce the cost of the units sold.

As you might expect, for most businesses such tagging would create a substantial additional bookkeeping cost. Think of the supermarket not just trying to keep track of how many cans of peas are sold, but also the specific cans. Can any type of business go to this effort? Certainly some can—typically those firms that keep close track of serial numbers for the items sold. For example, a car dealership only buys a few units at a time. The invoice the dealership receives for each car indicates a serial number. When the dealer sells a car he also records the serial number. At the end of the accounting period, it is not overly burdensome for the dealer to determine specifically which units are on hand and which were sold.

First-In, First-Out (FIFO). The second most common cost-flow approach is called first-in, first-out, and is almost always referred to by the shorthand acronym FIFO. This method allows you to keep track of the flow of inventory without tagging each item. It is based on the fact that in most industries inventory moves in an orderly fashion. We can think of a factory or a warehouse as a building with a front door and a back door. Raw materials or new deliveries of merchandise are received at the back door and put on a conveyor belt. They move along the conveyor belt and right out the front door. We would never have occasion to skip one unit ahead of the other items already on the conveyor belt ahead of it.

A good example of FIFO is a dairy. It is clear that the dairy would always prefer to sell the milk that comes out of the cow today, before they sell the milk that the cow produces tomorrow. We've all seen in the supermarket that the fresh milk is put on the back of the shelf so that we will purchase the older milk from the front of the shelf first. Of course, we know the fresh milk is in the back so we sometimes reach back to get it. But then, they know we know so they sometimes. . . . Nevertheless, the point is clear—their desire is for us to buy the oldest milk first; they want to sell the milk in a FIFO fashion.

In most industries there is a desire to avoid winding up with old, shopworn, obsolete, dirty goods. Therefore, FIFO makes reasonable sense as an approach for processing inventory.

Weighted Average (W.A.). The weighted average approach to inventory cost-flows assumes that all of our inventory gets commingled and there is no way to determine which units we are selling. For example, consider a gas station that fills up its underground tanks with gasoline costing $1.20 per gallon. A week later when the tanks are half full they are refilled with additional gasoline costing $1.40 per gallon. When we now sell gasoline to a customer, are we selling gallons that cost the gas station $1.20 or $1.40? Because there is really no way to know, the weighted average method assumes that all of the gasoline has been thoroughly mixed, and therefore the gas being sold cost $1.30 per gallon. This method would be appropriate whenever the inventory gets stirred or mixed together and it is physically impossible to determine what has been sold.

Last-In, First-Out (LIFO). The last of the four methods of cost-flow for inventory is last-in, first-out, which has received much attention in the last decade. The LIFO method is just the reverse of the FIFO method. It assumes that the last goods we receive are the first goods we ship. In the case of the dairy it would mean that we always would try to sell the freshest milk first and keep the older, souring milk in our warehouse.

Does the LIFO method make sense for any industries at all? Yes. In fact it is the logical approach to use for any industry that piles their goods up as they arrive, and then sells from the top of the pile. For example, a company mining coal or making chemicals frequently piles them up and then simply sells from the top of the pile. However, for most firms it doesn't provide a very logical inventory movement. Nevertheless, a large number of firms have shifted from the FIFO method to the LIFO method. Why?

COMPARISON OF THE LIFO AND FIFO COST FLOW ASSUMPTIONS

Financial statements are not ideally suited for inflationary environments. During inflation we have problems trying to report inventory without creating distortions in at least one key financial statement.

Consider an example in which we buy one unit of inventory on January 2 for $10 and another unit of inventory on December 30 for $20. On December 31, we sell a unit for $30. What happens to the financial statements if we are using the FIFO method of inventory tracking? The FIFO method means that the inventory that is first-in is the inventory that is the first-out. The January 2 purchase was the first one in, so the cost of the unit sold is $10 and the cost of the unit remaining on hand is $20 (the December purchase). Is the balance sheet a fair representation of current value? It says that we have one unit of inventory that cost $20. What would it cost to buy a unit of inventory near year-end? Well, we bought one on December 30 for $20, so the balance sheet seems pretty accurate.

However, consider the income statement under FIFO. We presumably sold the first-in, which cost $10, for a selling price of $30, leaving us with a $20 profit. Is that a good indication of the profit we could currently earn from the purchase and sale of a unit of inventory? Not really. At year-end we could have bought a unit for $20 and sold it for $30, leaving a profit of only $10. Thus, during periods of rising prices, the FIFO method does not give users of financial statements a current picture of the profit opportunities facing the firm.

We do not have that problem with LIFO. Under LIFO, the last-in is the first-out, which means that we sold the unit that was purchased on December 30. That unit had cost us $20, and by selling it for $30 we realize a profit of $10. When we tell our stockholders that our profit was $10, we are giving them a reasonably current picture of the profit we can currently make by buying and selling a unit.

Unfortunately this gives rise to another problem. Under LIFO, we have sold the unit which cost $20, so we must have held onto the unit that cost $10. Therefore, the inventory number to be shown on the balance sheet is $10. Is it true that we could currently go out and buy more inventory for $10 a unit? No, by year-end the price we pay was already up to $20. So, under LIFO the value of inventory on the balance sheet is understated.

There is no readily available solution to this problem. The weighted average method simply leaves both the balance sheet and income statements somewhat out of whack, instead of causing a somewhat bigger problem with respect to one or the other, as results under LIFO and FIFO. In the face of this problem, firms have shifted to LIFO for a very simple reason: to save taxes.

Let's take a second to consider the implications of our example. If we use a FIFO system during inflationary periods, we report a pretax profit of $20 because we have sold a unit that cost $10 for $30. Under LIFO, we report a pretax profit of only $10 because we have sold a unit that cost $20 for $30. Therefore, by being on the LIFO system, we can reduce our tax payments. Are the tax savings worth the fact that we will be reporting lowered profits on our financial statements? That question is a complex one and the response requires the following example of LIFO-FIFO, Inc.

In order for you to fully grasp the issues, you are hereby promoted to president and sole owner of LIFO-FIFO, Inc. For some reason, managers often worry that although something makes good sense to them the owners won't like it. By viewing this problem from the point of view of the owner of the firm as well as manager, you can more immediately understand whether LIFO is in the best interests of the owners of the firm. Exhibits 11-1 through 11-3 give the balance sheet for LIFO-FIFO, Inc. at the beginning of 1992, a detailed listing of purchases and sales for 1992, and income statements for 1992 under the LIFO and FIFO alternatives.

The Exhibit 11-1 balance sheet allows us to think of LIFO-FIFO, Inc., as if it had just been formed at the beginning of the year and has a clean slate. You, the owner, have invested $500 cash in exchange for all of the common stock of the firm. The firm does not owe anyone any money, and its assets are all in cash. As an owner, you hope that the firm will be more valuable at the end of the year than it is at the beginning.

EXHIBIT 11-1.
LIFO-FIFO, Inc.
Balance Sheet
January 1, 1992

ASSETS		EQUITIES	
Cash	$500	Liabilities	$ 0
		Contributed Capital	500
		TOTAL LIABILITIES &	
TOTAL ASSETS	$500	STOCKHOLDER'S EQUITY	$500

EXHIBIT 11-2.
LIFO-FIFO, Inc.
1992 Purchases and Sales

March 15	Purchase 1 Unit for $100
August 1	Purchase 1 Unit for 200
November 10	Sell 1 Unit for 300

According to Exhibit 11-2, on November 10, the firm has sold one unit for $300. This is true whether we use LIFO or FIFO. Under FIFO, the expense for the unit sold was $100 because the first one in (the March 15 purchase) cost $100, and that is the first one out. Under LIFO, the expense for the unit sold is $200 because the last one in (the August 1 purchase) is the first one out.

As a result of the difference in expense, the pretax profit differs under the two methods (Exhibit 11-3). This leads to a different amount of taxes payable to the government. We probably all agree that LIFO is superior to the extent that it allows us to pay less taxes. The LIFO firm pays $34 in taxes while the FIFO firm has to pay $68.

But what about the bottom line? It appears that the LIFO firm is less profitable. This is not actually the case. Using FIFO the

EXHIBIT 11-3.
LIFO-FIFO, Inc.
Income Statement
For the Year Ending December 31, 1992

	FIFO APPROACH	LIFO APPROACH
Revenue	$300	$300
Expense	100	200
Income Before Tax	$200	$100
Tax @ 34%	68	34
NET INCOME	$132	$ 66

firm has net income of $132, while the LIFO firm only has net income of $66 (assuming a tax rate of 34 percent). This does mean lower reported profits, but it doesn't mean lower profitability. In fact, this is an instance where looks may be quite deceptive. The key is to understand what the accountant really means, which is not necessarily what he or she says.

In order to understand how profitability may differ from net income or profits, let's put together a balance sheet for LIFO-FIFO, Inc. for the end of 1992. Before we can make a year-end balance sheet, we'll need the cash balance. Exhibit 11-4 provides a 1992 cash summary for LIFO-FIFO, Inc.

In both instances, the firm starts with $500 in cash and spends $300 on its March and August purchases. In both instances, the firm receives $300 from its November sale. You'll notice that in Exhibit 11-4 under both methods the firm has exactly the same cash balance before taxes. The only difference in the year-end cash balance is caused by the difference in the amount of taxes paid under the two methods. LIFO results in a higher cash balance. Is that alone enough to support the contention that the firm is better off under LIFO?

Let's look at Exhibit 11-5 for additional support. This exhibit gives the LIFO-FIFO year-end balance sheet. Clearly the firm is better off under LIFO. Well, perhaps it still isn't quite

EXHIBIT 11-4.

LIFO-FIFO, Inc.
1992 Cash Summary

	FIFO METHOD	LIFO METHOD
Balance Jan. 1, 1992	$500	$500
March Purchase	(100)	(100)
August Purchase	(200)	(200)
November Sale	300	300
Cash Balance Before Taxes	$500	$500
Tax Payment	(68)	(34)
Balance Dec. 31, 1992	$432	$466

EXHIBIT 11-5.

LIFO-FIFO, Inc.
Balance Sheet
December 31, 1992

FIFO APPROACH

ASSETS		LIABILITIES & STOCKHOLDERS' EQUITY	
Cash	$432	Liabilities	$ 0
Inventory	200	Stockholders' Equity	632
TOTAL ASSETS	$632	TOTAL LIABILITIES & STOCKHOLDERS' EQUITY	$632

LIFO APPROACH

ASSETS		LIABILITIES & STOCKHOLDERS' EQUITY	
Cash	$466	Liabilities	$ 0
Inventory	100	Stockholders' Equity	566
TOTAL ASSETS	$566	TOTAL LIABILITIES & STOCKHOLDERS' EQUITY	$566

crystal clear. Certainly $466 of cash is better than $432 of cash, but it still looks like the FIFO firm has more total assets and a higher stockholders' equity. Ah, but that's it. It looks like that. But it isn't really so. You see, this is the accountant's world of make-believe.

The game of make-believe is played this way. The accountant asks which is greater, your ego or your desire for wealth. If your ego is greater you should use FIFO and report to your stockholders and the government a high income and a high amount of total assets. On the other hand, if your ego is modest the accountant can show you a way to make-believe. The way you make-believe is by saying that you are poor and cannot afford to pay very much tax. If you are willing to make-believe (which, by the way, is legal), then the world will think you are poor, and you won't have to pay much tax. And that is the only thing that will be different!

Look back at the three transactions that LIFO-FIFO, Inc. had this year (Exhibit 11-2). What if you were told that the sale did not take place on November 10, but actually took place on April 1. In other words, purchases and sales for the year were as follows:

March 15	Purchase 1 unit for $100	
April 1	Sell 1 unit for	300
August 1	Purchase 1 unit for	200

FIFO is unaffected because the March purchase is the first in and the first out under FIFO, the same as before. But what about LIFO? Now the expense for goods sold is $100 because the March unit was the last one in prior to the April sale. Right? No, wrong. The unit shipped to our customer on April 1 was the one we purchased and received in August.

The accountant knows that obviously this can't physically be so. But that's okay. We'll just make-believe that that's what happened. Under LIFO there is no need for us to actually move our inventories on a LIFO basis. We don't have to throw our conveyor belt into reverse, or keep milk on hand until it turns sour. If our product is dated, there is no need to feel we can't be on a LIFO system because we can't afford to keep stock on hand past the expiration date.

The firm on LIFO can continue to behave all year long as if it were on FIFO. Your managers should continue to make their product decisions based on the current cost of inventory items— and that usually requires a FIFO type approach. However, your accountant at year-end will make adjustments to your financial records to calculate your income *as if* you were shipping on a LIFO basis.

Let's recap the year for LIFO-FIFO, Inc. Under either inventory method they started with $500, then purchased two units at a total cost of $300 and sold one of the two units for $300. Under either method they physically shipped the first unit that they had purchased and they physically have on hand the unit that was the second one they purchased. From a standpoint of physical movement of goods, the FIFO income statement tells the truth. However, by making believe that we shipped a unit that we hadn't even received by the shipping date, we can report a higher cost of goods sold expense, and therefore pay the government $34 less. Thus, for the LIFO firm, a true measure of profitability would be the Exhibit 11-3 FIFO income statement up to the income before tax, followed by the tax calculated under the LIFO heading. That is, the LIFO firm really makes $200 of pretax profit, but pays only $34 of tax, leaving $166 of profitability.

What about the balance sheet? What assets does the FIFO firm have? Is the answer $432 of cash plus inventory of $200? It would be clearer if we said that the FIFO firm has $432 of cash plus one unit of inventory purchased on August 1. The LIFO firm, on the other hand, has $466 of cash plus the exact same unit of inventory purchased on August 1. Here again you can see the results of make-believe. Are you prepared to have the world believe your total assets are only $566 ($466 of cash plus $100 of inventory) even though they are really worth $666 ($466 of cash plus inventory reported at $100 but really worth $200); or, would you rather have only $632 ($432 of cash plus $200 of inventory), and have everyone know that you're worth $632, rather than think you're only worth $566? For firms that do report on a LIFO basis, there is no doubt that they understate their profitability on the income statement and they understate the value of their inventory on the face of their balance sheet. The amount by which the inventory is understated on the balance sheet of a LIFO firm is sometimes referred to as a *hidden LIFO reserve*.

In the face of this make-believe world, your faith in the so-called "bottom line" may be somewhat shaken, and rightfully so. Throughout the remainder of this book, there are many times when the firm will feel that there are good reasons to manipulate somewhat the bottom line figure to achieve some other end, such as increasing overall profitability. Remember, the only difference between LIFO and FIFO is that the LIFO firm has more cash to invest and use to make more profits. Everything else is exactly the same. We have purchased the same goods for the same prices. We have sold the same unit for the same amount. We have exactly the same unit left in our inventory. The only difference is that the LIFO firm pays less taxes and has more cash. As a result, it is more profitable. The only payment the firm had to make in order to be more profitable was to report to the world that they had lower net income! Just a teeny weeny lie.

One can't help at this point recalling the story about the chief executive officer (CEO) who called the head of Research and Development (R & D) into his office, and asked her how much $2 + 2$ was equal to. The head of R & D left, saying she would be right back. Two weeks later she returned with reams of scientific calculations and asked if any more information was available to help solve the problem. Then the CEO called in the head of Marketing and asked the same question. The Marketing Director said, "I happen to have a graph of that right here. As you can see from the trend line, although it's only 3.7 now, we expect it to go to 4.4 by next selling season." Finally the CEO called in the Chief Accountant and asked him how much $2 + 2$ was. The accountant looked around to see if anyone else was in the room, and seeing it empty turned to the CEO and said, "Well, how much would you like it to be?"

POSTSCRIPTS ON LIFO

Switching to LIFO

The Internal Revenue Service (IRS) is not exactly thrilled to have everyone using the LIFO method to reduce their taxes. For a while it was difficult for firms to get IRS approval to change from LIFO to FIFO. However, a significant number of firms hired lobbyists to put pressure on Congress and the result is that the shift to LIFO is now routinely approved by the IRS.

However, once you are on LIFO the IRS is not likely to let you shift back to FIFO if the whim hits you. The IRS says you can change inventory methods, but just this one time. Suppose that we were to experience deflation (an inflation rate of less than 0, not merely a slowing of the inflation rate). FIFO would give you lower taxes but the IRS would not let you shift to FIFO. You have to make two judgments: first, do you think we'll have deflation in the foreseeable future, and second, if we do, will the IRS, under pressure from lobbyists and Congress, let you switch back to FIFO, but just this one time?

The LIFO Conformity Rule

When we talked about depreciation, we noted that we could have our cake and eat it too. We could tell our stockholders what a good year we had, but we could also tell the government how miserable things had really been. This is not currently true with LIFO. The government, apparently in an effort to discourage use of LIFO, requires that the firm use the same method of inventory reporting to stockholders as it uses to report to the government. What are the implications of this policy?

Many firms that have not shifted to LIFO have not made the shift because it lowers reported earnings, and they fear that their stock price will drop in the face of lower reported earnings. Yet numerous studies by finance researchers have shown that for two comparable firms, one of which shifts to LIFO and one of which doesn't, the LIFO firm will report relatively lower earnings, yet its stock price will rise relative to that of the FIFO firm that is reporting relatively higher earnings. Each individual stockholder must be a lot more savvy than you thought.

Well, not quite. There are, however, thousands of financial analysts who make their living telling people what stocks to buy, and they do understand the positive implications of LIFO. They cause the stock to attain a reasonable price in light of its increased liquidity (less taxes paid means more cash available) and increased profitability (more cash means more investment and profits). Think of this from your own point of view as owner of LIFO-FIFO,

Inc. Would you decide in favor of FIFO with its higher reported earnings, or LIFO with its decreased taxes and therefore higher profitability?

Who Shouldn't Use LIFO

Many, many firms could benefit from LIFO, but there are some that would not. LIFO is not necessarily advantageous if the cost of your inventory is highly uncertain, and veers downward as often as upward. For many firms dealing in commodities, weighted average remains a better bet. Firms whose inventory costs are actually falling (computer chips for example) will have lower taxes by staying on FIFO.

What if your inventory contains some items with rising cost and some items with falling cost? If you segment the inventory adequately, it is possible to report some of your inventory using one method and some of it based on another method.

LIFO Liquidations

The lower tax paid by a firm on LIFO is caused by reporting to the government that the most recent, high-priced purchases were sold while the old low-cost items were kept. If we ever liquidate our inventory and sell everything we have, we incur a high profit on the sale of those low-cost items and have to pay back the taxes we would have paid had we been on FIFO all along. However, in the meantime we have had an interest-free loan from the government.

If our year-end inventory is always at least as big as the beginning inventory, we will never have that problem and we will never have to repay those extra taxes to the government. Purchasing managers may get the word to stock up right before year-end to avoid a LIFO liquidation. Your inventory can drop below the beginning balance; it can even go to zero during the year. It can turn over completely ten times. As long as it is replenished before year-end you will not have a LIFO liquidation.

However, LIFO liquidations should not be avoided at any cost. During recessions the carrying costs of unneeded inventory may be quite high. In fact, we may pay more in warehousing and interest costs than we would pay in extra taxes if we reduced our inventory levels. The financial officers of the firm have to make a formalized decision as to when it pays to reduce the level of a LIFO inventory, and by how much it should be reduced.

Finally, must we liquidate inventory when we phase out a product-line? *No.* It is possible to use an advanced method (beyond the scope of this book) called dollar value LIFO that actually allows us to assign the costs of a phased out product to units of a new product. As we said, this is the world of accounting make-believe.

KEY CONCEPTS

The Inventory Equation:

$$\text{Beginning Inventory} + \text{Units Purchased} - \text{Units Sold} = \text{Ending Inventory}$$

Periodic vs. perpetual inventory—different methods for keeping track of how many units have been sold, and how many units are on hand.

Periodic—goods are counted periodically to determine the ending inventory. The number of units sold is calculated using the inventory equation.

Perpetual—the inventory balance is adjusted as each unit is sold so that a perpetual record of how many units have been sold and how many are on hand is maintained at all times.

Cost flow assumptions—inventory is valued at its cost. Therefore, it is necessary to know not only how many units were sold and how many are left on hand, but specifically which were sold and which are left. This determination is made via one of four different approaches.

Specific identification—we record and identify each unit as it is acquired or sold.

First-In, First-Out (FIFO)—we assume that the units acquired earlier are sold before units acquired later.

Weighted average—we assume that all units are indistinguishable and assign a weighted average cost to each unit.

Last-In, First-Out (LIFO)—we assume that the last units acquired are the first ones sold, even if this implies sale of a unit prior to its acquisition. During periods of inflation there are tax savings associated with LIFO.

Twelve

CAPITAL BUDGETING AND DISCOUNTED CASH FLOW ANALYSIS

Capital budgeting is the analysis of long-term projects. Long-term projects are worthy of special attention because of the fact that they frequently require large initial investments, and because the cash outlay to start such projects often precedes the receipt of profits by a significant period of time. In such cases, we are interested in being able to predict the profitability of the project. We want to be sure that the profits from the project are greater than what we could have received from alternative investments or uses of our money.

This chapter focuses on how managers can evaluate long-term projects and determine whether the expected return from the projects is great enough to justify taking the risks that are inherent in long-term investments. Several different approaches to capital budgeting are discussed. These are the payback method, the net present value method, and the internal rate of return method. The latter two of these methods requires us to acknowledge the implications of the "time value of money." We have indirectly alluded to such a time value of money previously, pointing out that we would prefer to defer tax payments to the future. Such deferment allows us the use of the money in the interim to earn additional profits.

Financial managers use a formalized approach to evaluate the time value of money. Such an approach is necessary because many of the problems we face in capital budgeting cannot be solved easily without a definite mechanical methodology. To give a rather elementary example, suppose that someone offered to buy your product for $250, and that they are willing to pay you either today, or one year from today. You will certainly prefer to receive the $250 today. At the very least, you could put the $250 in a bank and earn interest in the intervening year.

Suppose, however, that the buyer offered you $250 today or $330 in 22 months. Now your decision is much more difficult. How sure are you that the individual will pay you 22 months from now? Perhaps he or she will be bankrupt by then. What could we do with the money if we received it today? Would we put the $250 in some investment that would yield us more than $330 twenty-two months from today? These are questions that we have to be able to answer in order to evaluate long-term investment opportunities. But first let's discuss some basic issues of investment analysis.

INVESTMENT OPPORTUNITIES

The first step that must be taken in investment analysis is to generate various investment opportunities. Some firms choose to evaluate projects on an individual basis, accepting any project that can meet certain criteria. Other firms take the approach of comparing all of their alternative opportunities and selecting the best projects from among all of the alternatives.

In either case, the key first step is the development of the investment opportunity. Such opportunities fall into two major classes: new project investments, and replacement or reinvestment in existing projects. New project ideas can come from a variety of sources. They may be the result of research and development activity or exploration. Your firm may have a department solely devoted to new product development. Ideas may come from outside of the firm. Reinvestment is often the result of production managers pointing out that certain equipment needs to be replaced. Such replacement should not be automatic. If a substantial outlay is required, it may be an appropriate time to reevaluate the product or project to determine if the profits being generated are adequate to justify continued additional investment.

DATA GENERATION

The data needed to evaluate an investment opportunity are the expected cash flows related to the investment. Many projects have a large initial cash outflow as we acquire plant and equipment, and incur start-up costs prior to actual production and sale of our new product. In the years that follow, there will be receipt of cash from the sale of our product (or service) and there will be cash expenditures related to the expenses of production and sales. We refer to the difference between each year's cash receipts and cash expenditures as the net cash flow for that year.

You're probably wondering why we have started this discussion with cash flow instead of net income for each year. There are several important reasons. First, net income, even if it were a perfect measure of profitability, doesn't consider the time value of money. For instance, suppose that we have two alternative projects. The first project requires that we purchase a machine for $10,000 in cash. The machine has a ten-year useful life and generates revenue of $1,500 per year. If we depreciate on a straight-line basis for financial reporting, we have a depreciation expense of $1,000 per year. Assume for this simple example that there are no other expenses besides depreciation. Because we have revenues of $1,500 per year and expenses of $1,000 per year, we have a pretax profit of $500 each year.

Suppose that a totally different project requires that we lease a machine for $1,000 a year for ten years, with each lease payment being made at the start of the year. The leased machine produces revenues of $1,500 a year, leaving us with a pretax profit of $500 per year. Are the two alternative projects equal? No, they aren't. Even though they both provide the same pretax profit, they are not equally as good. One project requires us to spend $10,000 at the beginning. The other project only requires an outlay of $1,000 in the first year.

In this second project, we could hold on to $9,000 that had been spent right away in the first project. That $9,000 can be invested and can earn additional profits for the firm.

This issue stems from the generally accepted accounting principle that requires a matching of revenue and expense. Because the machine generates revenue for each of ten years, we must allocate the expense over the ten-year period when we report to our stockholders. The income statement for a firm that matches (that is, uses the accrual basis of accounting) is not based on how much cash it receives or spends in a given year.

There is another problem with the use of net income in this example. Although the pretax income is the same for each of the two projects, the amount of taxes paid by the firm would not be the same for these two projects. The first project provides us with ownership of a machine that has a ten-year useful life, but a 5-year life for tax depreciation under the Modified Accelerated Cost Recovery System (MACRS) discussed in Chapters 9 and 10. The depreciation reported to the IRS doesn't have to equal the depreciation reported to the stockholders. That means more depreciation will be reported to the government than to our stockholders in the early years of the asset's life. The result will be a tax deferment.

As we will see in Chapter 13, however, lease payments cannot provide us with tax deductions as great as the MACRS depreciation. Therefore, the project in which we lease instead of purchasing results in higher tax payments in the early years. The higher tax payments leave less money available for investment in profitable opportunities.

Even aside from these two problems, net income is not a very reliable figure on which to base project evaluation. Consider the LIFO inventory method of Chapter 11. Using LIFO, we intentionally suppress the reported net income in order to lower our taxes. But in determining whether a project is a good one or not, we want to know the true profitability—not the amount of profits we are willing to admit to when filling out our tax return. Cash is a good measure of underlying profitability. We can assess how much cash we put into a project and how much cash we ultimately get from the project. Just as importantly, we can determine when the cash is spent and when the cash is received to enable investment in other profitable opportunities.

The data needed for investment or project analysis is cash flow information for each of the years of the investment's life. Naturally we cannot be 100 percent certain about how much the project will cost and how much we will eventually receive. There is no perfect solution for the fact that we have to make estimates. However, we must be aware at all times that because our estimates may not be fully correct there is an element of risk. Project analysis must be able to assess whether the expected return can compensate for the risks we are taking.

Our analysis is somewhat simplified if we prepare all of our estimates on a pretax basis. Taxes can be quite complex and they add extra work on to the analysis. Unfortunately, we would be making a serious error if we didn't perform our analysis on an after-tax basis. Consider the previous example of two alternative projects. The tax payment is not the same for the two alternatives. In order to clearly see which project is better, we must analyze the impact of projects on an after-tax basis.

One final note prior to looking at the methods for assessing alternative investments. Our analysis should always attempt to consider firm-wide effects of a particular project. Too often we apply tunnel vision to a project. Most of the firm's products bear some relationship to the firm's other products. When we introduce a new product, its profitability can't be assessed in a vacuum. For instance, when a toothpaste manufacturer creates a new brand of toothpaste, the hope is that the new brand will gain sales from the competition. The total market for toothpaste is relatively fixed. Although new brands may increase the total market slightly, most of their sales will come at the expense of other brands already on the market. If the other brands are made by our competitors, great. But it's entirely probable that each of the brands of toothpaste our company already makes will lose some ground to our new brand. When we calculate the profits from the new brand, we should attempt to assess, at least qualitatively if not quantitatively, what the impact on our current brands will be.

On the other hand, consider a shoe manufacturer. If styles switch from loafers (shoelaceless) to wingtips (shoes that need shoelaces), then we can expect our shoelace division to have increased sales. For a sports equipment manufacturer, if a new aluminum baseball bat can expand the baseball bat market, then we can expect sales of baseballs and baseball gloves to increase. New products may have a positive or a negative effect on the rest of the company. In estimating the cash flows of the potential investment, this factor should be considered.

EVALUATION OF CASH FLOW INFORMATION: THE PAYBACK METHOD

The payback method of analysis evaluates projects based on how long it takes to recover the amount of money put into the project. The shorter the payback period, the better. Certainly there is some intuitive appeal to this method. The sooner we get our money out of the project, the lower the risk. If we have to wait a number of years for a project to "pay off," all kinds of things can go wrong. Furthermore, given high interest rates, the longer we have our initial investment tied up, the more costly it is for us.

Exhibit 12-1 presents an example for the payback method. Although there may be intuitive support for this method, we will note a number of weaknesses. In the exhibit, four alternative projects are being compared. In each project, the initial outlay is $400. By the end of 1994, projects one and two have recovered the initial $400 investment. Therefore, they have a payback period of three years. Projects three and four do not recover the initial

EXHIBIT 12-1.
Payback Method—Alternative Projects

| | PROJECT CASH FLOWS | | | |
	ONE	TWO	THREE	FOUR
January 1992	$(400)	$(400)	$(400)	$ (400)
1992	0	0	399	300
1993	1	399	0	99
1994	399	1	0	0
1995	500	500	500	5,000
TOTAL	$ 500	$ 500	$ 499	$4,999

investment until the end of 1995. Their payback period is four years, and they are therefore considered to be inferior to the other two projects.

It is not difficult at this point to see one of the principal weaknesses of the payback method. It ignores what happens after the payback period. The total cash flow for project four is much greater than the cash received from any of the other projects, yet it is considered to be one of the worst of the projects. In a situation where cash flows extend for 20 or 30 years, this problem might not be as obvious, but it could cause us to choose incorrectly.

Is that the only problem with this method? No. Another obvious problem stems from the fact that according to this method, projects one and two are equally attractive because they both have a three-year payback period. Although their total cash flows are the same, the timing is different. Project one provides one dollar in 1993, and then $399 during 1994. Project two generates $399 in 1993 and only $1 in 1994. Are these two projects equally as good because their total cash flows are the same? *No.* The extra $398 received in 1993 from project two is available for investment in other profitable opportunities for one extra year, as compared to project one. Therefore, it is clearly superior to project one. The problem is that the payback method doesn't formally take into account the time value of money.

This deficiency is obvious in looking at project three as well. Project three appears to be less valuable than projects one or two on two counts. First, its payback is four years rather than three, and second, its total cash flow is less than either project one or two. But if we consider the time value of money, then project three is better than either project one or two. With project three, we get the $399 right away. The earnings on that $399 during 1993 and 1994 will more than offset the shorter payback and larger cash flow of projects one and two.

Although payback is commonly used for a quick and dirty project evaluation, problems associated with the payback period are quite serious. As a result, there are several methods commonly referred to as discounted cash flow models that overcome these problems. Later in this chapter, we will discuss the most commonly used of these methods, net present value and internal rate of return. However, before we discuss them, we need to specifically consider the issues and mechanics surrounding time value of money calculations.

THE TIME VALUE OF MONEY

It is very easy to think of projects in terms of total dollars of cash received. Unfortunately, this tends to be fairly misleading. Consider a project in which we invest $400 and in return we receive $520 after three years. We have made a cash profit of $120. Because the profit was earned over a three-year period, it is a profit of $40 per year. Because $40 is 10 percent of the initial $400 investment, we have apparently earned a 10 percent return on our money. While this is true, that 10 percent is calculated based on simple interest.

Consider putting money into a bank that pays a 10 percent return "compounded annually." The term *compounded annually* means that the bank calculates interest at the end of each year and adds the interest onto the initial amount deposited. In future years, interest is earned not only on the initial deposit, but also on interest earned in prior years. If we put $400 in the bank at 10 percent compounded annually, we would earn $40 of interest in the first year. At the beginning of the second year we would have $440. The interest on the $440 would be $44. At the beginning of the third year, we would have $484 (the $400 initial deposit plus the $40 interest from the first year, plus the $44 interest from the second year). The interest for the third year would be $48.40. We would have a total of $532.40 at the end of three years.

The 10 percent compounded annually gives a different result from the 10 percent simple interest. We have $532.40 instead of $520 from the project. The reason for this difference is that in the case of the project, we did not get any cash flow until the end of the project. In the case of the bank, we were essentially given a cash flow at the end of each year. We reinvested that cash flow in the bank, although we could have withdrawn the interest from the bank and invested it elsewhere. The crucial fact is that the total amount we wind up with is different in these two cases.

The implication of this difference is that we cannot compare two projects that pay the same total return and surmise that they are equal. Two projects requiring investments of $400 are not equally as good if one pays $520 in three years while the other pays $40 after the first year and $40 after the second year and $440 after the third. In both cases the total is $520, but in the latter case $40 is available for investment after the first year and another $40 after the second. We must determine not only how much cash will be received from each project, but also when it will be received. The project that provides the cash flow sooner gives us an opportunity to earn additional profits. What we need is a method that can compare cash flows coming at different points in time and consider the implications of *when* the cash is received.

Consider a cash amount of $100 today. We refer to it as a present value (PV or P). How much could this cash amount accumulate to if we invested it at an interest rate (i) or rate of return (r) of 10 percent for a period of time (N) equal to two years? Assuming that we compound annually, the $100 would earn $10 in the first year (10 percent of $100). This $10 would be added to the $100. In the second year our $110 would earn $11 (that is, 10 percent of $110). The future value (FV or F) is $121. That is, two years in the future we would have $121.

Mechanically this is a simple process—multiply the interest rate times the initial investment to find the interest for the first period. Add the interest to the initial investment. Then multiply the interest rate times the initial investment plus all interest already accumulated to find the interest for the second year.

While this is not complicated, it can be rather tedious. Suppose we invest money for 30 years in an investment that compounds monthly. At the end of each month, we calculate interest and add it to the investment balance. For a period of 30 years we have to make this computation 360 times (monthly compounding requires 12 calculations per year for each of the 30 years, or a total of 360 computations).

To simplify this process, mathematical formulas have been developed to solve a variety of "time value of money" problems. The most basic of these formulas states that:

$$FV = PV(1 + i)^N$$

We will not derive this formula here. Many years ago the time value of money calculations could not be performed without an ability to derive, memorize, or look up the formulas. Even once you had the formulas and plugged in the appropriate variables, the mathematical calculation was still somewhat arduous. Later, tables were developed that made the process somewhat easier. A *financial* manager should have a good understanding of both the formulas and the tables. However, even the tables are somewhat cumbersome and limited.

Modern technology has made our calculations substantially simpler. For the nonfinancial manager, project analysis can be done with the aid of a hand held business-oriented calculator. The formulas are built right into the memory of the calculator. If we supply the appropriate raw data, the calculator performs all of the necessary interest computations.

Traditionalists will be disappointed to discover that this book contains neither tables nor derivations of the formulas. For those who desire such an approach, a number of references are listed at the end of this book. However, tables and formulas really aren't necessary either for understanding what we are doing, or for computing the results. Calculators, tables, and formulas all require the same level of understanding from the users—an ability to determine what information is available and what information is being sought.

For instance, if we wanted to know what $100 would grow to in two years at 10 percent, we would simply tell our calculator that the present value, P or PV (depending on the brand of calculator you use), equals $100; the interest rate, %i or i or r, equals 10 percent; and the number of periods, N, equals 2. Then we would ask the calculator to compute F or FV, the future value.

Can we use this method if compounding occurs more frequently than once a year? Bonds often pay interest twice a year. Banks often compound quarterly on savings accounts. On the other hand, banks often compound monthly to calculate mortgage payments. Using our example of $100 invested for two years at 10 percent, we could easily adjust the calculation for semi-annual, quarterly, or monthly compounding. For example, for semi-annual compounding, N becomes 4 because there are two semi-annual periods per year for two years. The rate of return, or interest rate, becomes 5 percent. If the rate earned is 10 percent for a full year, then it is half of that, or 5 percent for each half year.

For quarterly compounding, N equals 8 (four quarters per year for two years) and i equals 2½ percent (10 percent per year divided by four quarters per year). For monthly compounding, N equals 24 and i equals 10 percent/12. Thus, for monthly compounding, we would tell the calculator that PV = $100, i = 10%/12, and N = 24. Then we would tell the calculator to compute FV. We need a calculator designed to perform present value functions in order to do this.

If we expect to receive $121 in two years can we calculate how much that is worth today? This question calls for a reversal of the compounding process. Suppose we would normally expect to earn a return on our money of 10 percent. What we are really asking here is, "How much would we have to invest today at 10 percent, to get $121 in two years?" The answer requires unraveling compound interest. If we calculate how much of the $121 to be received in two years is simply interest earned on our original investment, then we know the present value of that $121. This process of removing or unraveling the interest is called *discounting*. The 10 percent rate is referred to as a discount rate. Using the calculator, this is a simple process. We again supply the i and the N, but instead of telling the calculator the PV and asking for the FV, we tell it the FV and ask it to calculate the PV.

Earlier in this chapter, we posed a problem of whether to accept $250 today, or $330 in 22 months. Assume that we can invest money in a project with a 10 percent return and monthly compounding. Which choice is better? We can tell our calculator (by the way, if you have access to a business-oriented calculator, you can work out these calculations as we go) that FV = $330, N = 22, and i = 10%/12. If we then ask it to compute PV, we find that the present value is $275. This means that if we invest $275 today at 10 percent compounded monthly for 22 months, it accumulates to $330. That is, receiving $330 in 22 months is equivalent to having $275 today. Because this amount is greater than $250, our preference is to wait for the money, assuming there is no risk of default. Looking at this problem another way, how much would our $250 grow to if we invested it for 22 months at 10 percent? Here we have PV = $250, N = 22, and i = 10%/12. Our calculation indicates that the FV = $300. If we wait, we have $330 22 months from now. If we take $250 today and invest it at 10 percent, we only have $300 22 months from now. We find that we are better off to wait for the $330, assuming we are sure that we will receive it.

Are we limited to solving for only the present or future value? No, this methodology is quite flexible. Assume, for example, that we wish to put $100,000 aside today to pay off a $1,000,000 loan in 15 years. What rate of return must be earned, compounded annually, for our $100,000 to grow to $1,000,000? Here we have the present value, or $100,000, the number of periods, 15 years, and the future value, or $1,000,000. It is a simple process to determine the required rate of return. If we simply supply our calculator with the PV, FV, and N, the calculator readily supplies the i, which is 16.6 percent in this case.

Or, for that matter, if we had $100,000 today and knew that we could earn a 13 percent return, we would calculate how long it would take to accumulate $1,000,000. Here we know PV, FV, and i, and we wish to find N. In this case, N = 18.8 years. Given any three of our four basic components, PV, FV, N and i, we can solve for the fourth. This is because the calculator is simply using our basic formula stated earlier and solving for the missing variable.

So, far, however, we have considered only one single payment. Suppose that we don't have $100,000 today, but we are willing to put $10,000 aside every year for 15 years. If we earn 12 percent, will we have enough to repay $1,000,000 at the end of the 15 years? There are two ways to solve this problem. We can determine the future value, 15 years from now, of each of the individual payments. We would have to do 15 separate calculations because each succeeding payment earns interest for one year less. We would then have to sum the future value of each of the payments. This is rather tedious. A second way to solve this problem is using a formula that accumulates the payments for us. The formula is:

$$FV = PMT \left[\frac{(1+i)^N - 1}{i} \right]$$

In this formula, PMT represents the payment made each period, or annuity payment. Although you may think of annuities as payments made once a year, an annuity simply means payments that are exactly the same in amount, and are made at equally spaced intervals of time, such as monthly, quarterly, or annually. For example, monthly mortgage payments of $321.48 per month represent an annuity.

To solve problems with a series of identical payments, we have five variables instead of the previous four. We now have FV, PV, N, i, and PMT. However, PV doesn't appear in our formula. There is a separate formula that relates present value to a series of payments. This formula is:

$$PV = PMT \left[\frac{1 - \left[\frac{1}{(1+i)^N} \right]}{i} \right]$$

Annuity formulas are built into business calculators. With the calculator, you can easily solve for PV or i or N or PMT, if you have the other three variables. Similarly, you can solve for FV or i or N or PMT given the other three. For instance, how much would we pay monthly on a 20-year mortgage at 12 percent if we borrowed $50,000? The present value (PV) is $50,000, the interest rate (%i) is 1 percent per month, the number of months (N) is 240. Given these three factors, we can solve for the annuity payment (PMT). It is $551 per month.

Annuity formulas provide you with a basic framework for solving many problems concerning receipt or payment of cash in different time periods. Keep in mind that the annuity method can only be used if the amount of the payment is the same each period. If that isn't the case, each payment must be evaluated separately. The remainder of this chapter and Chapter 13 give an opportunity to work with these concepts.

EVALUATION OF CASH FLOW INFORMATION: THE NET PRESENT VALUE (NPV) METHOD

The net present value (NPV) method of analysis determines whether a project earns more or less than a stated desired rate of return. The starting point of the analysis is determination of this rate.

The Hurdle Rate

The rate of return required in order for a project to be acceptable is called the required rate of return or the hurdle rate. An acceptable project should be able to hurdle over, that is, be higher than this rate.

The rate must take into account two key factors. First, a base profit to compensate for investing money in the project. We have a variety of opportunities in which we could use our money. We need to be paid a profit for foregoing the use of our money in some alternative venture. The second element concerns risk. Any time we enter a new investment, there is an element of risk. Perhaps the project won't work out exactly as expected. The project may turn out to be a failure. We have to be paid for being willing to undertake these risks. The two elements taken together determine our hurdle rate.

The hurdle rate for project analysis differs for different companies. There is no one unique standard required rate of return that can be used by all companies. Different industries tend to have different base rates of return. Further, within an industry one firm may have some advantage over other firms (for example, economies of scale) that allow it to have a higher base return. On top of that, different firms, and even different projects for one firm, have different types and degrees of risk. Buying a machine to use for putting Coca-Cola in bottles involves much less risk than developing new soft drink products.

Historically, U.S. government obligations, particularly treasury bills, have provided a benchmark for rates of return. These short-term government securities provide both safety and liquidity for the investor. Adjusted for inflation, the rate of return on treasury bills has historically been around two to three percent. A firm must be able to do better than this in order to attract any investor's money. This is true even if there is no risk in investing in the firm. We can therefore consider two to three percent to be a lower bound or a base, or "pure" rate of return. By pure rate of return we mean before we consider any risk. Because most firms are more risky than the government, they must also pay their investors for being willing to take the chance that something may go wrong and that they may lose money rather than make a profit. This extra payment is considered to be a return for having taken risks.

One of the most prevalent risks that investors take is loss of purchasing power. That is, price level inflation makes our money less valuable over time. Suppose we could buy a TV for $100, but instead we invest that money in a business. If the firm uses that money to generate a pretax profit of $10 in a year when the inflation rate is 10 percent, did we have a good year, bad year, or neutral year? Because we have to pay some taxes to the government on our $10 pretax profit, we had a bad year. After paying taxes we have less than $110 at the end of the year. But, due to inflation, it costs $110 to buy a TV set. This means that in deciding if a project is worthwhile, we have to consider whether the rate of return is high enough to cover our after-tax loss of purchasing power due to inflation.

We must also consider a variety of business risks. What if no one buys the product, or they buy it, but fail to pay us? If the product is made or sold internationally, we incur foreign exchange risk and foreign political risk. The specific types of risks faced by a company depend on its industry. The company's past experience with projects like the one being evaluated should be a guide in determining the risk portion of the hurdle rate. For example, if you found that historically one out of every 21 projects you invest in is a complete failure, then you should add 5 percent to your required rate of return. In that way, the total of the 5 percent extra profit you earn on each of the 20 successful projects exactly equals the 100 percent you lose on the unsuccessful project. Some firms build more than 5 percent into that calculation—they don't want to just break even on the risks they take. They feel they should make extra profits to pay for having been willing to take risks.

When we add the desired base or pure profit return to all of the risk factors, the total is the firm's hurdle rate. In most firms, the top financial officers determine an appropriate hurdle rate or rates and inform nonfinancial managers that this hurdle rate must be anticipated for a project to receive approval. Therefore, you will not usually have to go through a complete calculation of the hurdle rate yourself.

NPV Calculations

Once we know our hurdle rate, we can use the NPV method to assess whether a project is acceptable. The NPV method compares the present value of a project's cash inflows to the present value of its cash outflows. If the present value of the inflows is greater than the outflows, then the project is profitable because it is earning a rate of return that is greater than the hurdle rate.

For example, suppose that a potential project for our firm requires an initial cash outlay of $10,000. We expect the project to produce a net after-tax cash flow (cash inflows less cash outflows) of $6,500 in each of the two years of the project's life. Suppose our after-tax hurdle rate is 18 percent. Is this project worthwhile?

The cash receipts total $13,000, which is a profit of $3,000 overall, or $1,500 per year on our $10,000 investment. Is that a compounded return of at least 18 percent? At first glance it would appear that the answer is "no" because $1,500 is only 15 percent of $10,000. However, we haven't left our full $10,000 invested for the full two years. Our positive cash flow at the end of the first year is $6,500. We are not only making $1,500 profit, but we are also getting back half ($5,000) of our original investment. During the second year, we earn $1,500 profit on a remaining investment of only $5,000. It is not simply how much money you get from the project, but when you get it that is important.

The present value of an annuity of $6,500 per year for two years at 18 percent is $10,177 (PV = ?; PMT = $6,500; N = 2; i = 18%). The present value of the initial $10,000 outflow is simply $10,000 because it is paid at the start of the project. The NPV is the present value of the inflows, $10,177 less the present value of the outflows, $10,000, which is $177. This number is greater than zero, so the project does indeed yield a return greater than 18 percent, on an annually compounded basis.

It may not be intuitively clear why this method works, or indeed, that it works at all. However, consider making a deal with your friend who is a banker. You agree that you will put a sum of money into the bank. At the end of the first year, the banker adds 18 percent interest to your account and you then withdraw $6,500. At the end of year two, the banker credits interest to the balance in your account at an 18 percent rate. You then withdraw $6,500, which is exactly the total in the account at that time. The account will then have a zero balance. You ask your friend how much you must deposit today in order to be able to make the two withdrawals. He replies, "$10,177."

If we deposit $10,177, at an 18 percent rate, it will earn $1,832 during the first year. This leaves a balance of $12,009 in the account. We then withdraw $6,500, leaving a balance of $5,509 for the start of the second year. During the second year, $5,509 earns interest of $991 at a rate of 18 percent. This means that the balance in the account is $6,500 at the end of the second year. We then withdraw that amount.

The point of this bank deposit example is that when we earlier solved for the present value of the two $6,500 inflows using a hurdle rate of 18 percent, we found it to be $10,177. We were finding exactly the amount of money we would have to pay today to get two payments of $6,500 if we were to earn exactly 18 percent. If we can invest a smaller amount than $10,177, but still get $6,500 per year for each of the two years, we must be earning more than 18 percent because we are putting in less than would be needed to earn 18 percent, but are getting just as much out. Here, we invest $10,000, which is less than $10,177, so we are earning a rate of return greater than 18 percent.

Conversely, if the banker had told us to invest less than $10,000 (that is, if the present value of the two payments of $6,500 each at 18 percent was less than $10,000), then it means that by paying $10,000 we were putting in more money than we would have to in order to earn 18 percent, therefore we must be earning less than 18 percent.

The NPV method gets around the problems of the payback method. It considers the full project life, and considers the time value of money. Clearly, however, you can see that it is more difficult than the payback method. Another problem with it is that you must determine the hurdle rate before you can do any project analysis. The next method we will look at eliminates the need to have a hurdle rate before performing the analysis.

EVALUATION OF CASH FLOW INFORMATION: THE INTERNAL RATE OF RETURN METHOD (IRR)

One of the objections of the NPV method is that it never indicates what rate of return a project is earning. We simply find out whether it is earning more or less than a specified hurdle rate. This creates problems when comparing projects, all of which have positive net present values.

One conclusion that can be drawn from our net present value (NPV) discussion is that when the NPV is zero, we are earning exactly the desired hurdle rate. If the NPV is greater than zero, we are earning more than our required rate of return. If the NPV is less than zero, then we are earning less than our required rate of return. Therefore, if we want to determine the exact rate that a project earns, all we need to do is to set the NPV equal to zero. Because the NPV is the present value (PV) of the inflows less the present value of the outflows, or:

$$NPV = PV\ inflows - PV\ outflows$$

then when we set the NPV equal to zero,

$$0 = PV\ inflows - PV\ outflows$$

which is equivalent to:

$$PV\ inflows = PV\ outflows.$$

All we have to do to find the rate of return that the project actually earns, or the "internal rate of return," (IRR) is to find the interest rate at which this equation is true.

For example, consider our NPV project discussed earlier that requires a cash outlay of $10,000 and produces a net cash inflow of $6,500 per year for two years. The present value of the outflow is simply the $10,000 (PV = $10,000) we pay today. The inflows represent a two-year (N = 2) annuity of $6,500 (PMT = $6,500) per year. By supplying our calculator with the PV, N, and PMT, we can simply find the i or r (IRR). In this case, we find that the IRR is 19.4 percent.

Variable Cash Flow

This calculation is simple for any business calculator that can handle time value of money, frequently called discounted cash flow (DCF) analysis. However, this problem was somewhat simplistic because it assumed that we would receive exactly the same cash inflow each year. In most capital budgeting problems, it is much more likely that the cash inflows from a project will change each year. For example, assume that our $10,000 investment yields

$6,000 after the first year and $7,000 at the end of the second year. The total receipts are still $13,000, but the timing of the receipts has changed. The return is not as high because we are receiving $500 less in the first year than we had been in the earlier situation (that is, we get $6,000 instead of $6,500). Although we get $500 more in the second year ($7,000 instead of $6,500), that $500 difference could have been profitably invested if we had it for that intervening year. Are we still over our hurdle rate? What is the current IRR?

From a NPV point of view, it is still rather simple for us to determine whether this reviewed project is still acceptable. We need only find the present value of $6,000 evaluated with an N equal to one year, using our 18 percent hurdle rate, and add that to the present value of $7,000 evaluated with an N equal to two years at 18 percent. The sum of these two calculations is the present value of the inflows. We compare this calculation to the $10,000 outflow to see if the NPV is positive. In this case, the present value of the first inflow is $5,085 and the present value of the second inflow is $5,027. Their sum is $10,112, which is still greater than $10,000, so the project is still acceptable.

But what is the project's internal rate of return? The NPV solution was arrived at by two separate calculations. But the IRR method evaluates the one unique rate of return for the entire project. From a mathematical perspective, we run into difficulties if the cash inflows are not the same each year. This creates a situation in which we must solve for the missing i or r by trial and error! There is no better way to do this than to keep trying different rates until we find one rate at which the present value of the inflows is exactly equal to the present value of the outflows. Fortunately, the more advanced of the business calculators can do this trial and error process for you. However, in purchasing a calculator, you should be sure that it can handle internal rate of return with uneven or variable cash flow. Such a calculator can handle the complexity of having cash receipts and expenditures that differ in amount from year to year over the project's life.

In fact, as you watch such a calculator solving this type of problem, you will see numbers flashing across the display for several moments, or even several minutes, before the answer finally appears. This is a result of the calculator trying different interest rates, looking for the correct answer. It uses trial and error, just as we would do by hand. Calculators aren't smarter than we are, just faster.

PROJECT RANKING

The NPV method is quite adequate to determine if a project is acceptable or not. Often, however, we may be faced with a situation in which there are more acceptable projects than the number that we can afford to finance. In that case, we wish to choose the best projects. A simple way to do this is to determine the internal rate of return on each project and then to rank the projects from the project with the highest IRR to the lowest. We then simply start by accepting projects with the highest IRR and go down the list until we either run out of money, or reach our minimum acceptable rate of return.

In general, this approach allows the firm to optimize its over-all rate of return. However, it is possible for this approach to have an undesired result. Suppose that one of our very highest yielding projects is a parking lot. For a total investment of $50,000, we expect to earn a return of $20,000 a year for the next 40 years. The internal rate of return on that project is 40 percent. Alternatively, we can build an office building on the same site. For an investment of $10,000,000 we expect to earn $3,000,000 a year for 40 years, or an IRR of 30 percent. We can only use the site for the parking lot or the building but not both. Our other projects have an IRR of 20 percent.

If we build the parking lot because of its high IRR, and therefore bypass the building, we will wind up investing $50,000 at 40 percent and $9,950,000 at 20 percent instead of $10,000,000 at 30 percent. This is not an optimal result. We would be better off to bypass the high-yielding parking lot and invest the entire $10,000,000 at 30 percent.

This contrary outcome is not a major problem. Assuming that we have ranked our projects, if we don't have to skip over any projects because they conflict with a higher-yielding project that we have already accepted, the problem doesn't arise. If we have to skip a small project because we accepted a large project, we still don't have a problem. It is only in the case that we would be forced to skip over a large project (such as a building) because we accepted a small project (such as a parking lot) that causes us concern. In that case, our decision should be based on calculating our weighted average IRR for all projects that we accept. For instance, suppose we have $15,000,000 available to invest. We can invest $50,000 in a parking lot at 40 percent and $14,950,000 in other projects at 20 percent, for a weighted average internal rate of return of 20.1 percent, or we can invest $10,000,000 at 30 percent and $5,000,000 at 20 percent for a weighted average IRR of 26.7 percent. Here we decide to accept the $10,000,000 building at 30 percent, skipping the parking lot. Although the parking lot itself has a higher IRR, the firm as a whole has a higher IRR for all projects combined if it uses the land for a building.

SUMMARY

Capital budgeting represents one of the most important areas of financial management. In essence, the entire future of the company is on the line. If projects are undertaken that don't yield adequate rates of return, it will have serious long-term consequences on the firm's profitability—and even on its viability.

To adequately evaluate projects, discounted cash flow techniques should be employed. The two most common of these methods are NPV and IRR. The essential ingredient of both of these methods is that they consider the time value of money. A nonfinancial manager doesn't necessarily have to be able to compute present values. It is vital, however, that all managers understand that when money is received or paid can have just as dramatic an impact on the firm as the amount received or paid.

KEY CONCEPTS

Capital budgeting—analysis of long-term projects with respect to risk and profitability.

Net cash flow—the difference between cash receipts and cash disbursements. Cash flow is more useful than net income for project evaluation because net income fails to consider the time value of money.

Time value of money—other things equal, we would always prefer to receive cash sooner, or pay cash later. This is because cash can be invested and earn a return in exchange for its use. The total cash generated directly by a project is insufficient for evaluation—we must know the timing of cash flows as well as the amount.

> *Compounding*—calculation of the return on a project, including the return earned on cash flows generated during the life of the project.
>
> *Discounting*—a reversal of the compounding process. Discounting allows us to determine what a future cash flow is worth today.
>
> *Annuities*—cash flows of equal amounts, paid or received at evenly spaced periods of time, such as weekly, monthly, or annually.

Project Evaluation

> *Payback*—a method that assesses how long it will take to receive enough cash from a project to recover the cash invested in that project.
>
> *Discounted cash flow (DCF) analysis*—methods that consider the time value of money in evaluating projects.
>
> a. *Net present value*—method determining whether a project earns more than a particular desired rate of return, also called the hurdle or required rate of return. The hurdle rate is based on a return for the use of money over time, plus a return for risks inherent in the project.
>
> b. *Internal rate of return*—method that finds the specific rate of return a project is expected to earn.

Thirteen

LEASE OR BUY?
A TAXING QUESTION

While taxes are a pervasive element in all business decisions, in few areas are their impact as significant as in leasing. A large number of leasing arrangements are made in which the key, or even the sole purpose of the lease is tax avoidance. Bear in mind that while tax evasion is illegal, tax avoidance is not only legal, but it is considered to be an inalienable right guaranteed by the Constitution.

This chapter is divided into three major sections. The first examines the accounting issues and mechanics of leasing. The second section considers some of the pros and cons of leasing from a strictly managerial perspective, ignoring tax issues. Finally, the chapter focuses on the tax aspects of leasing.

ACCOUNTING ISSUES

Operating vs. Capital Leases

Leases are classified as either operating leases or capital leases. Operating leases are treated by the lessee (the party leasing the asset from the lessor) on a strictly rental basis. Rental payments are expenses. The asset is not considered to be owned by the lessee and it doesn't show up on the balance sheet. In contrast, a lessee treats a capital lease as if he bought the property and financed it with a mortgage. The leased property appears as an asset on the balance sheet. There is also a liability on the balance sheet to account for future payments to be made on the lease.

Short-term leases are always treated as operating leases. This stems from the fact that there is no strong ownership displayed by a lessee, when he leases the property for only a short period of time. In contrast, long-term leases may be treated as capital leases if there appears to be a significant ownership interest in the property on the part of the lessee.

Consider a firm that issues bonds to the general public. Why might a corporation issue bonds instead of simply borrowing from the bank? This is an example of cutting out the middleman. By borrowing from the public directly, the corporation gets a lower interest rate. But the bank's profit is not the only adjustable element of the interest rate the corporation pays. The rate on the bonds is directly affected by the riskiness of the firm. If the firm can reduce risk, it can borrow money at a lower rate.

In light of this, many firms make covenants, or agreements, as part of the bond offering. These covenants restrict management from taking certain risky actions. A common type of covenant is to agree to maintain a certain amount of assets relative to the amount of liabilities. For instance, a firm may agree that it will always have two dollars of assets on the balance sheet for every dollar of liabilities. This reduces risk because if the firm does get into financial difficulty, creditors will be fully protected if the firm can get at least 50 cents for every dollar of assets it owns.

Suppose a firm had made such an agreement, and that it currently has $20,000,000 in assets and $10,000,000 in liabilities. At this point, the president of the company sees a building that is the perfect building for the firm. The firm has been looking for a building like this one for years. The price is $5,000,000, which the president plans to pay by borrowing $4,000,000 from a bank on a twenty-year mortgage, and paying $1,000,000 in cash. Unfortunately, that would result in assets of $24 million (the original $20 million + $5 million building – $1 million cash down payment), and liabilities of $14 million (the original $10 million + $4 million mortgage). But to sustain $14 million of liabilities, the firm would need $28 million in assets. The firm cannot buy the building without defaulting on the bond agreement.

However, what if the firm merely rents the building? What if the firm takes out a twenty-year lease, with a provision that the property automatically becomes theirs at the end of the twenty years? In that case, if the lease were an operating lease, the firm wouldn't be in violation of the letter of their agreement with the bondholders! They would, however, certainly be violating the spirit of the agreement. Leasing property rather than buying it, with the main purpose being to avoid showing the asset and liability on the balance sheet is referred to as "off-balance sheet financing." It gets that name because you have effectively financed a purchase without explicitly showing the long-term commitment the firm has made.

Criteria for Capital Leases

As one might suspect, bondholders weren't too pleased with this type of behavior. Ultimately, the accountants modified their generally accepted accounting principles (GAAP) to handle this type of situation. Current GAAP specify that long-term, noncancellable leases must be treated as capital leases if they were entered into with the lessee intending to have an ownership interest in the property. Cancellable leases could be cancelled in the event that the firm has financial difficulties, so they don't cause as much concern with respect to committing the firm to long-term obligations.

How can we determine what the lessee intended? To handle this problem, accountants established four criteria. If any one of the four criteria is met, then it is assumed that ownership was intended, and the lease must be treated as a capital lease.

First, if the lessee owns the property at the end of the lease, it is a capital lease. For a firm using property from now until a future date at which time they will own the property, it is difficult to believe ownership was not intended. A way to avoid this rule would be to not automatically transfer ownership, but to leave an option for the lessee to buy the property for $1. To avoid this, a second criterion is that leases that have an option for purchase at a bargain price are capital leases. But what is a bargain? $1? $1,000? The accountants' definition is more or less as follows: If anybody but a fool would buy the item at the option price at the termination of the lease, it's a bargain. If a reasonable, prudent individual might, or might not, buy it at that price, then it isn't a bargain.

The third criterion concerns the life of the asset. If the lease covers 75 percent or more of the useful life of the asset, then it is a capital lease. This rule results from the fact that many assets are sold by their owners around that point in their useful life.

The fourth and final rule concerns the amount the lessee pays for leasing the property. If the present value of the payments the lessee is making is 90 percent or more of the fair market value of the property leased, then it is a capital lease.

One of the reasons for lease popularity was the ability to effectively own assets, but at the same time not show a liability on the balance sheet. Given these currently existing rules, this is no longer easily accomplished. Therefore, financial managers have looked for other pros and cons of leasing versus purchasing assets. Some of these considerations follow.

MANAGEMENT CONSIDERATIONS FOR LEASING

Many financial managers are strong supporters of leasing due to the added flexibility it provides. If you know you'll need a piece of equipment for only half of its useful life, a lease can eliminate the effort required to dispose of the asset after you no longer need it. If you're afraid that technology will make the item obsolete, a cancellable lease can protect you.

A lease also provides a greater degree of financing. Purchases financed by a mortgage typically require a down payment of perhaps 20 percent or more. Banks are quite reluctant to lend 100 percent of the cost for any item they use as collateral. Therefore, the firm with a great idea but no cash may not be able to get started. A lease provides an alternative way to start production with less equity financing.

Leases, however, tend to cost more than mortgages. We would expect that considering the risk and return issues. Certainly the leasing company bears more risk than a mortgagor, if only because the company bears all of the normal risks of ownership, such as assuring that fire insurance is maintained. Further, while the lessee has more flexibility to avoid technological obsolescence, the lessor charges a higher rent because he now bears that risk. The same thing is true with respect to 100-percent financing. The potential loss due to lessee default is greater to the lessor than the mortgagor because there is no sizeable down payment to absorb losses on foreclosure sales.

In some cases, leasing may be more efficient. Consider the firm that needs two autos. If they lease the autos, they may pay more for the autos than if they bought them outright, but they might get a wholesale service contract with the lease. The leasing company is willing to give a discount on service to get the lease. On the other hand, if the firm needs 2,000 autos, all in one geographic area, it might pay to buy them and open their own auto repair shop, thus maintaining the autos at cost, rather than wholesale or retail rates.

One final point. Who owns the property at the end of the lease? Well, unless it is specified one way or the other in the lease contract, the property belongs to the lessor. The lessor stands to gain from any increase in the value of the property. Frequently, the right of ownership upon termination of the lease is given to the lessee for "free." In such leases, the monthly or annual lease payments are higher than they would have to be if the lessor retained ownership of the property.

None of these managerial considerations provides absolute weight in favor of or against leasing. There are some benefits for the lessee, but they tend to raise the risk to the lessor, who therefore charges a higher price. Clearly, by adding a lessor instead of buying direct, we have brought in a middleman who will want to earn a profit. This profit must come from the lease payments. As we turn to our next section, however, it will become apparent that tax considerations can provide a situation in which the lessor and the lessee may both clearly benefit from a lease arrangement.

TAX CONSIDERATIONS FOR LEASING

Up until now, our discussion of taxes has predominantly focused on the deferral of taxes into the future. An important issue with respect to leasing is the shifting of taxes between taxpayers in different tax brackets. For example, suppose that you are in a 31 percent tax bracket, and that your 15-year-old child is in a 15 percent tax bracket. You could give your child a gift of some money. The income earned on that money will be taxed at only 15 percent. Had you earned the income it would have been taxed at 31 percent. The tax savings is permanent, rather than just a deferral to the future.

Suppose that a taxpayer in a low tax bracket—perhaps 15 percent, was anticipating buying a machine directly versus leasing it from a taxpayer in the 34 percent tax bracket. Every dollar of depreciation taken as a deduction by the taxpayer in a 15 percent tax bracket would reduce taxes paid by him or her to the government by 15 cents. If the taxpayer in the 34 percent bracket takes that same dollar of depreciation as a tax deduction, it will reduce his or her taxes by 34 cents. Therefore, there is a tax savings if a high tax bracket individual buys property and leases it to a lower tax bracket individual. The high tax bracket individual gets the depreciation deduction, and can share the benefit with the low tax bracket payer through lower lease rental charges.

This arrangement can be profitable for both parties even if the asset is later sold for a profit resulting in a taxable gain. For example, if a $50 million jet is purchased by a physician (all right—one physician can't afford a $50 million jet—assume a syndicate of physicians is formed). So the two physicians in the syndicate buy a jet, and lease it to an airline. Not only may the physicians be in a higher tax bracket than the airlines, but they also will be able to take advantage of the Modified Accelerated Cost Recovery System (MACRS) discussed in Chapters 9 and 10.

That means they depreciate the jet quickly, getting large tax write-offs in the early years. It is perfectly conceivable to show a paper loss, even if there is a positive cash flow. Eventually, however, the jet will be so depreciated that there will be no tax benefit to keeping it, so they sell it. Because they depreciated it much faster than its useful life, there will probably be a taxable gain on the sale. However, in the meantime they have had a substantial deferral of taxes. Further, that deferral can be maintained if they rollover into a new tax shelter. (Note that the value of this approach has been lessened substantially by IRS Passive Activity Loss rules, which limit allowable deductions.)

We can get even sneakier than that. Earlier we noted that land cannot be depreciated. However, what if we leased land rather than owning it? Leases are intangible assets that expire over time. Therefore, it is quite possible to lease land, and amortize that lease, getting a tax deduction. (Note that leases, as intangible property are amortized on a straight-line basis.) Of course the owner of the land receives rental payments and thus has a taxable gain. It seems to net out, with the tax savings of one individual being offset by increased taxes of another individual. But what if the owner of the land was losing money, and the lessee was very profitable. Then the rental payments received by the owner of the land might merely reduce his losses without causing any tax to be due, while the amortization of the lease would actually reduce the taxes of the profitable individual. Care should be exercised in setting up such a lease, to assure that the Internal Revenue Service does not interpret the lease as an installment purchase of the property. A tax expert should be consulted for specific details regarding installment purchase rules.

One of the features of the tax law that has made leasing particularly interesting is the investment tax credit. In order to encourage capital investment in plant and equipment, the federal government at times subsidizes some purchases through a tax credit. For example, if you were to purchase a new machine with a five-year MACRS life, then the government would allow you to reduce your taxes by a specified percent of the cost of the machine, such as 10 percent. Notice that the government will not "pay" any cash, it will just allow you to reduce your tax payment to them. What if a company were losing money? It wouldn't benefit from this equipment subsidy because it wouldn't be paying any taxes. However, leasing can help.

Suppose that ordinarily an airline might have arranged with a bank to buy an airplane and take a mortgage from the bank for

$50,000,000 for 15 years at 16 percent. The bank earns 16 percent and the airline has a cost of 16 percent. If the airline were losing money, there would be no investment tax credit benefit. Alternatively, the bank can buy the airplane and lease it to the airline. In that case, the bank demands that it earn a return of 17 percent because of the extra risks associated with leasing. Can this benefit the airline? Absolutely!

The bank buys the plane and gets a 10 percent credit. This reduces the net cost of the jet to $45 million. If the present value is $45 million, and the rate of return is 17 percent, and the lease is for 15 years, then the airline would have to pay the bank $8.5 million per year. From the airline's perspective, however, if they bought the jet, it would have cost them $50 million. Had they borrowed $50 million and made payments of $8.5 million per year for 15 years, then the effective interest rate they would be paying would be 15 percent. By interjecting the lease, the bank earns 1 percent more than its usual 16 percent and the airline pays 1 percent less than the 16 percent it would pay without the lease. This is because paying 17 percent on $45 million is better than paying 16 percent on $50 million. They are both better off because of the benefit of the investment tax credit.

Congress tends to enact and repeal the investment tax credit (ITC) in response to the existing economic conditions. At the time this Second Edition was written, the ITC was not in effect for new purchases. However, it is quite possible that the ITC will be reinstated at some future point in time, when the economy is weak.

The Alternative Minimum Tax also has interesting implications for leasing. However, it is an extremely complicated area, and is beyond the scope of this book. In general, tax issues with respect to leasing are extremely complex. There are a number of potential pitfalls. The discussion here should whet your appetite to the fact that even if a lease doesn't have strong managerial rationale, the tax consequences may make it attractive. However, you must seek out the advice of a tax expert to review the specifics of any potential lease. The tax law in this area is extremely volatile. Congress closes loopholes as fast as it opens them. You cannot be advised strongly enough that a lease should not be undertaken without a tax expert specifically reviewing the tax consequences of the lease.

KEY CONCEPTS

Accounting Issues

Operating leases —leases treated as rental arrangements in which no asset or liability appears on the balance sheet of the lessee.

Capital lease —leases treated as if the lessee had acquired the property. An asset and liability appear on the lessee's balance sheet.

Criteria requiring treatment as a capital lease —if any one of these four criteria apply to a long-term, noncancellable lease, it is a capital lease:

1. Transfer of ownership to lessee.
2. Bargain purchase option.
3. Lease extends for at least three-quarters of useful life.
4. Present value of payments is at least 90% of fair market value.

Managerial Issues

Advantages of leasing —flexibility, ease of disposal, protection against technological change, 100 percent financing, lower risk.

Disadvantages of leasing —higher cost (you pay for risk shifted to lessor, and for middleman profit). The lessor gets the residual value unless the contract specifies otherwise.

Tax Issues

Shifting deductions —to taxpayers in higher tax brackets; effective depreciation of land; salvaging investment tax credits that might be lost.

Consultation of experts —whenever managerial decisions are made on the basis of generating tax savings, a tax expert should be consulted regarding the current tax law and the specific situation involved.

Fourteen

COST ACCOUNTING

Cost accounting is a major subfield of accounting. Large firms have staffs of cost accountants that work full time on collection and analysis of costs. This chapter focuses on the terminology of cost accounting and how cost information can be used for improved managerial decisions.

The role of cost accounting is to collect cost information to report what costs have been and to use that information for making decisions about the future. We are going to focus on both retrospective and prospective uses of cost information for managerial decisions. We must know how much each unit of our product costs us to make so that we can charge a high enough price to make a profit. If we can't sell a particular product at a price greater than its cost, then we should assess whether we should eliminate production of that product.

COST VS. EXPENSE:
THE INVENTORY PROCESS

The words *cost* and *expense* are often casually used interchangeably. However, they are very distinct in their underlying meaning. From an accounting perspective, the cost of an item is what is paid to acquire it. Expense refers to costs that have been matched to revenues they are responsible for generating. In essence, an item is a cost before it becomes an expense. If we purchase clay to make statuettes, we can refer to the cost of the clay. However, if we have not yet used the clay to make the statuettes, nor sold any statuettes, then the matching principle of accounting does not allow us to consider that cost to be an expense. Using Generally Accepted Accounting Principles (GAAP), we can only treat a cost as an expense in the period in which we record the revenues associated with that cost. Until a cost becomes an expense, it is generally treated as an asset, such as inventory.

This creates some rather interesting problems. Assume that we started the hypothetical Statuette Corporation on the last day of 1991. The owners purchased common stock in exchange for $1,000 cash. Statuette purchased 100 pounds of clay in 1992 for $1 per pound. Each statuette they make requires one pound of clay. By the end of 1992, they had started 80 statuettes and had 20 pounds of unused clay. Only 70 of the statuettes had been completed, and of those 70, a total of 60 statuettes had been sold for $2 each. What was the expense for clay for 1992?

The answer to this question requires an understanding of the inventory process. See Exhibit 14-1. When Statuette initially bought the clay, it was recorded as $100 of raw materials inventory (RMI). The 20 pounds that were not used remain as a $20 inventory balance for the raw materials account at the end of 1992. When we started to make statuettes, the clay was transferred from the raw materials inventory into production. From an accounting point of view, the cost of that portion of clay was transferred from the RMI account into a separate work in process (WIP) account. Thus, during 1992, $80 was transferred from RMI into the WIP account. Other production costs, such as labor and the various elements of overhead, also go into the WIP account and ultimately become expenses. Here, however, we are focusing only on how much of the cost of clay ultimately becomes an expense this year.

EXHIBIT 14-1.
The Inventory Process

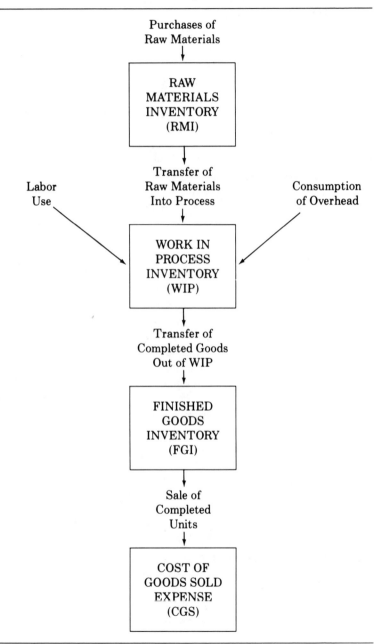

EXHIBIT 14-2.
Inventory Journal Entries

Assets + Expenses + Dividends = Liabilities + Revenues + Contributed Capital

---

1. Purchase of 100 pounds of clay for $100.
   Cash   − 100   = No change on right side.
   RMI   + 100

2. Transfer of 80 pounds of clay from RMI to WIP.
   RMI   − 80   = No change on right side.
   WIP   + 80

3. Transfer of 70 one-pound statuettes from WIP to FGI.
   WIP   − 70   = No change on right side.
   FGI   + 70

4. Sale of 60 one-pound statuettes for $2 each.
   a.) FGI   − 60   CGS +60 = No change on right side.
   b.) Cash + 120   =   Sales +120

Of the clay put into production, work was finished on 70 pounds, causing a transfer from WIP into a finished goods inventory (FGI) account. Then 60 units were sold, so they were transferred into a cost of goods sold (CGS) expense account. It is the $60 related to the final transfer that becomes an expense. At the end of 1992, $40 of cost is still in the raw materials, work in process, and finished inventory accounts. We can trace through the journal entries involved in a manner similar to that presented in Chapter 6 based on the modified basic equation of accounting, as shown in Exhibit 14-2.

If we were to look at a ledger for the accounts involved in this inventory process, we would see the following:

LEDGER ACCOUNT	BEGINNING BALANCE	TRANSACTION 1	2	3	4	ENDING BALANCE
Cash	1,000	−100			+120	1,020
RMI	0	+100	−80			20
WIP	0		+80	−70		10
FGI	0			+70	−60	10
CGS	0				+60	60
Sales	0				+120	120

The only portion of the cost that becomes an expense is the $60 that relates to the units which have been sold, thus generating $120 of revenue. The integrity of the matching principle has been preserved.

This process represents a manufacturing operation. For a wholesale or retail company, goods enter a merchandise inventory account when they are acquired. Their cost is transferred to cost of goods sold expense when the units are sold.

PERIOD COSTS VS. PRODUCT COSTS

In the previous example, we looked only at the cost of direct materials. In fact, there is a wide variety of costs. We must be concerned with labor, rent, administration, and marketing. We divide all costs into two broad categories: period costs and product costs. All costs directly associated with the product itself are considered to be product costs. All other costs are period costs.

For a merchandising firm, which simply buys and sells, the cost of the units purchased is the product cost. In a manufacturing firm, all costs associated with the manufacture of the product are considered to be product cost. This means that materials, labor, and factory rent are all treated as part of the cost of the product. Consider the implications of this for labor or factory rent. When we pay our factory workers, we cannot directly charge the labor expense account. This would imply that the labor generated revenue this period. However, it might be that the workers made units of product that have not yet been sold. To charge labor costs to expense directly would violate the matching principle. Instead, we add the cost of the labor to the work in process (WIP) inventory account. Similarly, the factory rent will be added to WIP. In this way, only a proportionate share of the labor and rent winds up being an expense this period. This proportion depends on how much of the product we work on this period is finished and sold. The remainder of these costs resides in the WIP and FGI accounts until all of this year's production is finally sold.

Any costs that are not product costs are automatically period costs. For all period costs, such as selling, general and administrative costs, there is no matching. These costs are charged to expense in the year incurred. Generally this is because it would be too difficult to determine which future sales result from bookkeeping, administrative, and selling efforts of this year. Thus, all depreciation on an office machine is an expense in the year the depreciation is incurred. But not all of the depreciation on a factory machine is an expense this year, unless all of this year's production is sold. When we see cost of goods sold on an income statement, it represents all elements of product cost: Direct labor (the hands-on labor in the production process), direct materials (the raw materials used to make the product), and factory overhead (all other elements of the production process such as supervisory labor, electricity, rent, depreciation, etc.).

MANIPULATION OF PRODUCT COSTS

The division between period and product cost can lead to some interesting manipulations of accounting information. Two principal areas of manipulation are in terms of classification between period and product cost, and in terms of the impact of changes in production levels.

Like many areas of accounting, there isn't necessarily always a correct classification of a cost as a period cost or a product cost. This is important because it has a direct impact on the net income of the firm. Suppose that one corner of the factory building is used as a payroll office. If we treat this office separately, its depreciation and other costs are all period costs reducing the current period income. On the other hand, if our accounting system doesn't draw that fine a line in the use of our factory space, many of those costs may become commingled with the factory and become product costs. In that way, some of this cost winds up in inventory at the year-end, and thus shows up as an asset rather than an expense. If the firm wants to maximize reported profits, this might be a desirable simplification. On the other hand, if the firm wants to minimize taxes, they may be very concerned with separately reporting all period expenses as such.

Another implication of this distinction between period and product costs is that it is possible to change income without necessarily changing sales. Consider what would happen if we were making and selling 100 units each year, and our factory rent was fixed at $2,000,000. Suppose that we were reporting an annual net income of exactly zero. What would happen if one year we doubled our production without changing our sales? The $2,000,000 of rent would be allocated to our 200 units of production. In the past, the entire $2,000,000 became an expense because we sold all of our production. Now we are only selling half of our production. Therefore half of the $2,000,000 remains as part of the 100 units of finished goods inventory that we didn't sell. Our expenses will be $1,000,000 lower (because only half of our rent is treated as an expense this year), so our pretax profit will be $1,000,000 higher!

While this may seem like a good idea, we really haven't gained any profits, we have just postponed the day of reckoning. We now have an entire year's worth of sales in inventory. Assuming we had to borrow some money to carry our inventory, our carrying costs are substantially higher than they would have been without the increased production. Meanwhile, we are still incurring factory rental cost of $2,000,000 per year. We didn't save $1,000,000, we just postponed recognition of the expense. While this practice doesn't provide any definite benefits for the firm other than short-term improvement in reported earnings, it has been used on occasion by managers whose incentive structure was improperly oriented toward short-term rather than long-term profit maximization. Issues of motivating managers to act in the best long-term interests of the firm are discussed in Part IV.

COST SYSTEMS: PROCESS, JOB-ORDER, AND STANDARD COSTS

The main focus of cost accounting is to be able to come up with a figure for the cost of each unit produced or acquired. The two most rudimentary systems for calculating this cost per unit are process and job-order actual costing. In both of these methods, we collect actual cost information and assign it directly to the units. Standard costs are the next step in the costing picture. Standard costs can simplify the costing process substantially.

Let's first consider process costing. This approach represents one extreme costing method. Under this approach a firm that makes a large quantity of an individual product keeps track of both the cost of the various components of the production process, and of the number of units made. For example, an aspirin manufacturer could keep track of the total amount of acetylsalicylic acid, labor, and so on used for a batch, and the number of bottles of aspirin produced in that batch. By dividing the total costs by the number of units, we find the cost per unit. This calculation can be done on a batch basis, or for continuous operations, on a monthly basis.

At the opposite extreme is the job costing or job-order costing approach. Consider the manufacturer of customized items, such as furniture. We can think of a custom furniture house receiving an order for six rosewood tables and another order for six knotty pine tables. The rosewood lumber is far more expensive than the knotty pine lumber. We might use skilled craftsmen on the rosewood tables and apprentices on the knotty pine tables. Clearly, the firm cannot get a good estimate of costs if it simply adds the total lumber and labor costs for the month and divides by 12 tables. Because each job is different, we need to gather information separately for each job.

Job-order costing is inherently more expensive from a bookkeeping standpoint than process costing. We need to keep track of how much of each type of lumber was used for each job. We need time cards to keep track of how much time each type of worker spent on each job. Pricing decisions cannot effectively be made without this information if the labor and materials truly are different for each job.

Many hybrid methods are possible. For example, it might well be that our furniture manufacturer has substantially different material costs depending on whether tables are oak or rosewood or knotty pine. But if all tables are alike from the point of view of labor, then regardless of which lumber we use, the labor requirements are identical. In that case, we could use job-order cost accounting to keep specific track of the materials used on each job. But we could use process-cost accounting for labor. We could simply total our labor cost and divide by the number of tables to get the labor cost per table.

What about standard costs? In using process and job-order accounting, one approach is to collect costs as you go and assign them periodically (often monthly) to the units produced. This provides very accurate information. Information, however, is costly. Managerial accountants are always attempting to find ways to provide an adequate amount of information at a lower cost. Do we really need the accuracy gained from actual process or actual job-order costing? Standard costs are a simplification that often provide enough information, but at a lower cost.

Suppose that our aspirin manufacturer produces a wide variety of pharmaceuticals, and the workers are used interchangeably among the various products. Further, there are materials that are used in common by many of the products. Process costing is no longer reasonable because there are so many different products using the same resources. Job-order costing is expensive because of the extra detail of material records and time cards. The standard costing alternative uses industrial engineering estimates and past experience to determine how much of our various resources we expect each unit of each product to consume, and what we expect those resources to cost.

For example, we have a standard cost card for aspirin showing how much of each material and how much labor and how much overhead we expect each bottle (or hundred bottles or thousand bottles) to consume, and the price we expect to have to pay for each material, type of labor, and so on. At the end of any month, as long as we know the number of units we have produced and sold, we can multiply the standard cost per unit times the number of units produced to get our total estimated production costs.

Use of standard costs does not relieve us from collecting actual cost information. The pharmaceutical house still needs to know the actual cost of labor for instance. But, by using standards, we can estimate a cost for each product individually, yet collect labor costs for all of our production in total. This significantly lessens the cost of collecting information about our expenditure on labor. At the same time, it increases our ability to control our operations significantly. Now we can compare our labor cost to what it should have cost (according to the standard cost) for the quantity of production we actually had.

If we actually spent more than we expected for that volume (an unfavorable variance) we can investigate to determine what the cause was. Possible causes include unexpected overtime, use of inferior materials, pay raises not included in the standard, or simply laxity on the part of workers and supervisors. Variances between actual production costs and estimated production costs based on standards require adjustments to the income statement so that we correctly report based on actual expenses. However, the inventory shown at year-end on the balance sheet is generally shown at its standard cost. This is much simpler than trying to calculate the actual costs for each product-line and assigning that value to year-end inventory. The ability to use standard cost information both for financial reporting, and as a tool to assess what has happened and improve control over future costs, makes it particularly valuable.

ACTIVITY BASED COSTING (ABC)

At the end of the 1980s and the beginning of the 1990s, a growing literature developed which is critical of traditional cost accounting methods. One major criticism concerns accounting for overhead. Many have suggested solving the overhead problem by moving to Activity Based Costing (ABC). Activity based costing proposes examination of overhead costs to see whether they can be directly related to specific activities.

Production costs are classified as being either direct or indirect. The direct costs generally consist of direct labor and direct materials. Direct labor is the labor directly associated with the production of a specific product. Direct materials are the materials specifically used to make a product. Anything that does not fall into a direct category is indirect, and is considered to be overhead. Direct costs for each product are measured and assigned directly to that product on a cause and effect basis. Indirect (overhead) costs are aggregated, and then allocated to products, not necessarily proportionately to the products that caused them to be incurred.

In determining the costs of a product, we would like to directly associate with the product all of the costs it is responsible for causing to be incurred. If more costs of production could be classified as direct, and fewer items as indirect, the costing would be more accurate. More accurate costs provide managers with better information for pricing and other product decisions. However, more accurate costing is usually more expensive.

For example, labor that is used to make a product or provide a service is often easily associated with the product. On the other hand, consider the labor of supervisors. Their labor is more difficult to associate with individual products. It might be extremely costly to track their time. Therefore their cost is considered to be indirect labor, and it is placed in an overhead pool. Overhead costs are then allocated to individual units of product.

Historically, most costs of production have consisted of direct materials and direct labor. Overhead has been a relatively minor component of total cost. As long as total overhead costs are relatively minor, the distortion caused by an arbitrary allocation of an overhead item is not important. In recent years, however, overhead has been a substantially growing portion of the overall cost of producing products and services. With the growth of the overhead component, a growing proportion of the cost assigned to each product is allocated arbitrarily rather than being directly measured.

For example, the cost of supervisory labor may be assigned to different products based on the proportion of direct labor hours worked on each project. Assume that a department's supervisory labor costs $100,000, and that in total the department's workers work 50,000 hours. The supervisory overhead cost is $2 per direct labor hour ($100,000 of cost divided by 50,000 direct labor hours). Assume further that the department makes 10,000 units of product A and 10,000 units of product B. Product A units each require 4 direct labor hours to make, and product B units each require 1 direct labor hour to make. Therefore, product A used 40,000 direct labor hours and product B uses 10,000 hours. At $2 per hour, product A is assigned supervisory labor overhead cost of $80,000, and product B is assigned $20,000 of overhead cost. This seems to be a fair allocation.

However, what if the supervisors spend most of their time setting up the production process? Suppose that they do an equal number of setups for A and B, and that they spend an equal amount of time for any set-up. In other words, in terms of actual supervisor time consumed, each product has used the exact same amount of that resource. Then each product should be assigned $50,000 of supervisory cost (i.e., half of the total). The existing system, which allocates supervisory cost based on direct labor hours, rather than based on the number of set-ups for each product has created a distortion in the cost of each product.

The focus of activity based costing is to review the various elements of overhead to determine whether they are related to an activity that can be measured. If so, then those overhead elements can become direct costs rather than overhead costs. They can be assigned directly to products. If set-ups is a good activity measure for supervisors, then we can measure the number of set-ups for each product and assign supervisory costs on a direct basis, without having to keep constant track of each supervisor's time.

Activity based costing will probably be gradually introduced to most organizations throughout the 1990s. Those organizations with a greater proportion of overhead will be the first to adopt this useful concept.

THE UNIT COST PROBLEM

The previous section focused on the ways to collect information concerning what it cost to produce units of various products. This is basically a retrospective approach. For prospective decisions, we often need to be able to predict costs. We must exercise some degree of care because historical costs may not clearly reflect the level of costs that would be incurred in the future. There are several problems of which we should be aware.

First of all, average cost information should always be viewed with suspicion. Very often we hear someone speak of the "cost per unit," of a product. In recalling the discussion of fixed and variable costs (from Chapter 8), we can see the problem with making decisions based on a cost per unit. Recall that fixed costs are those that do not change with changes in the volume of production. Variable costs change in direct proportion to production. For example, if we produce more units in our existing factory, the rent wouldn't rise, so rent would be a fixed cost. The amount of raw materials we use would increase, thus being a variable cost.

Suppose we currently are manufacturing 10,000 units at a cost of $10,000. Our cost per unit is $1. Suppose further that the variable costs for the 10,000 units are a total of $2,000, while the fixed costs are $8,000. If we are selling our units for 80 cents each, and they have a cost per unit of $1, then we are losing 20 cents on each unit we sell. We've all laughed at the story of the individual, faced by such a situation, who decided to increase production and make it up on volume! However, that is exactly the correct strategy. This is because our cost per unit is $1 *at a volume of* 10,000 units.

What happens to our cost per unit if we produce and sell 20,000 units? Our variable cost of $2,000 for 10,000 units doubles to $4,000 for 20,000 units, but the fixed cost remains $8,000. Thus the total cost for 20,000 units is $12,000, and the cost per unit is 60 cents. Suddenly our loss of 20 cents per unit becomes a profit of 20 cents per unit! This assumes that we could sell 20,000 units at the same price of 80 cents. The key is that because some costs are fixed, the cost per unit declines as volume increases. Thus, some products that look marginal or downright unprofitable at certain volumes might be very profitable at higher volumes. Of course, this only helps if you can sell the higher volume of units.

We can go even one step further. What if we were making 10,000 units at a cost of $1 per unit at that volume. However, now suppose that we were selling them for $1.20, so we are making a profit. Along comes a potential high volume customer who offers to buy 10,000 units for 50 cents per unit. We assume that this additional sale of 10,000 units does not affect our original sales at $1.20. Should we take the offer?

First we must understand how it might be possible for this new order not to affect our current sales. In order for this to be possible, we must be able to segment the market we face into distinct groups. This task generally belongs to the marketing department. The airlines have commonly charged several distinct prices for the same product. However, the lower super-saver fares usually have restrictions that make them undesirable to business traffic. Another form of segmentation is geographic. Another form is separation by wholesale and retail. For example, a firm normally selling a cleaner for home use might sell the same product at a substantially different price to a high volume industrial user.

Assuming that we can segment our market adequately to prevent our current customers who are paying $1.20 from demanding and receiving a 70 cent discount, should we sell an extra 10,000 units at 50 cents each? At first thought, we might say no. Even if we double our production from 10,000 units to 20,000, our average cost only falls to 60 cents. We would lose 10 cents on every unit sold. Or would we?

We are already making and selling 10,000 units. What will happen to the firm if it accepts this order, versus what would happen if it rejects the order? For every extra unit produced, we are going to generate an additional 50 cents of revenue. For every extra unit we make, we are going to spend an extra 20 cents on variable costs. How about fixed costs? How much extra fixed costs will we have for each extra unit we make? By definition, fixed costs are fixed in total. Assuming that we have sufficient excess capacity of plant and equipment to make the extra 10,000 units without incurring any additional fixed cost, our total fixed costs will not change. In that case, the total extra cost of producing an extra unit is only 20 cents. This variable cost is often referred to as the out-of-pocket or incremental or marginal cost. As long as the extra revenue received from each unit sold exceeds the variable cost, we are better off to make the additional sales.

Basically this constitutes a short-run strategy. In the long-run, the firm cannot survive unless it has some sales that not only cover variable cost, but also pay for the fixed costs. However, once the firm has committed itself to its fixed costs, all of the short-term decisions should consider those costs to be irrelevant. This is frequently referred to as a contribution margin approach. The extra revenue less the extra variable cost is called the contribution margin. This margin is the amount that a given project or department or product or contract contributes toward paying the firm's fixed costs and toward profits. In the short-run, the firm is better off by undertaking projects, products, etc., that have a positive contribution, even if they operate below average cost. That is, the accounting system allocates a variety of fixed overhead costs to a given project or product. Including these costs, that project or product may well be operating at a loss. However, if the firm would incur those allocated costs even if it doesn't do the project or make the product, then the allocated costs are irrelevant to the decision.

Thus, it should not be surprising that financial managers sometimes make decisions that seem perverse on the surface. They insist on allocating costs, even if those costs exist anyway. This is done because the financial reporting for historical purposes requires that total costs be shown. On the other hand, the same financial officers may require that you offer a product, even at a loss, because its contribution margin is positive. The firm's loss would be even greater if the project were not undertaken or the product was not offered. Although it may put the nonfinancial manager in a bind, it makes perfect sense to the accountant. The costs are allocated for proper retrospective reporting. The contribution approach is taken for proper prospective profit-maximizing decision-making.

The chief problem with all of this centers around the way that managers are rewarded. If your bonus depends on the income or return on investment of your division, you can have serious problems of goal congruence. What is in the best interests of the firm may not be in your own personal best interests. It may help the firm, but hurt you as a manager if a job with a positive contribution margin is accepted at below average cost. This topic is discussed in greater depth in Chapter 18 when we look at ratios that give performance measures for the firm and its managers.

KEY CONCEPTS

Cost accounting—the collection of information for reporting the costs incurred related to the acquisition or production of our product or service, and for making decisions regarding future production and product strategy.

The manufacturing inventory process—when inventory is acquired its cost is recorded as raw materials inventory (RMI). The costs of RMI that enter into the production process are transferred into the work in process inventory account (WIP). Other production costs are also added to WIP. When production is completed, the costs in WIP related to that production are transferred to the finished goods inventory account (FGI). When goods are sold, their cost is transferred from FGI to the cost of goods sold (CGS) account.

Product cost vs. period cost—product costs are all of the costs of manufacturing or acquiring the product. These costs become an expense only in the year in which the units of product are sold. Period costs are all costs that are not product costs. They become expenses in the year in which they are incurred.

Cost systems —process, job-order, and standard costs

Process costing—the determination of unit costs by comparing the number of units made to the total cost for a large amount of production, such as an entire month's output. Appropriate for mass production of similar units.

Job-order costing—the costs of each particular job are accumulated separately, and the cost per unit is assessed based on resources consumed for each particular job. More costly than process costing, but appropriate when individual jobs vary significantly in resource consumption.

Standard costing—use of a predetermined estimate of the cost per unit for each product. Any differences between actual and standard costs are adjusted in the year-end income statement.

Activity based costing—a method of examining overhead costs to see whether they can be related to specific activities. If so, then they can be assigned to products as direct costs, rather than being arbitrarily allocated as part of general overhead.

Cost per unit—the average cost of production for a specific volume of production. If any of the production costs are fixed, the cost per unit will fall as production volume increases.

Contribution margin pricing—the contribution margin is the difference between the revenue and variable costs. In the short run, when we have committed ourselves to a certain level of fixed costs, any job with a positive contribution margin (extra revenue exceeding extra variable costs) should be accepted, as long as it doesn't negatively impact on current sales or our long-run relations with our regular customers.

Fifteen

BUDGETING

DEFINITION AND ROLE OF BUDGETS

A budget is simply a plan. Despite any unpleasant connotations the term has picked up over time, a budget is simply a plan. In business, budgets are formalized (that is, written down) and quantitative (expressed in dollars).

One key reason for having a budget is to provide the firm with goals. If we have no initial plan, we have no idea of what we hope to achieve during a period of time. A second key reason for having a budget is to allow for effective evaluation. If we don't know where we're going, it's hard to tell whether or not we've arrived. A third key reason for having budgets is to force managers to think ahead. When plans are made well in advance, more choices are generally available than when decisions are made on a firefighting or crisis basis. Advance planning provides the necessary lead time for effective decisions. Once decisions are made, they must be acted upon by the organization. The fourth key use for budgets is as a tool of communication and coordination. Even if the chief executive officer has great plans for the organization, they can only be put into operation if they are communicated to the appropriate individuals in the firm. The budget serves this purpose.

THE MASTER BUDGET

The master budget contains a projection of each of the key financial statements: The income statement, the balance sheet, and the statement of cash flows. In addition, there are a variety of supporting schedules giving the assumptions and calculations used as a basis for the components of each statement.

The master budget is generally broken down into an operating budget and a financial budget. The operating budget provides all the information necessary to prepare a budgeted income statement. It includes revenue projections; cost of goods sold projections, which include the projected costs of materials, labor, and overhead for a manufacturing firm, or cost of purchases for a merchandising firm; selling expenses; administrative expenses; and finally financing (interest cost) expenses. These separate elements are combined into a projected income statement. The financial budget includes the cash budget and financial statement projections other than the income statement.

In addition to the operating and financial budgets, there are often special capital budgets that review all of the capital projects the firm is considering. These projects are evaluated according to the methods discussed in Chapter 12. Furthermore, the master budget includes performance reports. The area of budgeting is primarily thought of in terms of planning because the definition of a budget is a plan. However, budgeting differs from a budget in that budgeting encompasses both planning and control. By adding the -ing ending, we have added a substantial element. A budget by itself is useful because it forces managers to think ahead and set goals. But budgeting makes the budget much more valuable, in that it makes the budget a useful tool to help us achieve our goals. This is accomplished by frequent comparison of actual and budgeted results, with investigation and correction of problems when we stray from our budget.

Budgets are generally prepared annually. Within the annual budget, we usually prepare monthly projections. This allows us to make evaluations after each month and to make necessary adjustments throughout the year. Recently, many firms have started to use continuous budgets. Under this system, each month the annual budget is projected one month further into the future. One of the main reasons we have budgets is to see our plan into the future. Consider the firm that prepares their budget in October for the next calendar year. At that point, they have a fourteen month horizon (November of this year through December of next year). But by next June their horizon is only six months, and by the beginning of October it is only three months. This decreasing horizon problem is avoided with continuous budgeting. At all times there is a plan for at least one full year into the future. Furthermore, continuous budgeting relieves the massive problem of doing a whole year's budget in just a few months.

BUDGET PREPARATION

Preliminaries

The first step in budget preparation is the completion of an environmental statement. The firm cannot effectively plan for the coming year without a clearly stated idea of what their position is vis-a-vis their suppliers, competitors, and customers. An annual evaluation of industry trends, changes in customer base, technological changes, and so on can help the firm to better determine where it should be going.

The next step is for top management to develop a set of general objectives and policies. This statement should be a broad-based look at what the firm hopes to achieve. Is the coming year one of holding the line against competitors, or is it to be a year of rapid growth? Is the firm looking for domestic expansion, or establishment of foreign markets? Does the firm expect to increase the market share in existing products, or to be aggressive in the introduction of new products? If top management communicates the desired direction of the firm, middle management can set out to move in that direction.

Before the actual budget can be developed, a set of assumptions must be adopted. What will inflation be in the coming year? What actions do we expect competition to take that might affect our sales or the price of our product? Will suppliers be raising their prices? Will new sources of raw materials become available? Are there going to be more significant shifts in consumer demand? All of these and many more questions must be answered, but there is no way to know the answer, so assumptions must be made and communicated to those directly involved in the budget preparation process.

Finally, specific, measurable goals should be established. Here we are not dealing simply with the general direction of the firm, but with the actual operating objectives. For example, sales should increase by 10 percent and profits by 15 percent. These are two ambitious objectives—more often than not, a firm that doesn't budget, or that doesn't control the budget, will not have much success in achieving such goals.

Forecasting

At this point forecasting can begin. Once we have decided what we are trying to accomplish, we have to set up a specific plan to meet those goals. This specific plan requires a forecast of what would happen under a variety of alternatives. What if we raise our price? What if we import partially assembled parts? What if we automate? What if we don't formally change anything? In all of these cases, how much will we sell, at what price, and at what cost?

Forecasts can be quite simple. They may simply be a projection that what happened last year will happen again next year. Or they can be based on extremely complex mathematical formulas. We can statistically review trends and seasonal patterns. Most forecasting is based, to a major extent, on historical patterns. Of course, an accurate forecast must also consider any changes that may make the future different from the past. These changes can be due to improved technology, initiatives by competitors, changes in laws, etc.

In the last few years sophisticated forecasting techniques have become available for non-financial managers. Specifically, a number of forecasting software programs have been developed for personal computers. Generally, these programs can be used by managers with little or no experience in forecasting.[1] Some programs allow the user to select from a range of statistical forecasting methods, or to simply allow the computer to automatically select the best forecasting method for your data, from among a group of methods.

The computer forecasting programs generate graphs and tables of forecasts. Some of the programs can generate forecasts that are curvilinear. One of the limitations of most forecasting done in businesses is that the forecasts are linear. They are based on straight lines. However, if there are seasonal patterns for the firm (times of the year that are generally very busy or unusually slow for production or sales or both), a curved line would generate a more accurate forecast. Curvilinear forecasting is rarely done by hand because of the extreme complexity of the mathematics. However, with computer programs, generating more accurate curvilinear forecasts is within the easy grasp of both financial and nonfinancial managers alike.

The most important feature of forecasts that a nonfinancial manager should be aware of is that they are guesses about the future. These guesses are primarily made by mechanical rather than judgmental means. Unfortunately, there are always a number of variables that cannot be captured by mechanical approaches. Therefore, a manager should never be afraid to question the accuracy of a forecast. As a manager of your business, you know more than any formula, and you should rely on your judgment to modify formulas or projections for factors that you feel the formulas have ignored. Once forecasts of sales and production costs have been made, the budgets can be prepared.

Departmental Budgets

Having completed the preliminary budget activities, and having prepared forecasts for the key elements of the budget, the next step is the actual preparation of the budget. The organizational budget consists of a compilation of the operating and capital budgets for

[1] One example of a popular forecasting program for nonfinancial managers is Smart-Forecasts II. Information on SmartForecasts II is available from the vendor, Smart Software Inc., 4 Hill Road, Belmont, MA 02178.

the various departments. Based on the total requirements for each department, cash flow projections can also be made.

Each department must compile its budget based on the specific costs that it expects to encounter, and if it is a revenue center, the revenues that it projects as well. Budgets should be as detailed as possible, to ensure that all relevant items have been included. The budgeting task sometimes seems very complicated because of the specific forms that any given organization requires to be completed. However, the essential process is not complicated. Each organization strives to get an itemization of the various costs that it will encounter for the coming year, and the associated revenues.

Once these itemizations are completed, there is a process of evaluation. Are the requests reasonable? Do the departments need all of the resources they are requesting, or are they building fat into the budget? If the budget is carried out as specified, will it result in a satisfactory outcome for the organization? Will sales be high enough? Will costs be low enough?

Even if a department's budget is reasonable, there may still be limitations on what the organization can, or will, approve. It is possible that a series of capital expenditures, even if profitable in the long term, will require more cash than the organization believes will be available. Thus there is an interplay between the operating and capital budgets prepared by departments, and the resulting projections of cash flows prepared by the financial office. All of the elements of the master budget must come together to result in a satisfactory outcome for the organization before the individual components can be approved.

USING BUDGETS FOR CONTROL

Static Budgets

The usual master budget is a "static" budget. The static budget is used to compare expected results with actual results. Any difference is called a variance. If the amount actually spent on an expense item is greater than the budgeted amount, it is considered to be an unfavorable variance. On the other hand, if less was spent than anticipated, it is a favorable variance.

EXHIBIT 15-1.
Total Manufacturing Variance
Bud Jet Corporation

BUDGETED TOTAL COSTS	ACTUAL TOTAL COSTS	VARIANCE FAVORABLE/ (UNFAVORABLE)
$2,000,000	$2,200,000	$(200,000)

Within this framework, the more detailed the budget is, the greater the amount of control we can exercise. For example, if we know only the total budget, we have very little information. Consider the case of hypothetical Bud Jet Corporation. In Exhibit 15-1 we see that Bud Jet had total manufacturing costs of $200,000 more than expected for a particular month. Why? From the information in this exhibit it is hard to tell. If we had information by department, we would have a better idea of what has occurred.

From Exhibit 15-2, we can see that although the polishing department had a good year, the Processing, Assembly, and Packing departments were substantially over budget. This gives the first step toward discovering what has happened. Now we can begin to investigate why cost overruns occurred so that we can hopefully

EXHIBIT 15-2.
Manufacturing Department Variances
Bud Jet Corporation

DEPARTMENT	BUDGETED COSTS	ACTUAL COSTS	VARIANCE
Purchasing	$1,000,000	$1,010,000	$ (10,000)
Processing	200,000	280,000	(80,000)
Assembly	400,000	460,000	(60,000)
Polishing	100,000	90,000	10,000
Packing	300,000	360,000	(60,000)
TOTALS	$2,000,000	$2,200,000	$(200,000)

avoid them in future months. Specifically, we can focus our attention on the departments where the largest variances occurred.

Yet, we still don't really have adequate information. Consider the large Processing Department variance. We do know who to ask about the variance. We want the manager of the Processing Department to explain what happened. But the financial officers haven't given the manager of that department much to go on. He simply knows he was $80,000 over budget. If the static budget is broken down even further by line item for each department, such as personnel cost, materials, and overhead, it becomes easier to determine why excess costs occurred. Exhibit 15-3 presents such an analysis for the Processing Department at Bud Jet.

Note that the entire variance occurred in the area of materials. Investigation might show that this was unavoidable due to a significant unexpected rise in the price of raw materials used. On the other hand, we might find that employees had been quite careless in the use of materials, resulting in significant waste. This latter possibility makes clear the fact that budget variances should be calculated and investigated frequently. Although there may be little that can be done about rises in the prices of raw materials, we should catch waste and correct it long before year-end.

Line-item analysis of variances can, of course, be quite detailed. We can calculate the variance with respect to each type of labor or raw material input. However, even that still does not help us to isolate the cause of the variance as much as we would like. Did

EXHIBIT 15-3.
Processing Department Line-Item Variances
Bud Jet Corporation

	BUDGETED COSTS	ACTUAL COSTS	VARIANCE
PROCESSING DEPT.			
Personnel	$ 80,000	$ 80,000	$ 0
Materials	100,000	180,000	(80,000)
Overhead	20,000	20,000	0
TOTALS	$200,000	$280,000	$(80,000)

the processing department go over on its materials budget because it wasted materials or because the price of materials had risen? We have gone as far as we can with the static budget. In order to gain additional information about the cause of variances, we now have to turn our attention to flexible budgeting.

Flexible Budgeting

The key problem with static budgets is that they provide an expected cost for one particular volume, hence the name *static*. At the end of a reporting period such as a month or a year, it is highly unlikely that we will have attained exactly the expected output level. If we produce more units than we had planned, because sales are up substantially over our expectations, then it is logical to assume that we will have to go over our budget. On the other hand, if volume is down, then costs should be under budget. Flexible budgets are an after-the-fact device to tell what it should have cost for the volume level actually attained. The flexible budget is derived by adjusting the static budget for the actual production volume achieved.

Flexible Budget Variance and Volume Variance

Suppose we expect the variable cost per unit to be $10. If we expect to produce 100,000 units, then we expect a total variable cost of $1,000,000. What if we only produced 85,000 units, and we had a total variable cost of $900,000? The static budget comparison would be that we had a budgeted variable cost of $1,000,000, and we only spent $900,000, so we had a favorable variance of $100,000. But it should have cost only $850,000 to produce 85,000 units. We actually spent more than we should have, given the level of actual production. We should have noted an unfavorable variance! In this example, the actual cost was $900,000, the static budget was $1,000,000, and the flexible budget was $850,000.

The total variance between the actual cost of $900,000 and the static budget of $1,000,000 is a favorable variance of $100,000, as noted earlier. Exhibit 15-4 shows that we can decompose this total variance into two parts. The first part, on the right side of the exhibit, is the difference between the static budget and the flexible

EXHIBIT 15-4.
Flexible Budget Variance and Volume Variance

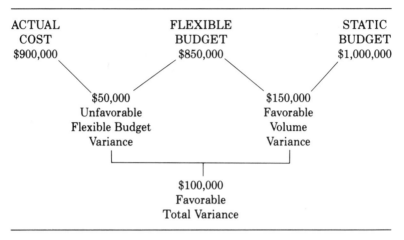

budget. This is a $150,000 favorable variance. However, by favorable we simply mean we spent less than expected. This variance is called a volume variance: it is caused because our volume varied from what was expected. It is likely that because volume was below that expected this is an unfavorable event, even though the accountant calls it a favorable variance.

On the left side of Exhibit 15-4 is the difference between the actual cost and the flexible budget, which gives rise to an unfavorable flexible budget variance of $50,000. That is, we actually spent $50,000 more than we would have budgeted for the level of production attained. The flexible budget variance and the volume variance in total are equal to the total variance.

Price and Quantity Variances

We can still get more information from variance analysis. For each variable cost item, we can calculate not only the volume and flexible budget variances, but also a price, and quantity variance.

The difference between the flexible budget and the actual costs incurred makes up the flexible budget variance. It is possible for the accountant to break down this flexible budget variance into two components—the part of the total variance caused because we paid a different price for our inputs, and the part of the difference caused because we used more or less of an input than we expected, for the actual volume of production. See Exhibit 15-5. The total of the price, quantity, and volume variances makes up the total variance between actual costs and the original static budget.

When we consider materials, we refer to the price variance simply as a price variance, and we refer to the quantity variance as a use variance. While the term *price* is adequately clear, the word *use* allows us to visualize that the variance refers to how much material we used to make the amount of product. With respect to variances in the cost of labor, we generally refer to these variances as rate and efficiency variances. The term *rate* is based on the rate we pay labor. The term *efficiency* is based on the fact that frequently, when we consume more labor than expected to produce a given level of output, inefficiency exists. However, this may not always be the case.

We should be especially careful in interpreting variances. The accountant uses the word *favorable* to imply that less money was spent than was expected. The term *unfavorable* is used to mean that more money was spent than was expected. There is no sense of good or bad or efficient or inefficient implied by the terms *favorable* and *unfavorable* in an accounting context. If we have an unfavorable labor efficiency variance, this doesn't necessarily

EXHIBIT 15-5.
Price, Quantity and Volume Variances

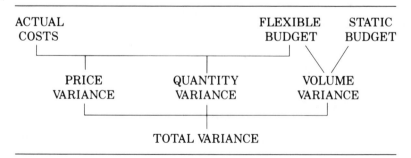

imply that labor worked inefficiently. There may have been a machine breakdown, or a stockout of a key material. It is possible the purchasing department bought inferior materials that required more labor input.

The benefit of using price and quantity variances is that it can help to very narrowly pinpoint the specific areas where we went over or under budget. However, the variances themselves should not be considered causes for punishment or congratulations. All that variances can do is point the direction for investigations to take to determine the underlying causes for variances. But by undertaking such investigations on a timely basis, we can convert a budget into budgeting, and thus convert a plan into an ability to both plan and control results, so that we come as near to achieving or surpassing the plan as possible.

KEY CONCEPTS

Budget—a formalized (written), quantitative (in dollars) plan.

Uses of budgets—set goals; evaluate results; improve the effectiveness of decision making by planning ahead; and for communication and coordination.

Master budget—a projection of the key financial statements, cash flow, and capital projects. The master budget also describes performance reports to be used.

Budget preparation

Preliminaries—an environmental statement should be developed to determine the position of the firm relative to customers, suppliers, and creditors. General objectives should be set, specific assumptions made, and measurable goals established.

Forecasts—the essential ingredient for compilation of budgets is a set of forecast information. Generally, forecasts use such mechanical means as statistics and computers to project the past into the future. Managers must be aware that judgment should be used to modify forecast results.

Departmental Budgets—the organization budget consists of the aggregation of budgets from each department. The departmental budgets itemize revenues and expenses in detail.

Static budget—a budget prepared before the year begins, establishing what it should cost for the anticipated output level.

Flexible budget—an after-the-fact budget establishing what it should have cost for the actual attained output level.

Variance—a difference between an actual result and a budgeted amount:

Volume variance—the difference between the static budget and the flexible budget.

Price variance—the portion of the difference between the flexible budget and actual costs caused by paying a different price for each unit of raw material or hour of labor than had been anticipated.

Quantity variance—the portion of the difference between the flexible budget and the actual costs caused by using more raw materials or labor for each unit produced than had been anticipated.

Total variance—the volume variance, plus the price variance, plus the quantity variance make up the total variance for the variable inputs. This is equal to the difference between the static budget and the actual costs.

Part IV

FINANCIAL STATEMENT ANALYSIS

Sixteen

A CLOSER LOOK AT FINANCIAL STATEMENTS

Earlier this book examined the source of financial statements. We discussed the basic definitions of assets, liabilities, stockholders' equity, revenues, and expenses. We traced through a variety of journal entries, and saw how ledger balances can be used to derive key financial statements. In order to understand financial information, it is vital to have an understanding of where this information comes from.

We now turn our attention to trying to get as much useful information as possible from a set of financial statements. There are a variety of reasons for wanting to be able to do this. First and foremost is to enable us to manage our firm better. Second, we want to be able to review the financial statements of close competitors to evaluate our performance as compared to theirs. Third, we may want to evaluate the financial statements of a firm in which we wish to invest. Fourth, we want to evaluate the financial statements of firms we are considering extending credit to.

We may be looking for different types of information in each case. Before extending credit, we want to assess a firm's liquidity and solvency. Before investing in a firm, we wish to know about its potential profitability. The goal of financial statement analysis is to derive from financial statements the information needed to make informed decisions.

We do this primarily through examination of the notes that accompany the financial statements, and through the use of a technique called ratio analysis. Generally accepted accounting principles, in recognition of many of the limitations of financial numbers generated by accounting systems, require that clarifying notes accompany financial statements. The information contained in these notes may be more relevant and important than the basic statements themselves. Ratio analysis is a method for examining the numbers contained in financial statements to see if there are relationships among the numbers that can provide us with useful information.

Chapter 17 focuses on the notes to the financial statements. Chapter 18 discusses ratio analysis. For the remainder of this chapter we will present a hypothetical set of financial statements to use as a basis of discussion for the remainder of the book.

THE BALANCE SHEET

Exhibit 16-1 presents the balance sheet for the hypothetical Pacioli Wholesale Corporation (PW) that will be the subject of our analysis. The information is provided for two years. In recognition of the fact that information in a vacuum is not very useful, accountants generally provide comparative data. In the case of PW, the financial statements present the current fiscal year ending June 30, 1992 and the previous fiscal year ending June 30, 1991. Some financial reports contain the current year and the two previous years for comparison.

All the numbers on the PW financial statements are rounded to the nearest thousand dollars. For large corporations, it is not uncommon to round numbers to the nearest hundred thousand or even million. This is done to avoid giving the impression of a higher degree of accuracy than really exists. Keep in mind that the auditor of a firm's financial statements is concerned with the generally accepted accounting principle (GAAP) of materiality. That is, the auditor wants to make sure that significant errors are uncovered and corrected.

EXHIBIT 16-1.

Pacioli Wholesale Corporation
Statement of Financial Position
As of June 30, 1992 and June 30, 1991

ASSETS	1992		1991	
Current Assets				
Cash		$ 8,000		$ 7,000
Marketable Securities		12,000		9,000
Accounts Receivable, Net of Uncollectible Accounts		22,000		30,000
Inventory		49,000		40,000
Prepaid Expenses		3,000		2,000
Total Current Assets		$ 94,000		$ 88,000
Fixed Assets				
Buildings and Equipment	$150,000		$120,000	
Less Accumulated Depreciation	40,000		30,000	
Net Buildings and Equipment	$110,000		$ 90,000	
Land	50,000		50,000	
Total Fixed Assets	$160,000		$140,000	
Goodwill		$ 45,000		$ 50,000
TOTAL ASSETS		$299,000		$278,000

LIABILITIES AND STOCKHOLDERS' EQUITY	1992		1991	
Current Liabilities				
Wages Payable		$ 3,000		$ 2,000
Accounts Payable		29,000		25,000
Taxes Payable		15,000		12,000
Total Current Liabilities		$ 47,000		$ 39,000
Long-Term Liabilities				
Mortgage Payable		$ 45,000		$ 50,000
Bond Payable		100,000		100,000
Deferred Taxes		39,000		35,000
Total Long-Term Liabilities		$184,000		$185,000
Stockholders' Equity				
Common Stock, $1 Par, 1000 shares		$ 1,000		$ 1,000
Common Stock—Excess over par		24,000		24,000
Preferred Stock, 10%, $100 Par, 100 shares		10,000		10,000
Retained Earnings		33,000		19,000
Total Stockholders' Equity		$ 68,000		$ 54,000
TOTAL LIABILITIES & STOCKHOLDERS' EQUITY		$299,000		$278,000

The accompanying notes are an integral part of these statements.

The large number of journal entries made by a firm during the course of the year creates a probability that a number of errors have been made. As long as the errors are relatively minor, the firm and its auditor are willing to live with them. The cost of detecting every error would be enormous. Furthermore, a number of estimates are made in the accounting process. Accounting is far from being an exact science. By rounding off the numbers presented on the financial statements, we can convey, at least to some extent, the fact that the statements cannot give a perfectly accurate reflection of the firm's position and the results of its operations.

Current Assets

The first group of assets on the balance sheet are the current assets. These are the most liquid of the firm's resources. Earlier, as a simplifying assumption, we defined current assets as those that would become cash or be used up within a year. A more formalized definition would be that current assets are assets that will become cash or will be used up within the firm's operating cycle. The operating cycle is the period of time from when a firm pays cash to buy the raw inputs for providing its goods and services, until it finally receives cash in payment for its sales. The operating cycle is often assumed to be one year for purposes of preparing financial statements. However, some firms clearly have a longer operating cycle. For example, a whiskey manufacturer buys raw materials and puts them into process at least several years before the sale of the aged whiskey and the collection of revenue on the sale. In such cases, the inventory is considered to be a current asset (you might even call it a liquid asset), even though it will be on hand for a number of years.

The current assets are presented on the balance sheet in order of liquidity. Cash, the most readily available asset for use in meeting obligations as they become due, is listed first. Cash includes amounts on deposit in checking and savings accounts as well as cash on hand. The next item is marketable securities that are intended to be liquidated in the near term. They can be converted to cash in a matter of a few days. Marketable securities that the firm intends to hold as long-term investments shouldn't be listed with current assets, but instead under a long-term investment category, after fixed assets.

The next current asset listed would be accounts receivable, net of uncollectible accounts. It is usually the case that we do not expect to collect what is due us from all of our customers. In fact, it is a correct business decision to incur bad debts. Often we find ourselves faced with a choice of whether or not to extend credit to a customer who we know is facing some financial difficulty. Suppose that we make a unit of our product for a cost of $600 and that we sell it for $1,000. If there is a 20 percent chance of default by a customer, should we refuse the sale? Probably not. If we were to sell to five such customers, each with a 20 percent chance of default, the probabilities indicate that one of them would default on the payment. The total sale to the five customers would be $5,000 and the cost of the goods sold would be $3,000. If we collect from four of the five customers, we collect $4,000 as compared to our cost of $3,000. We are $1,000 better off than if we refused to sell to any of the five customers. Your accountant can calculate the relevant margins, but the trick here is to have a credit manager who can accurately predict how likely it is that a customer will default.

Inventory is not as liquid as receivables because we first have to sell the goods in order to generate receivables. Prepaid expenses are generally small, relative to the rest of the balance sheet. They would include such items as prepaid rent or insurance. Prepaid expenses are grouped with current assets even though they will not generally generate any cash to use for paying current liabilities.

Long-Term Assets

All assets the firm has that are not current assets fall into the general category of long-term assets. Prominent among the long-term assets are fixed assets, which include the property, plant, and equipment used to process or produce the firm's product or service. A variety of other long-term assets may appear on the balance sheet. There would be a category for investments if we had marketable securities that we anticipated keeping for more than one year.

In the case of PW, there is an asset called goodwill. Goodwill is an intangible asset that may arise through the acquisition of another company. Most firms have some goodwill: they have customer loyalty and a good relationship with their suppliers. However, goodwill is an intangible asset that accountants usually leave off the balance sheet because of the difficulty in measuring it. When one company takes over another, if they pay more for the company they are acquiring than can reasonably be assigned as the fair market value of the specific identifiable assets that they are buying, then the excess is recorded on the balance sheet of the acquiring company as goodwill. This follows the accountant's philosophy that people are not fools. If we pay more for a company than its other assets are worth, then there is a presumption that the various intangibles we are acquiring that can't be directly valued, must be worth at least the excess amount we paid. GAAP require us to reduce (amortize) a portion of the goodwill each year, and to charge that reduction as an expense on our financial report to the stockholders.

Liabilities

The firm's current liabilities are those that exist at the balance sheet date, which have to be paid in the next operating cycle— usually considered to be one year. Common current liabilities include wages payable, accounts payable, and taxes payable. The taxes payable would include only the portion to be paid in the near term, not the taxes that have been deferred more than one year beyond the balance sheet date.

Long-term liabilities include any recorded liabilities that are not current liabilities. There may be a variety of commitments that the firm has made that will not be included with the liabilities. For example, if the firm has operating leases (see Chapter 13), they will not appear on the balance sheet, even though they may legally obligate the firm to make large payments into the future. The notes to the financial statements are especially important in disclosing material commitments.

Stockholders' Equity

The stockholders' equity section of the balance sheet contains a number of elements not previously discussed. Instead of simply having contributed capital and retained earnings, there are a number of separate items that comprise contributed capital. In addition, there is a distinction between amounts paid representing *par* value and amounts in excess of par. *Par value* is a new term that is discussed in this section.

In the case of PW, there are two general classes of stock. There is common stock and preferred stock. Both types of stock represent contributed capital. Individuals have given the firm cash or other valuable resources in exchange for an ownership interest in the firm. Preferred shareholders have rights to get dividends prior to common shareholders. In the event of bankruptcy, they will get paid before the common shareholders. However, common shareholders generally have a greater say in running the company, and while they bear a greater risk in the case of bankruptcy, they stand to earn a greater return on their money if the firm is very successful.

Par value is a legal concept. In many states, firms are required to set an arbitrary amount as the par value of their stock. Creditors can rely on the fact that for each share of stock outstanding, the stockholders of the firm have risked their own money. The amount the stockholders have risked must be at least the par value for each share issued.

One of the primary reasons many firms incorporate is to achieve a limited liability for their owners. Unlike a proprietorship or a partnership, in which the owners are personally responsible for all of the business' debts, owners of corporations have limited liability. They can lose the entire amount that they've invested, but creditors can't come to the owners personally and take their house, car, etc. That is, assuming that the corporation's stock was originally issued for at least its par value. If stock is issued below the par value—let's say that $10 par value stock is issued for $7, then the owner could be liable for the difference between the issue price and the par value should the firm go bankrupt. Given that situation, the par value of a corporation's stock is generally set low enough so that all stock is issued for at least the par value. Recall that par value is an arbitrary value set by the firm.

There is no connection between the par value and any underlying *value* of the firm. There is no reason to believe that the arbitrarily selected par value is a good measure of what a share of stock is worth. In fact, because most firms are very careful to set par low enough so that there is no extra liability for the corporation's owners, par value has become almost meaningless. Therefore, some states now allow corporations to issue stock without assigning a par value.

From an accounting perspective, we wish to be able to show the user of financial statements whether there is some potential additional liability to the stockholders. For example, what if 100 shares of $10 par value stock had been issued for $7 and another 100 shares had been issued for $13. Legally we can not average these amounts and say that all shares were issued for $10 each. The first 100 shares were issued below par value and therefore there is a $3 per share exposure to risk for the owners of those shares. To show this, the accountant will have one account to show amounts received for stock up to the par value amount. Anything paid above par for any share will go into a separate account with a name such as "excess paid over par" or "additional paid-in capital."

In the case of the PW, we see that it has 1,000 shares of $1 par value common stock. The balance in the common stock par account is $1,000, meaning that all 1,000 shares were issued for at least $1 each, the par value. There are 100 shares of $100 par value preferred stock and the balance in the preferred stock par account is $10,000, indicating that each of the 100 shares was issued for at least $100. Therefore, we know that the stockholders of PW have limited liability. They can lose everything they've paid for their stock, but if the firm goes bankrupt, the creditors cannot attempt to collect additional amounts from the stockholders personally.

As is quite commonly the case, PW's stockholders have paid more than the par value for at least some of the stock issued by the corporation. The common stock excess over par account has a balance of $24,000. Together with the $1,000 in the common stock par account, this indicates the investors paid $25,000 (or gave the firm resources worth $25,000) for 1,000 shares of stock. On average, investors have paid $25 per share for the common stock. There is no excess over par account for the preferred stock. Therefore, we know that the preferred stockholders each paid exactly $100 per share for the preferred stock.

The preferred stock is referred to as 10 percent, $100 par stock, indicating that the annual dividend rate on the preferred stock is 10 percent of the $100 par value. Each preferred share must receive a $10 dividend before the firm can pay any dividend to the common stock shareholders.

The retained earnings, as discussed earlier in the book, represent the profits that the firm earned during its existence that have not been distributed to the stockholders as dividends, and therefore have been retained in the firm. Remember that this category, like the others on the liability and owners' equity side of the balance sheet, represent claims on assets. There is no pool of money making up the retained earnings. Rather, the profits earned over the years and retained in the firm have likely been invested in a variety of fixed and current assets.

THE INCOME STATEMENT

The income statement of PW (Exhibit 16-2) does not overtly raise as many new concepts and issues as the balance sheet did. PW uses the common multiple step statement in which various expenses are shown separately. For instance, product costs are all grouped under the heading "Cost of Goods Sold." The gross margin provides information about the margin of profitability when sales are compared to the direct product costs of the firm.

Operating income is derived by subtracting the various other day-to-day operating costs from the gross margin. By operating costs, we mean the various selling, administrative, and general costs of the firm. These costs include everything except product costs, financing costs, and taxes. Financing costs are isolated as a separate figure because of the specific financial leverage decisions (see Chapter 8) the firm makes. There is a much greater degree of control over whether interest expense exists than, say, selling expenses. Management can decide whether money is to be borrowed—thus generating interest expense, or whether money should be raised through the issuance of stock.

Management can choose to use a single step statement in which far less information is given about individual types of expenses. In this latter case, less information is provided to stockholders and creditors. On the other hand, less information is also given to competitors. The single step approach cannot be used if it would mask information that the auditor believes is necessary for a fair representation of the firm's position and results of operations.

The line following net income in Exhibit 16-2 contains earnings per share data. GAAP require inclusion of information on a per share basis for common stock. It is felt that this type of information

EXHIBIT 16-2.

Pacioli Wholesale Corporation
Income Statement and Analysis of Retained Earnings
For the Years Ending June 30, 1992 and June 30, 1991

		1992		1991
Sales		$297,000		$246,000
Less Cost of Goods Sold		162,000		143,000
Gross Profit		$135,000		$103,000
Operating Expenses				
Selling Expenses	$30,000		$25,000	
General Expenses	12,000		10,000	
Administrative Expenses	49,000		40,000	
Total Operating Expenses		91,000		75,000
Operating Income		$ 44,000		$ 28,000
Interest Expense		12,000		10,000
Income Before Taxes		$ 32,000		$ 18,000
Income Taxes		13,000		7,000
Net Income		$ 19,000		$ 11,000
Earning Per Share Common	$ 18.00		$ 10.00	
Less Dividends 1992 and 1991		5,000		3,000
Addition to Retained Earnings		$ 14,000		$ 8,000
Retained Earnings July 1,				
1991 and 1990		19,000		11,000
Retained Earnings June 30,				
1992 and 1991		$ 33,000		$ 19,000

The accompanying notes are an integral part of these statements.

may be more relevant than net income for many users of financial information. Consider an individual who owns 100 shares of common stock of a large corporation. The corporation reports that its profits have risen from $25,000,000 to $30,000,000. On the surface, we would presume that the stockholder is better off this year. What if, however, during the year the firm issued additional shares of stock, thereby creating additional owners. Although total profits have risen $5,000,000 or 20 percent, because of the additional shares of stock outstanding, our investor will find that his share of earnings increased by less than 20 percent. In fact, it is quite possible that the profits attributable to each individual share may have fallen, even though the total profit for the firm has increased.

Therefore, we must show not only net income for the firm, but also net income per share of common stock. Although there are 1,000 shares of common stock for PW, and the net income was $19,000, the earnings or income (the two terms are used interchangeably) per share is $18.00, rather than the expected $19.00 This is because $1,000 has to be paid as a 10 percent dividend to the preferred shareholders. This portion of the income of the firm doesn't belong to the common shareholders. The remaining $18,000 does.

For PW, the balance in the common and preferred stock accounts didn't change during the year (Exhibit 16-1). However, upon looking at the stockholders' equity section of the balance sheet, we see that the retained earnings has changed. Furthermore, the change is not exactly equal to the firm's income for the year. Somewhere in the financials we need some way of reconciling this change. In PW's case they have chosen one of the most common approaches—retained earnings are reconciled as part of the income statement.

In order to accomplish this reconciliation, the first step is to subtract any of this year's dividends from this year's net income. The difference is in the amount of this year's earnings that are being retained in the firm. This year's earnings that are retained in the firm, plus the balance of retained earnings at the start of the year gives us the retained earnings balance at year-end. This number should, and does, reconcile directly with the number that appears on the balance sheet as the year-end retained earnings.

THE STATEMENT OF CASH FLOWS

The statement of cash flows is the newest of the required financial statements, having been a required part of an audited annual report only since the late 1980s. The income statement focuses on the operations of the firm. Specifically, what did it cost to make and sell the product or service, what did it cost to operate the firm, and how much revenue did the firm get for the product or service? The statement of cash flows focuses on financial rather than operating aspects of the firm. Where did the money come from, and how did the firm spend it? While the major concern of the income statement is profitability, the statement of cash flows is very concerned with viability. Is the firm generating and will it generate enough cash to meet both short-term and long-term obligations?

PW's statement of cash flows is presented in Exhibit 16-3. The first element of the statement is cash flows from operating activities. This is a key focal point, because it provides information on whether the routine operating activities of the firm generate cash, or require a cash infusion. If the operating activities generate a surplus of cash, the firm is more financially stable and viable, than if they consume more cash then they generate. This does not mean that negative cash from operating activities is bad. It may be indicative of a growing, profitable firm that is expanding inventories and receivables as it grows. However, it does provide a note of caution. Overly rapid expansion, without other adequate cash sources, can cause financial failure.

The cash flows from operating activities are first approximated by the net income of the firm. Revenue activities are generally generators of cash, and expenses generally consume cash. That is not always the case, however, and a number of adjustments are needed. First of all, there are certain expenses that do not consume cash. In Exhibit 16-3 note that there are several expenses that are added to net income. Depreciation and amortization reflect a current year expense for a portion of fixed assets and goodwill that are being used up during the year. These assets were mostly purchased in earlier years, and paid for at that time. The income statement charges part of their cost as an expense in the current year. However, that does not necessarily require any cash. Therefore, net income is an imperfect measure of cash flow. It treats all expenses as if they consumed cash. Since depreciation and amortization did not consume cash, they are added back. To the extent that cash was actually spent this year on fixed asset purchases, it will show up in the investing activity portion of the statement of cash flows.

Taxes are another expense that do not necessarily require cash. As noted earlier (Chapter 10) some tax expense may be deferred for a number of years into the future, requiring no current

EXHIBIT 16-3.

Pacioli Wholesale Corporation
Statement of Cash Flows
For the Years Ending June 30, 1992 and June 30, 1991

	1992	1991
Cash Flows from Operating Activities		
Net Income	$ 19,000	$ 11,000
Add Expenses Not Requiring Cash:		
Depreciation	10,000	8,000
Amortization of Goodwill	5,000	5,000
Increase in Taxes Payable and Deferred Taxes	7,000	3,000
Other Adjustments:		
Add Reduction in Accounts Receivable	8,000	1,000
Add Increase in Wages Payable	1,000	0
Add Increase in Accounts Payable	4,000	0
Subtract Decrease in Accounts Payable	0	(3,000)
Subtract Increase in Inventory	(9,000)	(2,000)
Subtract Increase in Prepaid Expenses	(1,000)	0
Net Cash from Operating Activities	$ 44,000	$ 23,000
Cash Flows from Investing Activities		
Increase in Marketable Securities	$ (3,000)	
Sale of Fixed Assets	0	$ 2,000
Purchase of New Equipment	(30,000)	(20,000)
Net Cash Used for Investing Activities	$(33,000)	$(18,000)
Cash Flows from Financing Activities		
Payment of Mortgage Principal	$ (5,000)	$ (5,000)
Payment of Dividends	(5,000)	(3,000)
Net Cash from Financing Activities	$(10,000)	$ (8,000)
NET INCREASE/(DECREASE) IN CASH	$ 1,000	$ (3,000)
CASH, BEGINNING OF YEAR	7,000	10,000
CASH, END OF YEAR	$ 8,000	$ 7,000

The accompanying notes are an integral part of these statements.

cash payment, even though they are currently recorded as an expense. Additionally, some taxes that are due for the current year, may not be actually paid until the tax return is filed, several months after the end of the year. These taxes also show up as an expense, even though the cash payment has not yet been made. Thus, these increases in taxes which are recorded as expenses, but don't require cash payments, must be added back to net income to arrive at a clearer picture of actual cash flows.

In addition to these expense items, there are a variety of other activities related to operations that consume or provide cash, but are not adequately approximated by net income. For example, when the firm purchases more inventory than it uses, the extra inventory is not an expense. Nevertheless, we must pay for it, so there is a cash flow. Increases in inventory must therefore be subtracted to show that they consume cash. On the other hand, if wages payable increase, that indicates that less cash was currently paid than we would expect based on the expenses we had for the year.

These adjustments can become complicated. However, for the nonfinancial manager it is not necessary to be able to make the various adjustments. Nonfinancial managers should focus on interpretation of the numbers. It is more important to be aware of the fact that these components show us what is impacting on cash from operating activities. For instance, increases in accounts receivable require a subtraction from net income. This is because net income assumes that all revenues have been received. If accounts receivable are rising, the firm is not collecting all of its revenues from the current year. If we note a large increase in accounts receivable, it warns the managers that perhaps greater collections efforts are in order.

The second part of the statement of cash flows is cash from investing activities. We note here that PW increased its marketable securities, using $3,000 of cash, and purchased new equipment for $30,000. In the prior year, some equipment had been purchased, and some equipment had been sold.

The third section of the statement is cash flows from financing activities. In this case there were no cash inflows from financing activities in either year. No new stock was issued by the corporation, nor were there increases in debt. The only financing activities relate to paying off an existing mortgage to creditors, and paying dividends to shareholders.

Combining the cash flows from operating, investing, and financing activities, yields the net increase or decrease in cash for the year. Added to the cash balance at the beginning of the year, this provides the cash balance at the end of the year. This is the same balance as that appearing on the balance sheet (Exhibit 16-1).

For PW the final cash balance has not been varying substantially. At the end of 1992 the balance is $8,000. The prior year it was $7,000. The prior year it was $10,000 (this is seen on Exhibit 16-3 from the opening cash balance of the June 30, 1991 fiscal year). More important than the stability in the closing balance each year, is the fact that the investments made by PW are being financed from operating activities. Not only are operations generating a positive cash flow, but further this cash flow is generally sufficient, or nearly sufficient, to cover the firm's investing and financing needs.

Right now, PW is relatively stable. They are growing, profitable, have twice as much current assets as current liabilities, and have sustained their cash balance. On the other hand, as growth continues they must carefully monitor this statement. Increases in fixed assets, inventory, and receivables which normally accompany growth may prevent them from remaining in balance. They should consider whether the cash being generated from activities will be sufficient to sustain planned growth. If not, they should start to plan for either increases in long-term debt, or the issuance of additional stock. A specific focus on the statement of cash flows can be a tremendous aid to management in preparing an orderly approach to meeting the financial needs of the firm.

THE NOTES TO THE FINANCIAL STATEMENTS

This chapter introduced you to the financial statements of PW. We discussed these statements in somewhat more detail than the statements we looked at in earlier chapters. However, no matter how closely you read the numbers in the financial statements, nor how well you understand the detail presented on the financial statements, in themselves they are an inadequate picture of the firm.

The balance sheet, income statement, and statement of cash flows of an audited set of financial statements each refers the reader to the "notes" that follow or accompany the financial statements. Accounting is not a science. It is a set of rules containing numerous exceptions and complications. Financial analysis requires an understanding of what the firm's financial position really is and what the results of its operations and cash flows really were. It is vital that the user of financials not simply look to the total assets and net income to determine how well the firm has done. The notes that accompany the financial statements really are an integral part of the annual report. It is to those notes for PW that we turn in Chapter 17.

KEY CONCEPTS

Financial statement analysis—techniques of analyzing financial statement information to find out as much about the firm's financial position and the results of its operations and its cash flows as possible. The focus is on the financial statements, the notes to the financial statements, and on ratio analysis.

Materiality—financial statements are not 100 percent accurate. Numerous undiscovered errors and inexact estimates are contained in the financial statements. Financial statements are only intended to be a reasonable representation of the firm.

Par value—a legal concept related to limited liability of stockholders. There is no relationship between par value and a fair or correct value of the firm's stock.

Earnings per share—rather than focus simply on net income or total earnings, GAAP require disclosure of the earnings available to common shareholders on a per share basis.

Seventeen

NOTES TO THE FINANCIAL STATEMENTS

The financial statements for Pacioli Wholesale (PW) Corporation tell a great deal about the company. We have information about the firm's resources, obligations, net worth (stockholders' equity), profitability, and cash flows. Yet financial statements are extremely limited in their ability to convey information.

We've discussed many of these limitations. Inventory may be stated using LIFO (last-in, first-out), FIFO (first-in, first-out), or weighted average cost-flow assumptions. Equipment and buildings are shown at their cost adjusted amount for depreciation, whether or not that is an accurate measure of the current worth of the assets. For the user of financial statements to really have a reasonable understanding of the firm's financial position and the results of its operations and cash flows, he or she must have more information than the financial statements themselves present. Therefore, audited financial statements must be accompanied by a set of *notes*. These notes explain the company's significant accounting policies and provide disclosure of other information not contained in the balance sheet, income statement, and statement of cash flows, which is necessary in order for the statements to be a fair representation of the firm's financial position and the results of its operations.

This chapter presents a hypothetical set of notes for the financial statements of PW. We will first present each note and then discuss it before moving on to the next note. This discussion will not be exhaustive. Each firm has notes that apply to its own unique circumstances. The reader should use this chapter to gain an insight to the general area of notes to the financial statements. Then, he or she will be in a reasonable position to ask financial officers questions about the firm's complex notes. Having read this book the reader will hopefully be in a much better position to understand the answers.

SIGNIFICANT ACCOUNTING POLICIES

The notes section generally begins with a statement of accounting policies. This is particularly important because of the alternative choices of accounting methods allowed, even within the constraints of generally accepted accounting principles (GAAP). Accountants have been unable to choose one set of rules that must be adhered to in all circumstances. The LIFO/FIFO choice mentioned previously is one such example. In cases where the firm has a choice of methods, that choice will likely have an impact on both the balance sheet and the income statement and possibly on the statement of cash flows. The financial statement figures are not meaningful unless we know what choices have been made by the firm.

NOTE A: Significant Accounting Policies
1. Sales —sales are recorded when title passes —for most sales this is at the time of shipment.

For some businesses, revenue can be recorded prior to the final sale. For example, a construction company can record some revenue on a partially completed building if they have a sales contract. Even though the title has not yet passed to the buyer, some revenue and expense might be reported in that situation. On the other hand, for some sales where there is great uncertainty about the collection of the sales price, revenue recognition is deferred until the time of cash receipt. For example, if a company sells swamp land in Florida for a vacation or retirement home, it can generally only record revenue as cash installments are received, because of the uncertainty surrounding receipt of future installments. For PW, which is a wholesale company, the normal rules of accrual accounting require revenue recognition when title passes, which is normally when the goods are shipped.

2. Short-term Investments—short-term investments are stated at the lower of their cost or their market value.

PW has $12,000 of marketable securities at the end of fiscal year 1992 (for your convenience the financial statements of PW from Chapter 16 have been repeated here as Exhibits 17-1, 17-2, and 17-3). Your expectation might well be that these securities *cost* PW $12,000 because that would correspond with the *cost* principle of accounting. What if the securities have gone up in value? The generally accepted accounting principle of conservatism creates a reluctance to raise the values shown on the financial statements. Upward adjustment is therefore not allowed. On the other hand, what if our portfolio has a total market value that is less than its cost?

Here the principle of recording at cost (based on objective evidence) conflicts with that of conservatism (adequate consideration of relevant risks). In this case, GAAP requires use of *lower of cost or market* value (LCM). If the market value exceeds cost, we use the cost. If the cost exceeds market value, we use the market value. Essentially we are willing to value the securities below their cost, but not above it.

3. Inventories—inventories are stated at cost, not to exceed market. Cost is calculated using the last-in, first-out method.

Inventories, like marketable securities, are stated using LCM because of the GAAP of conservatism. But how does PW measure the cost of their inventory? This note tells us that PW uses the LIFO method to determine inventory cost. If PW had significant international operations, it is likely that its foreign inventory would be maintained on a FIFO or weighted average basis because most

EXHIBIT 17-1.

Pacioli Wholesale Corporation
Statement of Financial Position
As of June 30, 1992 and June 30, 1991

ASSETS

	1992	1991
Current Assets		
Cash	$ 8,000	$ 7,000
Marketable Securities	12,000	9,000
Accounts Receivable, Net of Uncollectible Accounts	22,000	30,000
Inventory	49,000	40,000
Prepaid Expenses	3,000	2,000
Total Current Assets	$ 94,000	$ 88,000
Fixed Assets		
Buildings and Equipment	$150,000	$120,000
Less Accumulated Depreciation	40,000	30,000
Net Buildings and Equipment	$110,000	$ 90,000
Land	50,000	50,000
Total Fixed Assets	$160,000	$140,000
Goodwill	$ 45,000	$ 50,000
TOTAL ASSETS	$299,000	$278,000

LIABILITIES AND STOCKHOLDERS' EQUITY

	1992	1991
Current Liabilities		
Wages Payable	$ 3,000	$ 2,000
Accounts Payable	29,000	25,000
Taxes Payable	15,000	12,000
Total Current Liabilities	$ 47,000	$ 39,000
Long-Term Liabilities		
Mortgage Payable	$ 45,000	$ 50,000
Bond Payable	100,000	100,000
Deferred Taxes	39,000	35,000
Total Long-Term Liabilities	$185,000	$185,000
Stockholders' Equity		
Common Stock, $1 Par, 1000 shares		
Common Stock—Excess over par	$ 1,000	$ 1,000
Preferred Stock, 10%, $100 Par, 100 shares	24,000	24,000
	10,000	10,000
Retained Earnings	33,000	19,000
Total Stockholders' Equity	$ 68,000	$ 54,000
TOTAL LIABILITIES & STOCKHOLDERS' EQUITY	$299,000	$278,000

The accompanying notes are an integral part of these statements.

EXHIBIT 17-2.
Pacioli Wholesale Corporation
Income Statement and Analysis of Retained Earnings
For the Years Ending June 30, 1992 and June 30, 1991

		1992		1991
Sales		$297,000		$246,000
Less Cost of Goods Sold		162,000		143,000
Gross Profit		$135,000		$103,000
Operating Expenses				
Selling Expenses	$30,000		$25,000	
General Expenses	12,000		10,000	
Administrative Expenses	49,000		40,000	
Total Operating Expenses		91,000		75,000
Operating Income		$ 44,000		$ 28,000
Interest Expense		12,000		10,000
Income Before Taxes		$ 32,000		$ 18,000
Income Taxes		13,000		7,000
Net Income		$ 19,000		$ 11,000
Earning Per Share Common	$ 18.00		$ 10.00	
Less Dividends 1992 and 1991		5,000		3,000
Addition to Retained Earnings		$ 14,000		$ 8,000
Retained Earnings July 1,				
1991 and 1990		19,000		11,000
Retained Earnings June 30,				
1992 and 1991		$ 33,000		$ 19,000

The accompanying notes are an integral part of these statements.

foreign countries don't allow LIFO. In this case, the note would have to disclose that domestic inventories are calculated using the LIFO method, while foreign inventories are calculated using the FIFO or weighted average method.

LIFO/FIFO is a choice the firm is allowed under GAAP. Our inventory equation from Chapter 11 was stated in terms of units. In dollars it is

EXHIBIT 17-3.
Pacioli Wholesale Corporation
Statement of Cash Flows
For the Years Ending June 30, 1992 and June 30, 1991

	1992	1991
Cash Flows from Operating Activities		
Net Income	$ 19,000	$ 11,000
Add Expenses Not Requiring Cash:		
Depreciation	10,000	8,000
Amortization of Goodwill	5,000	5,000
Increase in Taxes Payable and Deferred Taxes	7,000	3,000
Other Adjustments:		
Add Reduction in Accounts Receivable	8,000	1,000
Add Increase in Wages Payable	1,000	0
Add Increase in Accounts Payable	4,000	0
Subtract Decrease in Accounts Payable	0	(3,000)
Subtract Increase in Inventory	(9,000)	(2,000)
Subtract Increase in Prepaid Expenses	(1,000)	0
Net Cash from Operating Activities	$ 44,000	$ 23,000
Cash Flows from Investing Activities		
Increase in Marketable Securities	$ (3,000)	
Sale of Fixed Assets	0	$ 2,000
Purchase of New Equipment	(30,000)	(20,000)
Net Cash Used for Investing Activities	$(33,000)	$(18,000)
Cash Flows from Financing Activities		
Payment of Mortgage Principal	$ (5,000)	$ (5,000)
Payment of Dividends	(5,000)	(3,000)
Net Cash from Financing Activities	$(10,000)	$ (8,000)
NET INCREASE/(DECREASE) IN CASH	$ 1,000	$ (3,000)
CASH, BEGINNING OF YEAR	7,000	10,000
CASH, END OF YEAR	$ 8,000	$ 7,000

The accompanying notes are an integral part of these statements.

| Beginning | | | Cost of | | Ending |
| Inventory | + | Purchases | − Goods Sold | = | Inventory |

At the end of 1991, the PW inventory was $40,000 (from **Exhibit 17-1**). Therefore, that must be the value of the beginning inventory for 1992. The inventory at the end of 1992 was $49,000 (from Exhibit 17-1). The cost of goods sold was $162,000 for 1992 (from Exhibit 17-2). In order for the inventory equation to balance, purchases must have been $171,000. The equation would appear as follows:

Beginning			Cost of		Ending
Inventory	+	Purchases	− Goods Sold	=	Inventory
$40,000	+	$171,000	− $162,000	=	$49,000

But what if PW had decided to use FIFO to calculate inventory cost? If PW had been on a FIFO system, suppose that their beginning inventory for 1992 would have been $45,000 and their ending inventory for 1992 would have been $58,000. The balance sheets would look different for the firm on FIFO because of the differences in beginning and ending inventories as compared to those balances under LIFO. What would happen to the income statement? We need to know the effect of these differences on the cost of goods sold to answer that question.

We can use the inventory equation to calculate the cost of goods sold under a FIFO approach. The amount of purchases for 1992 would be the same $171,000 under FIFO as it was under LIFO. The LIFO/FIFO choice focuses on which units were sold, not on how much was spent on purchases. Using the inventory equation, we know that beginning inventory of $45,000 plus purchases of $171,000 less cost of goods sold equals the ending inventory of $58,000. Then, the cost of goods sold must be equal to $158,000.

What would happen if PW had chosen to use the weighted-average method to calculate inventory cost? Suppose that using weighted average, the beginning inventory would have been $42,000 and the ending inventory would have been $53,000. Using the same approach we find that the cost of goods sold was $160,000. Recall that under the LIFO method that PW actually chose, the cost of goods sold was $162,000 (Exhibit 17-2).

Exhibit 17-4 presents the PW income statement for 1992 under the three alternative inventory methods. Clearly, we can see that we must know the inventory method being used to understand net income. Here the net income reported differs by as much as $2,000 depending on which system was used (assuming a total local, state, and federal marginal income tax rate of 50%). If we were evaluating identical LIFO and FIFO firms, the FIFO firm would look better if we didn't know that the two firms were using different inventory methods. This issue is further discussed in Note C below.

4. Property, Plant, and Equipment—property, plant, and equipment are recorded at cost, less depreciation. Depreciation taken over the useful lives of plant and equipment is calculated on the straight-line basis.

EXHIBIT 17-4.
Comparative Income Statements
Based on Alternative Inventory Methods

Pacioli Wholesale Corporation
Income Statement
For the Year Ending June 30, 1992

	(A)	(B) WEIGHTED	(C)
	LIFO	AVERAGE	FIFO
Sales	$297,000	$297,000	$297,000
Less Cost of Goods Sold	162,000	160,000	158,000
Gross Profit	$135,000	$137,000	$139,000
Operating Expenses	91,000	91,000	91,000
Operating Income	$ 44,000	$ 46,000	$ 48,000
Interest Expense	12,000	12,000	12,000
Income Before Taxes	$ 32,000	$ 34,000	$ 36,000
Income Taxes	13,000	14,000	15,000
NET INCOME	$ 19,000	$ 20,000	$ 21,000

For tax purposes, our depreciation choices are largely mandated by law. For financial reporting, however, we have a fair degree of latitude. We could use a declining balance or sum-of-the-years digits approach as an alternative to straight-line depreciation. For PW in 1992, operating costs included $10,000 of depreciation calculated on a straight-line (ST.L.) basis. Suppose that the double-declining balance (DDB) depreciation would have been $18,000, and that the sum-of-the-years digits (SYD) depreciation would have been $14,000. What would be the impact on the income statement had we used one of these alternative depreciation methods? Exhibit 17-5 shows net income for PW for 1992 under the various alternative inventory and depreciation choices. A 50% marginal tax rate for local, state, and federal income taxes is again assumed.

There are nine possible net incomes. Each of the three inventory methods can be matched with each of the three depreciation methods. If we didn't explain our choice of inventory and depreciation methods, there would be no way for the reader to determine if the firm's reported net income was based on relatively liberal or conservative approaches. In this case, we could have two firms with virtually identical operations and each report a different net income—net incomes as diverse as $15,000 for a LIFO/DDB firm and $21,000 for a FIFO/ST.L firm—a difference of 40 percent! A whole range of reportable incomes between these extremes is also possible. And you thought we were joking when we told the story about the controller who asked the president how much he wanted 2 + 2 to be. The firm's reported net income can be greatly affected by the choice of accounting methods.

5. Taxes on Income—income taxes reported on the income statement differ from taxes paid as a result of deferred income taxes. Deferred income taxes arise when there are differences between the year in which certain transactions, principally depreciation, affect taxable income and the year they affect net income. Taxes on income are reduced by investment tax credits in the year in which the qualifying assets are placed into service.

This note discusses two issues. The first issue concerns information regarding the source of deferred taxes. Based on our

EXHIBIT 17-5.

Comparative Income Statements
Based on Alternative Inventory and Depreciation Methods

Pacioli Wholesale Corporation
Income Statement
For the Year Ending June 30, 1992
(000's omitted)

	A LIFO ST.L	B WA ST.L	C FIFO ST.L	D LIFO SYD	E WA SYD	F FIFO SYD	G LIFO DDB	H WA DDB	I FIFO DDB
Sales	$297	$297	$297	$297	$297	$297	$297	$297	$297
Less Cost of Goods Sold	162	160	158	162	160	158	162	160	158
Gross Profit	$135	$137	$139	$135	$137	$139	$135	$137	$139
Operating Expenses	91	91	91	95	95	95	99	99	99
Operating Income	$ 44	$ 46	$ 48	$ 40	$ 42	$ 44	$ 36	$ 38	$ 40
Interest Exp.	12	12	12	12	12	12	12	12	12
Income Before Taxes	$ 32	$ 34	$ 36	$ 28	$ 30	$ 32	$ 24	$ 26	$ 28
Income Taxes	13	14	15	11	12	13	9	10	11
NET INCOME	$ 19	$ 20	$ 21	$ 17	$ 18	$ 19	$ 15	$ 16	$ 17

KEY: LIFO—Last-in, first-out
      WA—Weighted average
      FIFO—First-in, first-out
      ST.L—Straight-line
      SYD—Sum-of-the-years digits
      DDB—Double-declining balance

discussion in Chapter 10, we are already familiar with that issue. See Note B, below, for additional discussion. The other issue referred to is that of investment tax credits (ITCs). Note that at the writing of this second edition of this book, there was no ITC in effect. However, since Congress often enacts an ITC during recessions to encourage equipment purchases, discussion is warranted. This example assumes that an ITC was in effect, just for purposes of discussion. We talked about ITCs in Chapter 13, but did not discuss the GAAP choice with respect to them.

When equipment qualifying for an ITC is acquired, the tax benefit is all received in the year of acquisition. For example, PW bought $30,000 of new equipment with a 10-year useful life in 1992. If this equipment all qualifies for a 10 percent credit, then PW would get a $3,000 reduction in taxes paid for 1992. This is a permanent tax savings. Unfortunately, this raises a problem with the matching principle. Using straight-line depreciation, our depreciation expense related to this equipment would be $3,000 each year for the 10-year life.

Should the $3,000 ITC tax savings we realize by purchasing the equipment be assigned to this year's income statement as an expense reduction? If it is, then the depreciation expense will be exactly offset by the tax savings—effectively the equipment costs us nothing in the first year, but $3,000 for each of the next nine years.

An alternative approach would be to consider the $3,000 tax savings as if it were a reduction in the cost of the equipment. In that case, the equipment would have cost us $27,000, with an annual depreciation cost of $2,700. Each year we would show a $300 tax savings instead of the entire $3,000 savings in the first year. This latter method is called the deferral method because we defer recognition of some of the benefit of the ITC to future years. The former method is called flow-through because all of the tax benefit flows through for recognition in the current year.

PW is given its choice of these two methods under GAAP and chooses the flow-through method. Had they been on the deferral method, tax expenses for 1992 would have been $2,700 higher, and net income $2,700 lower. This would be true for any of our depreciation or inventory methods, so there are now 18 possible net incomes that this firm could report!

Keep in mind that the firm would have the tax benefit in 1992 (that is, $3,000 in reduced tax payments) whether it uses flow-through or deferral for ITCs. We aren't changing any cash flow or other substantive event. We are merely changing the amount of income we chose to report!

OTHER NOTES

In addition to a summary of accounting policies, the annual report contains other notes that provide additional disclosure of information needed for the financial statements to provide a fair representation of the financial position of the firm and the results of its operations.

Part 5 of Note A was concerned with the calculation of the amount of tax expense reported on the financial statements. Note B concerns the difference between taxes actually paid and the tax rate. PW is assumed to be in a 34 percent federal tax bracket, and an average 16 percent local and state income tax bracket (state and local income tax rates vary considerably around the United States, and a weighted average rate would be used), after adjusting for the federal tax benefit. This benefit arises from the tax deductibility of state and local income taxes on the federal tax return. Therefore, the combined rate is 50 percent of pretax income. Because our 1992 pretax income is $32,000 (Exhibit 17-2), we would expect tax payments of $16,000. However, the ITC under the flow-through method reduces both tax expense reported on the income statement and tax payments to the government by $3,000 in 1992. Thus the effect of the ITC would be to reduce the tax rate on net income by 9% (the $3,000 ITC divided by the $32,000 net income, times 100%). Therefore, tax expense is reduced from 50% to 41% of pretax income, or $13,000. However, PW did not pay $13,000 in 1992. Note B explains why.

NOTE B: Tax Payments —Differences between the effective tax rate and the statutory federal income tax rate are reconciled as follows:

IMPACT ON PRETAX INCOME	1992	1991
Statutory federal income tax rate	34%	34%
State and local income taxes net of the federal income tax benefit	16%	16%
Investment tax credits	(9%)	(11%)
Deferred tax increase	(13%)	(17%)
Taxes paid as a percentage of pretax income (effective tax rate)	28%	22%

We note from Exhibit 17-1 that deferred taxes increased by $4,000 in 1992. Based on Note A, Part 5, this must be attributed primarily to the use of accelerated depreciation for tax return purposes. In other words, only $9,000 of the $13,000 tax expense was paid or payable for 1992. $9,000 is only 28 percent of pretax income. This note makes it clear that the effective tax rate for PW for 1992 was not the statutory combined federal and state rate of 50 percent, nor the 41 percent of pretax income that was reported on the income statement as tax expense, but instead was only 28 percent.

NOTE C: Inventory—If the FIFO method of inventory had been used, inventories would have been $9,000 and $5,000 higher at June 30, 1992 and June 30, 1991, respectively.

The Internal Revenue Service (IRS) only allows a firm to use LIFO on its tax return if it uses LIFO for its income statement and balance sheet, which are included in its annual report to its stockholders. However, the Securities and Exchange Commission (SEC) requires publicly held firms to disclose their inventory on a FIFO basis if it differs significantly from inventory on a LIFO basis. This practice allows a financial analyst to convert income calculated on a LIFO basis to what it would have been if the firm were on a FIFO basis.

NOTE D: Commitments and contingent liabilities—Lease commitments and contingent liabilities stemming from pending litigation are not considered to be material in the opinion of management.

The firm is required to disclose any material obligations under noncancellable long-term leases, or other potential liabilities that are significant in amount. Recall that a financial transaction is not recorded unless there has been exchange. If PW has signed a contract raising its president's salary from $5,000 to $500,000 and guaranteeing that new salary for the next ten years, there would be no journal entry to record the new $5,000,000 total obligation. However, if that amount is material, disclosure would be required as a commitment or contingent liability.

NOTE E: Goodwill—The goodwill recorded on the balance sheet arose as a result of the acquisition of another company for

> *more than the fair market value of the identifiable assets of that*
> *company. Goodwill is being amortized over a 40-year life.*

When one firm acquires another for more than the value of the specific identifiable resources, the excess is grouped under the category of goodwill. It is very common for goodwill to arise when acquisitions occur. If the ongoing firm being acquired wasn't worth more than its specific assets, the purchaser might simply buy similar assets rather than acquiring the firm. Many intangibles arise over a firm's life, such as reputation for quality products and creditworthiness. Goodwill must be amortized over a period of not longer than 40 years. It may be amortized over a shorter period, but because goodwill amortization lowers income, most firms use the full 40-year period, therefore minimizing the impact on income.

> *NOTE F: Industry Segment Information—The firm has*
> *only one major type of operation—that of selling consumer goods*
> *to retail outlets. All of the firm's operations are domestic.*

One of the requirements of financial reporting is industry segment information. A major reason for this requirement is that many firms have diversified substantially, making it difficult for stockholders and other users of financial information to determine just what business the company is in. Therefore, firms are required to disclose their major lines of business, and where their business generated. While the intent is to protect and inform stockholders, the information provided can in fact hurt stockholders.

The type of information disclosed for a business with multiple types of operations includes not only a description of each type of business, but also sales, operating profit, net earnings, and assets for each segment. This means that a competitor can examine your financial statements (or for that matter, you can examine a competitor's financial statements) to determine which segments are the most profitable. This information can be a tremendous aid in planning competitive strategy. The same is true of geographic data. If it is disclosed that our growth is occurring primarily in Latin America, our competitors may use that information to decide that it is time for a push in Asia.

Management is far more answerable to the firm's stockholders about their mistakes, if the mistakes aren't buried among the successes. If the firm is losing some money in Latin America, or in one major line of business, it is harder to hide that fact from the firm's owners when disclosure is required by the line of business and geographic location. Therefore this disclosure is required for the benefit of stockholders and creditors, despite the potentially negative impact on the firm's competitive position.

OTHER INFORMATION (UNAUDITED)—PRICE LEVEL INFORMATION

The effect of changing prices (that is, inflation) tends to have a distorting effect on financial statement information. The financial statements for Pacioli Wholesale Corporation were compiled on the basis of generally accepted accounting principles, which do not completely adjust for the impact of inflation. In recognition of this problem, the Financial Accounting Standards Board passed a rule in the late 1970s which required large, publicly held firms to report supplementary information explaining the impact of changing prices on the firm's financial position and the results of its operations. Many users found the information to be confusing. When the rate of inflation declined during the 1980s, the requirement was eliminated. Now such information is reported only on a voluntary basis.

Information of this type is considered to be supplementary and is explicitly separated from the information that has been audited by the Certified Public Accountant who gives an opinion on the financial statements. Because the information is not calculated on the traditional historical cost basis, using objective, verifiable evidence, auditors do not want the user of the information to place too much reliance on its accuracy. This supplemental information is generally thought to provide a general idea about trends and the approximate impact of inflation on the firm. Including the information as part of the audited notes would imply a greater degree of reliability than accountants feel really exists.

SUMMARY

As mentioned earlier, this chapter does not present an all-inclusive listing of required notes to the financial statements. Depending on the exact circumstances of different companies, a wide variety of disclosures are required by generally accepted accounting principles, and by requirements of the Securities and Exchange Commission. The most important learning issue in this chapter is not the information contained in the notes discussed here. Rather, it is that the reader should have an awareness of the importance of the information that is contained in the notes to the financial statements.

In the simple case of Pacioli Wholesale Corporation, we showed how there were 18 possible net incomes that could be reported depending on which accounting choices were made. It is vital to read a firm's notes in order to understand which choices it did make, and what the likely impact of those choices was on the reported net income. Additionally, a good understanding of the financial position of a firm requires more information than the financial statements themselves can convey. What contingent liabilities does the firm have, and are they material in amount? Where does the firm get its profits—domestically or from foreign sources? Which general area of business is most important to the company?

Upon looking at the notes to the financial statements, they may at first seem both overwhelming and boring. They certainly don't make for light reading. You have to work through them slowly and carefully to understand the information that each note is trying to convey. Exactly which choices has the firm made, and what are the implications of each choice? Is the company reliant on one key customer? If so, that fact would have to be disclosed somewhere in the notes. Can the company use all of its cash, or does it have a "compensating balance" agreement with its bank that requires it to maintain a minimum balance? If so, its liquidity is somewhat overstated in the balance sheet. Compensating balance arrangements must be disclosed. Are there securities outstanding, such as convertible bonds, which can be converted into common stock? If so, then the firm's net income might have to be shared among more stockholders. Such potential dilution, if significant, is discussed in the notes.

We could continue with examples of the types of information relevant to creditors, investors, and internal management that is contained only in the notes to the financials. Not all notes are relevant to all readers. Some items are of more concern to employees than stockholders. Some items help creditors more than internal managers. Whatever your purpose in using a financial report, the key is that the financial statements by themselves are incapable of telling the full story. To avoid being misled by the numbers, it is necessary to supplement the information in the statements with the information in the notes that accompany the statements.

KEY CONCEPTS

Significant accounting policies —whenever generally accepted accounting principles (GAAP) allow a firm a choice in accounting methods, the firm must disclose the choice that it made. This allows the user of financial statements to better interpret the numbers such as net income contained in the financial statements.

Other notes —any information that a user of the financial statements might need in order to have a fair representation of the firm's financial position and the results of its operations in accordance with GAAP, should be included in either the financial statements themselves, or the notes that accompany the financial statements.

Eighteen

RATIO ANALYSIS

One of the most widely used forms of financial analysis is the use of ratios. They can provide information that is useful for investment decisions such as, "Should we acquire XYZ Corporation?" Ratios can provide information regarding whether we should sell to XYZ or lend money to XYZ. They can also help internal management of an organization gain an awareness of their company's strengths and weaknesses. And, if we can find weaknesses, we can move to correct them before irreparable damage is done.

What is a ratio? Basically, a ratio is simply a comparison of any two numbers. If we compare one number to another number, we have created a ratio. In financial statement analysis, we compare numbers taken from the financial statements. For instance, if we want to know how much Pacioli Wholesale Corporation (PW) had in current assets as compared to current liabilities at the end of fiscal 1992, we would compare its $94,000 in current assets (Exhibit 18-1) to its $47,000 in current liabilities. Or more briefly, it had $94,000 compared to $47,000. Mathematically, we could state

EXHIBIT 18-1.

Pacioli Wholesale Corporation
Statement of Financial Position
As of June 30, 1992 and June 30, 1991

ASSETS

	1992 %	1992 $	1991 $	1991 %
Current Assets				
Cash	2.7%	$ 8,000	$ 7,000	2.5%
Marketable Securities	4.0%	12,000	9,000	3.2%
Accounts Receivable, Net of Uncollectible Accounts	7.4%	22,000	30,000	10.8%
Inventory	16.4%	49,000	40,000	14.4%
Prepaid Expenses	1.0%	3,000	2,000	.7%
Total Current Assets	31.4%	$ 94,000	$ 88,000	31.7%
Fixed Assets				
Buildings and Equipment	50.2%	$150,000	$120,000	43.2%
Less Accumulated Depreciation	13.4%	40,000	30,000	10.8%
Net Buildings and Equipment	36.8%	$110,000	$ 90,000	32.4%
Land	16.7%	50,000	50,000	81.0%
Total Fixed Assets	53.5%	$160,000	$140,000	50.4%
Goodwill	15.1%	$ 45,000	$ 50,000	18.0%
TOTAL ASSETS	100.0%	$299,000	$278,000	100.0%

LIABILITIES AND STOCKHOLDERS' EQUITY

	1992 %	1992 $	1991 $	1991 %
Current Liabilities				
Wages Payable	1.0%	$ 3,000	$ 2,000	.7%
Accounts Payable	9.7%	29,000	25,000	9.0%
Taxes Payable	5.0%	15,000	12,000	4.3%
Total Current Liabilities	15.7%	$ 47,000	$ 39,000	14.0%
Long-Term Liabilities				
Mortgage Payable	15.1%	$ 45,000	$ 50,000	18.0%
Bond Payable	33.4%	100,000	100,000	36.0%
Deferred Taxes	13.0%	39,000	35,000	12.6%
Total Long-Term Liabilities	61.5%	$184,000	$185,000	66.5%
Stockholders' Equity				
Common Stock, $1 Par Com. Stock—Excess over par	.3%	$ 1,000	$ 1,000	.4%
Preferred Stock, 10%, $100 Par, 100 shares	8.0%	24,000	24,000	8.6%
Retained Earnings	3.3%	10,000	10,000	3.6%
	11.0%	33,000	19,000	6.8%
Total Stockholders' Equity	22.7%	$ 68,000	$ 54,000	19.4%
TOTAL LIABILITIES & STOCKHOLDERS' EQUITY	100.0%	$299,000	$278,000	100.0%

The accompanying notes are an integral part of this statement.

$94,000 compared to $47,000 as $94,000 divided by $47,000, which is equal to two. This means that there are two dollars of current assets for every one dollar of current liabilities. This would be referred to either as a ratio of 2 or a ratio of 2 to 1. This particular ratio is called the current ratio. In this chapter, we discuss many widely used ratios, but the discussion is not all inclusive. Each industry may have many ratios specially suited to its needs, which are not used by other industries, and which are not discussed in this book. For example, the key ratio for the airline industry is occupied seats compared to available seats, the load factor ratio. You can even create new ratios by simply comparing any one number to another, if some relationship between the two numbers exists.

BENCHMARKS FOR COMPARISON

Is the PW current ratio of two good or bad? Is it high enough? Is it too high? We don't want to have too little in the way of current assets, or we may have a liquidity crisis—that is, insufficient cash to pay our obligations as they become due. We don't want to have too much in the way of current assets because this implies that we are passing up profitable long-term investment opportunities. But there is no correct number for the current ratio. We can only assess the appropriateness of our ratios on the basis of some benchmark or basis for comparison.

There are three principal benchmarks. The first is the firm's history. We always want to review the ratios for the firm this year, as compared to what they were in the several previous years. This enables us to discover favorable or unfavorable trends that are developing gradually over time, as well as pointing up any numbers that have changed sharply in the space of time of just one year.

The second type of benchmark is to compare the firm to specific competitors. If the competitors are publicly held companies, we can obtain copies of their annual reports and compare each of our ratios with each of theirs. This approach is especially valuable for helping to pinpoint why your firm is doing particularly better or worse than a specific competitor. By finding where your ratios differ, you may determine what you are doing better or worse than the competition.

The third type of benchmark is industrywide comparison. Dun and Bradstreet and Robert Morris Associates are a few examples of firms that collect financial data, compute ratios by industry, and publish the results. Not only are industry averages available, but the information is often broken down both by size of firm and in a way that allows determination of relatively how far away from the norm you are.

For example, if your current ratio is 2, and the industry average is 2.4, is that a substantial discrepancy? Published industry data may show that 25 percent of the firms in the industry have a current ratio below 1.5. In this case, we may not be overly concerned that our ratio of 2.0 is too low. We are still well above the bottom quartile of firms in our industry. On the other hand, what if only 25 percent of the firms in the industry have a current ratio of less than 2.1? In this case, over three-quarters of the firms in the industry have a higher current ratio than we do. This might be a cause for some concern. At the very least, we might want to investigate why our ratio is particularly low, compared to our industry.

There are five principal types of ratios that we examine in this chapter. They are: 1) common size ratios; 2) liquidity ratios; 3) efficiency ratios; 4) solvency ratios; and 5) profitability ratios.

COMMON SIZE RATIOS

Common size ratios are used as a starting point in financial statement analysis. Suppose that we wished to compare our firm to another. We look to our cash balance and see that it is $10,000, while the other firm has cash of $5,000. Does this mean we have too much cash? Does the other firm have too little cash? Before we can even begin to consider such questions, we need more general information about the two firms. Are we twice as big as the other firm? Are we smaller than the other firm? The amount of cash we need depends on the size of our operations compared to theirs. Comparing our cash to their cash does not create a very useful ratio.

However, we can "common-size" cash by comparing it to total assets. If our cash of $10,000 is one-tenth of our total assets and their cash of $5,000 is one-tenth of their total assets, then relative to asset size, both firms are keeping a like amount of cash. This is much more informative. Therefore, the first step in ratio analysis is to create a set of common size ratios. Usually common size ratios are converted to percentages. Thus, rather than referring to cash as being one-tenth of total assets, we would refer to it as being 10 percent of total assets.

To find our common size ratios, we need a key number for comparison. On the balance sheet, the key number is total assets or total equities (that is, liabilities plus stockholders' equity). We calculate the ratio of each asset on the balance sheet as compared to total assets. We calculate the ratio of each liability and stockholders' equity account as compared to the total equities. For the income statement, all numbers are compared to total sales. Once we have calculated the common size ratios we can use them to compare our firm to itself over time, to specific competitors, and to industry-wide statistics.

The common size ratios for PW's balance sheet and income statement are presented in Exhibits 18-1 and 18-2. Very little ratio

EXHIBIT 18-2.
Pacioli Wholesale Corporation
Income Statement
For the Years Ending June 30, 1992 and June 30, 1991

	1992		1991	
Sales	100.0%	$297,000	100.0%	$246,000
Less Cost of Goods Sold	54.5%	162,000	58.1%	143,000
Gross Profit	45.5%	$135,000	41.9%	$103,000
Operating Expenses				
Selling Expenses	10.1%	$ 30,000	10.2%	$ 25,000
General Expenses	4.0%	12,000	4.1%	10,000
Admin. Expenses	16.5%	49,000	16.3%	40,000
Total Operating Expenses	30.6%	$ 91,000	30.5%	$ 75,000
Operating Income	14.8%	$ 44,000	11.4%	$ 28,000
Interest Expense	4.0%	12,000	4.1%	10,000
Income Before Taxes	10.8%	$ 32,000	7.3%	$ 18,000
Income Taxes	4.4%	13,000	2.8%	7,000
Net Income	6.4%	$ 19,000	4.5%	$ 11,000

analysis has been developed for the statement of cash flows, probably because the statement is relatively new. Over the next decade it is quite likely that researchers will develop a number of useful ratios based on that statement.

The Balance Sheet: Assets

Looking at the balance sheet, or statement of financial position (Exhibit 18-1), we can begin to get a general feeling about PW by comparing the common size ratios for two years. Note that there will typically be some rounding errors in ratio analysis. We could eliminate them by being more precise. For example, in 1992 the ratio of cash to total assets really is 2.6756 percent. We generally don't bother with such precision. Ratios can't give their users a precise picture of the firm. They are meant to serve as general conveyors of broad information. Our concern is if a number is particularly out of line—either unusually high or low. It is virtually impossible to interpret minor changes.

For PW, current assets have remained relatively stable, falling from 31.7 percent to 31.4 percent. Note, however, that accounts receivable have fallen while inventory has risen. Is this good or bad? If accounts receivable have fallen because sales are down this year or because there are more bad debts, and inventory has risen because PW is left with a lot of unsold goods, then this is bad. On the other hand, if accounts receivable are down because the firm has been successful in its efforts to collect more promptly, and inventory is up because it is needed to support growing sales, then this is a good sign.

Clearly, ratios can't be interpreted in a vacuum. The ratio merely points out what needs to be investigated. The ratio doesn't provide answers in and of itself. In the case of PW, the income statement (Exhibit 18-2) shows us that sales did indeed rise during the fiscal year ending June 30, 1992. It would appear that the changes in accounts receivable and inventory represent a favorable trend.

Fixed assets (Exhibit 18-1) for PW have increased, not only in absolute terms, but also as a percentage of total assets. After accounting for depreciation that has accumulated on buildings and equipment over their lifetime, we see a rise in net buildings and equipment from 32.4 percent to 36.8 percent of total assets.

Goodwill is declining in absolute amount as we write off to expense the excess we paid for an acquired company above the fair market value of its individual identifiable assets. Because total assets are increasing, goodwill is declining even faster as a percentage of total assets.

The Balance Sheet: Equities

The current liability common size ratios have remained fairly constant over time (Exhibit 18-1). Each has risen slightly, which might well have been anticipated given the rise in sales and inventory noted earlier. As our operations grow and become more profitable, we might expect some growth in current liabilities to match the increases in inventory. In any case, the changes here appear to be modest.

Long-term liabilities (Exhibit 18-1) have fallen as a percentage of total equities. This is primarily because the firm has not needed to raise funds from the debt market to finance its fixed asset growth. Deferred taxes have risen modestly, an indication that we are taking advantage of the Modified Accelerated Cost Recovery System which in effect creates interest-free government loans as we acquire additional equipment (see Chapter 10).

The common size ratio for stockholders' equity (Exhibit 18-1) has risen from 19.4 percent for 1991 to 22.7 percent for 1992. This is not surprising considering the absolute growth in profits retained in the firm (Exhibit 17-2).

The Income Statement

For the income statement (Exhibit 18-2), sales is the key figure around which all common size ratios are calculated. This year the cost of goods sold has fallen in relation to sales. Assuming that quality has been maintained, this is a favorable trend. By keeping production costs down relative to the selling price, profits should rise. Internal management of a firm should, nevertheless, be very interested in determining why this occurred. If the causes were related to improved efficiency, we want to know that so we can reward the individuals responsible and maintain the higher level of efficiency. On the other hand, if the improvement is caused by use of poorer quality raw materials, the long-run impact may be to hurt our reputation and long-run profits.

There is always a conflict between long-run and short-run profits. If we maintain our equipment, our short-run profits will be less than if we don't incur maintenance expense. But in the long-run, the repair bills from inadequate maintenance will exceed the cost of proper maintenance. From the firm's point of view, it pays to maintain the equipment. However, for the manager rewarded currently based on current profits, it is harder to focus on the long-run impact of actions. Therefore, even favorable trends such as reduced cost of goods sold should be viewed with caution. Investigation is needed to determine why that change occurred.

For PW, other operating expenses have remained fairly stable, increasing in relative proportion to the dollar increase in overall sales. Gross profit has risen from 41.9 percent to 45.5 percent, and operating income has risen from 11.4 percent to 14.8 percent, both as a result of the change in the cost of goods sold expense. The firm is making more profit on each dollar of sales than it had in the prior year. Of course, greater profits are associated with greater taxes. Because the pretax profit per dollar of sales has risen from 7.3 percent to 10.8 percent, the tax per dollar of sales has also risen from 2.8 percent to 4.4 percent.

Common Size Ratios: Additional Notes

The common size ratios give a starting point. You can quickly get a feel for any unusual changes that have occurred, adjusted for the overall size of assets and the relative amount of sales. Comparison with specific and industry-wide competition would point out other similarities and differences. For example, our firm has 31.4 percent of its assets in the current category. (See Exhibit 18-1). Is that greater or less than the industry average? If it's substantially greater or less than you might want to investigate why. Are we in a peculiarly different situation relative to other firms in our industry? An investor might be interested in our equities. For PW, 61.5 percent of the entire equity side of the balance sheet is in long-term liabilities. For some industries that is a very high proportion and would indicate significant risk. In other industries, that is quite common. As mentioned earlier, the key to interpretation of ratios is benchmarks. Without a basis for comparison, it is impossible to reasonably interpret the meaning of a ratio.

LIQUIDITY RATIOS

Liquidity ratios attempt to assess whether a firm is maintaining an appropriate level of liquidity. Too little liquidity raises the possibility of default and bankruptcy. Too much liquidity implies that long-term investments with greater profitability have been missed. Financial officers have to walk a tightrope to maintain enough, but not too much liquidity.

The most common of the liquidity ratios is the current ratio (see Exhibit 18-3), discussed earlier in the chapter. This ratio compares all of the firm's current assets to all of its current liabilities. A common misleading rule of thumb is that the current ratio should be two. A manufacturing industry needs inventories and receivables. Both of those items result in significant amounts of current assets. An airline, on the other hand, collects most payments in advance of providing service, so their receivables are low. Their product isn't inventoriable, so except for fuel, spare parts, and supplies, their inventory is low. You would expect the airline industry to have a very low current ratio. On the other hand a distillery, having whiskey aging for a period of years, will likely have a large inventory and therefore a high current ratio.

A second liquidity ratio exists that places even more emphasis on the firm's short-term viability—its ability to stay in business. This ratio is called the quick ratio. It compares current assets quickly convertible into cash to current liabilities (see Exhibit 18-3). The concept here is that while not all current assets become cash

EXHIBIT 18-3.
Liquidity Ratios

$$\text{Current Ratio} = \frac{\text{Current Assets}}{\text{Current Liabilities}}$$

$$\text{Quick Ratio} = \frac{\text{Cash} + \text{Marketable Securities} + \text{Receivables}}{\text{Current Liabilities}}$$

in the very near term, most current liabilities have to be paid in the very near term. For example, prepaid rent is a current asset, but it is unlikely that we could cash in that prepayment to use to pay our debts. Inventory, while saleable, takes time to sell.

The quick ratio compares the firm's cash + marketable securities + accounts receivable to its current liabilities. Accounts receivable are considered to be "quick" assets because there are factoring firms that specialize in lending money on receivables or actually buying them outright, so they can be used to generate cash almost immediately. For PW, the quick ratio fell from 1.2 in 1991 to .9 in 1992. While this trend may be disturbing, one should keep in mind that it largely resulted from an apparent increased efficiency in the collection of receivables.

Both of these ratios have commonly been used as measures of the firm's risk—how likely it is to get into financial difficulty. However, you should be extremely cautious in using these ratios. No one or two ratios alone can tell the entire story of a firm. They should be used like clues or pieces of evidence for the financial analyst who is really acting as a detective. Any one clue can point in the wrong direction.

For example, suppose a firm has large balances in cash and marketable securities, and its current ratio is 4 or 5. Is this an extremely safe company? The current ratio by itself leads us to believe that it is. The quick ratio might be 3. This ratio also leads us to believe that the firm is very safe. However, what if the company is losing money at a rapid rate, and the only thing that staved off bankruptcy was the sale of a major plant or investment. The sale generated enough cash to meet immediate needs and left an excess, resulting in the high current and quick ratios. How long will this excess last? If the cash and securities are large relative to current liabilities, but small relative to operating costs or long-term liabilities, then the firm may still be extremely risky.

On the other hand, a profitable firm, with careful planning, may be rapidly expanding. Due to cash payments related to the expansion, perhaps the current ratio falls to 1.5 and the quick ratio to .6 at year-end. However, within a month or two after the year-end, the firm may be receiving cash from the issuance of stock or debt that has already been arranged. This firm is probably stable. The point is that all of the ratios when taken together can supplement the financial statements and the notes to the financial statements. They can point out areas for specific additional investigation. No one or two ratios by themselves can in any way replace the information in the financial statements, the notes to the financial statements, and the other information possessed by management.

EFFICIENCY RATIOS

The firm wants to maximize its profits for any given level of risk. This requires the firm to operate efficiently. A number of ratios exist that can help a firm to assess how efficiently it is operating and allow for comparison between firms and over time. The principle efficiency ratios measure the efficient handling of receivables and inventory.

Receivables Ratios

One problem faced by most firms is the timely collection of receivables. Once receivables are collected, the money received can be used to pay off loans or it can be invested. This means that once the money is received, either we would be paying less interest, or we would be earning more interest. Therefore, we want to collect our receivables promptly.

The receivables turnover ratio (Exhibit 18-4) is a very common indicator of efficiency in collecting receivables. It measures

EXHIBIT 18-4.
Efficiency Ratios

$$\text{Receivables Turnover Ratio} = \frac{\text{Credit Sales}}{\text{Average Receivables Balance}}$$

$$\text{Days Receivable} = \frac{365}{\text{Receivables Turnover}}$$

$$\text{Inventory Turnover Ratio} = \frac{\text{Cost of Goods Sold}}{\text{Average Inventory Balance}}$$

$$\text{Days Inventory} = \frac{365}{\text{Inventory Turnover}}$$

how many times during the year our receivables are generated and then collected. To measure the turnover of receivables, we compare our sales on credit to our average accounts receivable balance. The average accounts receivable are simply the balance in accounts receivable at the beginning and the end of the year divided by 2. In the case of PW, the average accounts receivable are $22,000 plus $30,000 divided by 2, or $26,000. The turnover ratio for 1992 is sales of $297,000, divided by $26,000, which equals 11.4. This number by itself is not very meaningful.

We could directly compare the turnover to that of other firms or our own firm in prior years. However, we often think of receivables in terms of how long it takes from the sale to the collection. A useful aid in analysis is to convert our receivables turnover into a statistic referred to as "days receivable," or more simply, the average age of receivables (Exhibit 18-4). We arrive at this statistic by dividing the 365 days in a year by the receivables turnover ratio. For PW, the average age of receivables is 32 days (365/11.4).

This is much easier to relate to. Consider whether 32 days is a reasonable average length of time to wait for collection of receivables. If the industry average is 40 days we might be pleased with ourselves. If the industry average is 20 days we may be concerned. However, like the current ratio, we want the turnover of receivables or the average age to be neither too low nor too high. We are really striving for a middle ground, rather than as far to one extreme as possible. You might want to collect receivables as promptly as possible, given the interest savings we achieve as soon as we receive payment. That is in fact correct. However, this doesn't lead as directly to desiring extremely high receivables turnover, or low average age of receivables as you might think.

The problem is that in order to keep the age of receivables low, our credit manager may attempt to deny credit to any firm that typically pays slowly. This is not necessarily in the best interests of the company. Suppose that PW's borrowing cost is 18 percent per year. If we have a customer who pays after three months, waiting to collect costs us $4\frac{1}{2}$ percent as compared to receiving payment as soon as the bill is issued. If we operate on a 2 percent margin, we don't want that customer. But if we have a 20 to 30 percent margin, we don't want to lose the sale, even if we don't get prompt payment.

Therefore, we not only want to calculate the receivables turnover and age of receivables, but also we need to investigate that

ratio to see if a short average age of receivables indicates too re-
strictive a credit policy on whom we sell to, or if a long age indicates
too loose a credit policy or a lack of sufficient efforts to collect on a
timely basis.

Inventory Ratios

The same type of ratios calculated for receivables can also be calculated with respect to inventory (Exhibit 18-4). The inventory
turnover ratio is the cost of goods sold divided by the average inventory (beginning plus ending inventory divided by 2). For PW for
1992, the inventory turnover ratio is $162,000 (cost of goods sold
from Exhibit 18-2) divided by the average of $49,000 and $40,000
(1992 and 1991 ending inventory balances from Exhibit 18-1), which
is equal to 3.6. The average age of PW's inventory is 100.3 days,
calculated by dividing 365 days in a year by the inventory turnover.

If we keep inventory on hand for too long a period, we are
wasting money through lost interest that could have been earned, or
through extra interest paid on money borrowed to maintain the
inventory. Excessively large inventories also result in unnecessarily
high warehousing costs, property taxes, and spoilage. On the other
hand, if we don't maintain a sufficiently large inventory, we may
lose sales or have production-line stoppages due to stock-outs of
finished goods or raw materials, respectively.

Industry-wide statistics are usually available for total inventory turnover. However, it is especially useful to compute the
turnover and/or age of inventory separately for raw materials, work
in process, and finished goods for manufacturing concerns. For example, a common response to why inventory turnover is slow is that
the business is seasonal, and the firm must stockpile *finished goods*
for the busy season, often Christmas. On the other hand, if we examine the inventory ratios on a more detailed basis, we may find it is in
fact *raw materials* that are being held for excessive periods of time.

SOLVENCY RATIOS

One of the primary focuses on the firm's riskiness occurs through
examination of its solvency ratios. Unlike the liquidity ratios that

are concerned with the firm's ability to meet its obligations in the very near future, solvency ratios take more of a long-run view. They attempt to determine if the firm has overextended itself through the use of financial leverage. That is, does the firm have principal and interest payment obligations exceeding its ability to pay, not only now, but into the future as well.

Two of the most common of the solvency ratios are the interest coverage ratio and the debt to equity ratio (Exhibit 18-5). The former focuses on the ability to meet interest payments arising from liabilities. The latter focuses on the protective cushion owners' equity provides for creditors. If a bankruptcy does occur, creditors can share in the firm's assets before the owners can claim any of their equity. The more equity that the owners have in the firm, the greater the likelihood that the firm's assets will be great enough to protect the claim of all the creditors.

The interest coverage ratio compares funds available to pay interest to the total amount of interest that has to be paid. The funds available for interest are the firm's profits before interest and taxes. As long as the profit before interest and taxes (the operating income) is greater than the amount of interest, the firm will have enough money to pay the interest owed. The higher this ratio is, the more comfortable creditors feel. For PW in 1992, the operating income is $44,000 (Exhibit 18-2) and the interest is $12,000 (Exhibit 18-2). The interest coverage ratio therefore is 3.7. This is a relative improvement from 1991 when the operating profit was $28,000 and interest was $10,000. In that year, the interest coverage was 2.8.

However, we should be careful in our use of the term, *improvement*. From a creditor's point of view, this is an improvement because profits are up relative to interest, creating a greater cushion

EXHIBIT 18-5.
Solvency Ratios

$$\text{Interest Coverage} = \frac{\text{Income Before Interest \& Taxes}}{\text{Interest Expense}}$$

$$\text{Debt to Equity} = \frac{\text{Total Liabilities}}{\text{Total Liabilities} + \text{Stockholders' Equity}}$$

of safety. From the firm's point of view, whether this is an improvement or not depends on their attitude toward risk and profits. If the firm desires to be highly leveraged, this rise in the interest coverage ratio indicates that the firm could have paid more dividends to its owners, and financed more of its expansion through increased borrowing. This would have increased the rate of return earned by the owners, although they would have incurred a greater risk because of the increased leverage. (Review Chapter 8 for a discussion of financial leverage and its implications.)

Once again, this is a ratio that we try to maintain at a certain level, rather than maximizing or minimizing. The appropriate level depends on what is customary in our industry combined with whether we desire to be more or less highly leveraged than our industry. The same point holds true for the debt to equity ratio. There are several different debt/equity ratios. For example, we can compare long-term debt to stockholders' equity, or total liabilities to stockholders' equity. One common form of the debt/equity ratio compares the firm's total liabilities to its total equities (both liabilities and stockholders' equity). The greater the liabilities relative to the total, the more risky the firm.

For example, at the end of fiscal 1992, PW has $299,000 of total equities—liabilities plus stockholders' equity (Exhibit 18-1). By definition, this is equal to the total assets. These assets are available to repay our liabilities. The total liabilities of PW are $231,000, which consists of $47,000 of current liabilities and $184,000 of long-term liabilities. The debt to equity ratio of $231,000 to $299,000 is .77. If PW were to have financial difficulty, and perhaps even go bankrupt and sell off all of its assets, it would have to realize on average, 77 cents on every dollar of assets in order to fully pay its creditors.

As with most major ratios, a number of alternative ratios can be created. As mentioned above, debt-equity is sometimes used to refer to long-term debt compared to stockholders' equity. Debt-equity focuses on how much the long-term creditors have invested in the firm compared to the owners. Another approach is to compare the total liabilities to the stockholders' equity. None of these ratios is clearly superior in value to the others, but different industries tend to focus on one or the other as a standard industry practice for consistent comparison purposes.

It is important to bear in mind that the nature of the firm and its industry have a lot to do with what is an acceptable level of debt, relative to equity, and what level of interest payments can be considered reasonably safe. For a business with very constant sales and earnings, more debt is relatively safer than for a firm that has wide swings in profitability. This doesn't mean that one industry is better or worse than the other. It does mean, however, that an equal level of debt does not imply an equal level of risk for two firms in different industries. Therefore, any arbitrary rules of thumb commonly used, such as a debt to equity ratio of .5, are not terribly valuable.

PROFITABILITY RATIOS

When all is said and done, the key focus of accounting and finance tends to be on profits. How well did the firm do? Was the wealth of the owners improved by the actions the firm undertook during the year? Profitability ratios attempt to show how well the firm did, given the level of risk and types of risk it actually assumed during the year. Net income is not a satisfactory measure of profitability because it is a single number without an adequate benchmark.

Even if we compare net income to that of the competition, it is an inadequate measure. Suppose that the chief competitor of PW had earnings of $57,000 this year, while PW made only $19,000. Did the competitor have a better year? Not necessarily. They earned three times as much money, but perhaps it required four times as much resources to do it. Even earnings per share is inadequate. Suppose that PW's earnings per share of $18.00 were only one-third of the competitor's $54.00. If the investors in PW's competitor invested four times as much to buy each of their shares, they would have been better off investing an equal total amount of money in PW. Therefore, a number of profitability ratios exist to help in evaluating the firm's performance.

Margin Ratios

Margin ratios are one common class of profitability ratios. Firms commonly compute their gross margin, operating margin, and profit margin as a percentage of sales. These ratios (Exhibit 18-6) are nothing more than common size ratios we calculated earlier in the chapter. For PW in 1992, their gross margin was 45.5 percent, their operating margin was 14.8 percent, and their profit margin was 6.4 percent. These margins are often watched closely, as changes can be early warning signals of serious problems. A slacking off of a percentage or two in the gross margin can mean the difference between healthy profits or a loss in many industries. For instance, in the supermarket industry the profit margin is rarely more than one to two percent. A two percent change in the gross margin can totally wipe out the supermarket's profit.

Return on Investment (ROI) Ratios

Another broad category of profitability measures fall under the heading of return on investment (ROI). There are many definitions for return on investment, although individual firms usually select one definition and use that as a measure of both individual and

EXHIBIT 18-6.
Profitability Ratios

MARGIN RATIOS

$$\text{Gross Margin} = \frac{\text{Gross Profit}}{\text{Sales}} \times 100\%$$

$$\text{Operating Margin} = \frac{\text{Operating Income}}{\text{Sales}} \times 100\%$$

$$\text{Profit Margin} = \frac{\text{Net Income}}{\text{Sales}} \times 100\%$$

RETURN ON INVESTMENT (ROI) RATIOS

$$\text{Return on Assets (ROA)} = \frac{\text{Net Income}}{\text{Total Assets}}$$

$$\text{Return on Equity (ROE) or} \atop \text{Return on Net Assets (RONA)} = \frac{\text{Net Income}}{\text{Stockholders' Equity}}$$

---

firm performance. Because we cannot know the specific definition a firm has chosen, we will discuss a variety of ROI measures in this section. Even if none of the ones discussed here is exactly the same as that chosen by your firm, you should gain enough from the discussion to understand the strengths and weaknesses of whatever ROI measure(s) your firm uses.

The problem with using net income solely as a measure of performance is that it ignores resources invested to generate that income. Return on assets (ROA) is an ROI measure that evaluates the firm's return or net income relative to the asset base used to generate the income. If we could invest $100 in each of two different investments, and one generated twice as much income as the other, we would prefer the investment generating twice as much income (assuming the levels of risk had been the same). Similarly, if we could invest half as much in one project as in the other, and they had equal profits, we would prefer to invest half as much.

Therefore, the firm that generates more income, relative to the amount of investment, is doing a better job, other things equal. If we divide the profit earned by the amount of assets employed to generate that profit, we get the ROA. A high ROA is better than a small one. The ROA measure is particularly good for evaluating division managers. It focuses on how well they used the assets entrusted to them.

Is that what the firm's owners want to know? Not really. They are not as interested in the use of assets as they are with the return on their investment. They want to focus on how well the firm did in earning a return on the stockholders' equity. This is commonly called the return on equity (ROE) or the return on net assets (RONA). (See Exhibit 18-6.) Note that net assets are defined as being the assets less the liabilities. Net assets are equivalent to the firm's book value or net worth or stockholders' equity.

While ROA is good for evaluating managers, but inadequate for evaluating the firm, ROE is good for evaluating overall firm performance, but not for manager evaluation. Except for the very top officers of the firm, managers don't control whether the firm borrows money or issues stock to raise funds. Most managers are simply trying to use the funds that the finance officers have provided them most efficiently. If two managers operated their firms exactly the same, except that one firm was financed substantially with debt, while the other was financed almost exclusively with equity, the firms would have substantially different ROEs for two reasons. First of all, the stockholders' equity will be different for the two firms, because one firm issued more stock than the other, so the denominator of the ratio will be different. Second, the interest expense will differ because one firm borrowed less than the other, so the net income will not be the same. Therefore, the numerator of the ratio would be different. How can we evaluate what part of the firm's results was caused by reasons other than the leverage decision, and what part was caused by the specific decision regarding financial leverage?

ROE is a useful measure of the income that the firm was able to generate relative to the amount of owners' investment in the firm. ROE includes the effect caused by the firm's degree of leverage. To remove the impact of leverage from our evaluation, we should use ROA. This eliminates the problem with respect to the denominator of the ROE ratio. The asset base or denominator of the ROA ratio is the same whether the source of the money used to acquire the assets is debt or equity. However, it leaves a problem with the numerator. The return, or numerator (that is, the net income) is affected by the amount of interest the firm pays. For this reason, the measure of ROA often used for evaluation abstracting from the leverage decision is calculated using something called delevered net income.

Delevered net income means recalculating the firm's income by assuming that it had no interest expense at all. In doing this, we can put firms with different decisions regarding the use of borrowed money vs. owner contributed funds all on a comparable basis. We can see how profitable each firm was relative to the assets it used regardless of their source. We have completely separated any profitability (or loss) created by having used borrowed money instead of owner invested capital. The way we delever net income is to take the firm's operating margin (income before interest and taxes) and calculate taxes directly on that amount, ignoring interest. The result is a net income based on the assumption that there had been no interest expense.

This should not lead the reader to believe that all firms calculate ROA in exactly the same way. Some firms use assets net of depreciation as the basis for comparison. This is how the assets appear on the balance sheet. Some firms ignore depreciation and use gross assets as a base. The reason for this is to avoid causing a firm or division to appear to have a very high return on assets simply because its assets are very old and fully depreciated. Such fully depreciated assets cause the base of the ratio to be very low and therefore the resulting ratio to be very large. Along the same lines, some firms use replacement cost instead of historical cost to place divisions in an equal position.

Despite any of these adjustments, use of any of the ROA measures for evaluation of managers creates undesired incentives. Suppose the firm and its owners are happy to accept any project with an after-tax rate of return of 20 percent. One division of the firm currently has an ROA of 30 percent, and a proposed project that would have a 25 percent ROA is being evaluated. The manager of the division wants to reject the project entirely if he or she is evaluated based on ROA. The 25 percent project, even though profitable, and perhaps better than anything else the firm's owners could do with their money, will bring down that division's weighted average ROA, which is currently 30 percent. Even though the project is good for the firm and its owners, it would hurt the manager's performance evaluation.

It is for this reason that many professors of accounting and finance recommend an ROI concept called residual income (RI). Under this approach, the firm specifies a minimum required ROA rate, using one of the various approaches previously discussed. For each project being evaluated, we would multiply the amount of asset investment required for the project by the required ROA rate. The result would be subtracted from the profits anticipated from the project. If the project is expected to earn more than the proposed investment multiplied by the required rate, then there will be a residual left over after the subtraction. A division manager would be evaluated on the residual left over from all his or her projects combined.

For example, suppose that 20 percent was considered to be an acceptable rate to the firm. Currently all projects for the division earn 30 percent. Suppose further that a project requiring an investment of $100,000 of assets was proposed. If this new project would earn a profit of $25,000, or 25 percent ROA, it would be rejected by a manager evaluated on an ROA basis and accepted by a manager evaluated on an RI basis. From an ROA basis, the 25 percent would lower the currently achieved 30 percent average. For RI, we would multiply the $100,000 investment by the 20 percent ROA required rate, getting a result of $20,000. When the $20,000 is subtracted from the profit of $25,000, there is a $5,000 residual income. The manager is considered to have increased his or her RI by $5,000.

The advantage of this method is that if the firm would like to undertake any project earning a return of more than 20 percent, division managers will have an incentive to accept all such projects. This is because all projects earning more than 20 percent will cover the minimum desired 20 percent ROA and have some excess left over. This excess adds to the manager's total residual income. Thus, RI motivates the manager to do what is also in the best interests of the firm.

The reader can readily see that ROI is not a simple topic. The finance officers of most firms spend a fair amount of time considering the implications of various forms of ROI for both motivation and evaluation. Unfortunately, it is difficult for one ROI measure to provide effective evaluation of the performance of both a manager and the firm. It is even harder to use that same measure of performance to motivate managers to do what is in the best interests of the firm. However, many firms use just one ROI measure for the firm and its managers. In attempting to make the measure serve multiple roles, the ROI measures used often are so complex that they are difficult to understand. The net result often is that ROI measures do not motivate the way they are intended to and do not provide fair measures of performance.

KEY CONCEPTS

Ratio—any number compared to another number. Ratios are calculated by dividing one number into another.

Benchmarks—a firm's ratios can be compared to ratios for the same firm from prior years and/or to ratios of a specific competitor and/or to ratios for the entire industry.

Common size ratios —all numbers on the balance sheet are compared to total assets or total equities, and all numbers on the income statement are compared to total sales. This makes intercompany or interperiod comparison of specific numbers such as cash more meaningful.

Liquidity ratios —assess the firm's ability to meet its current obligations as they become due.

Efficiency ratios —assess the efficiency with which the firm manages its resources, such as inventory and receivables.

Solvency ratios —assess the firm's ability to meet its interest payments and long-term obligations as they become due.

Profitability ratios —assess how profitable the firm was and how well it was managed by comparing profits to the amount of resources invested in the firm and used to generate the profits earned.

Nineteen

SUMMARY AND CONCLUSION

This book has covered quite a bit of ground in a relatively short space. We've discussed materials from both accounting and finance that go beyond those offered simply in introductory courses. Yet we've done it in a book shorter and less detailed than an introductory text in either accounting or finance. This was possible because the goal of the book has not been to make you into a controller or a treasurer.

In completing this book, you should have gained an improved understanding of the nature of accounting and finance. You should have a wealth of vocabulary and should be aware of many concerns of financial managers, as well as some of the tools they use to manage their concerns. For example, by now you are well aware of the emphasis on profitability, but should also have an awareness of the risks that go along with profits, and the fact that financial managers are attempting to balance the level of profit with the level of risk.

You should be aware of the financial manager's concern for liquidity, and the many measures of liquidity that the accountant builds into financial statements. This information helps the financial officer compute ratios on liquidity and solvency to monitor the firm's viability and to enable adjustments to be made if problems arise.

Accounting and finance go hand in hand in the financial process of the firm. The accountant provides information, both historical and prospective, and the finance officer uses that information to make crucial decisions regarding how much the firm will invest and from where the invested resources will come.

Undoubtedly you have more questions. This book is not a comprehensive handbook on all the issues of accounting and finance. Such handbooks do exist, but unfortunately they are both cumbersome and overwhelming. It is their very nature to be so because of the fantastically huge amount of information they contain. The uninitiated attempting to get his or her first exposure to accounting and finance from such a book would soon give up because of the monumental task of reading and trying to absorb what is basically a dictionary or encyclopedia.

Such completeness in all detail was not the goal of this book. What the author hopes is that you have been taught a vocabulary, a language—the language of business. If this goal has been achieved, then the reader is now competent to research for him or herself any particular point. A list of references follows this chapter to give you a starting point. Essentially, you must know many words before you can use a dictionary to look up the meaning of a specific word. Nothing is more frustrating than to have a dictionary define one word you don't know with another, and when you look up this new word, its definition is the word you looked up in the first place.

Yet, until you have a basic vocabulary, every word you look up in a dictionary will be defined by other words you also don't understand. Having read this book, you should now be well on your way to the comfortable use of accounting and finance dictionaries. You may be comfortable using the handbooks that exist, or you might prefer to read a chapter in a textbook when you have a question about a specific issue. References to both types of sources are included in the reference section.

If you find that having finished this entire book, you still have questions, you shouldn't be disturbed. Especially if they are questions you hadn't even thought of before you started this book. That implies that this bit of knowledge the author conveyed here has focused your thoughts on key financial issues of concern or importance to you. Obviously a book such as this one can't answer all the specific questions of all the many readers of the book. But if it helps you formulate specific questions for further exploration, that in itself is an accomplishment. If you want to know more about the internal rate of return, the textbooks listed after this chapter contain long discussions on the topic. But before reading this book you may not have known much at all about internal rate of return, or at least not had the introductory background supplied that will make further reading on the topic easier.

The key focus of this book was to create an awareness that specific topics and methods exist—leverage, ratio analysis, net present value, tax advantages to leasing—and to provide you with the vocabulary to enable you to go further. Going further may simply mean asking your controller or treasurer a question and having a better ability to understand the answer. Or it may mean further reading. In either case, the answers you get should be a bit more intelligible to you now.

A final caveat. You are not a financial analyst after having read this book. You are not an accountant or a treasurer. Certain parts of the material covered in this book are so complex that they seemed complex as you read about them. Other parts of the book may have seemed very clear, but represented simplifications of complex problems and techniques. Don't think of this book as a how-to-do-it book. Don't attempt to do your own tax planning based on the tax discussions contained in this book. Accounting and finance are highly complex areas.

This doesn't mean that they should simply be left to the experts. Nonfinancial managers have a need to be able to understand the basic goals and techniques of financial officers. You should be able to understand what is going on and what is being said. Don't, however, gain an overconfidence that, "That's all there is to financial management." Rather, think of it this way: hopefully someone soon will write a book on operating management for staff and financial managers. It won't teach them all there is to know about line management, but they certainly could use it—communication, after all, is a two-way street.

REFERENCES

Anthony, Robert N., and David Young, *Management Control in Nonprofit Organizations,* 4th Edition, Richard D. Irwin, Inc., Homewood, IL, 1988.

Brigham, Eugene F., *Fundamentals of Financial Management,* 5th Edition, Dryden Press, Chicago, IL, 1989.

Davidson, Sydney, C. Stickney, and R. Weil, *Accounting: The Language of Business,* 8th Edition, Thomas Horton and Daughters, Inc., Glen Ridge, NJ, 1990.

Defliese, Philip L., Henry R. Jaenicke, Vincent O'Reilly, and Murray B. Hirsch, *Montgomery's Auditing,* John Wiley & Sons, New York, NY, 1990.

Dominiak, Geraldine F., and Joseph G. Louderback, *Managerial Accounting,* 5th edition, PWS-Kent Publishing Co., Boston, MA, 1988.

Eskew, Robert K., and Daniel J. Jensen, *Financial Accounting,* 3rd Edition, Random House, New York, NY, 1989.

Gitman, Lawrence, *Principles of Managerial Finance,* Harper Collins Publishers, New York, NY, 1990.

Guy, Dan M., C. Wayne Alderman, and Alan J. Winters, *Auditing,* 2nd Edition, Harcourt Brace Jovanovich, San Diego, CA, 1990.

Hansen, Donald B., *Management Accounting,* PWS-Kent Publishing Co., Boston, MA, 1990.

Horngren, Charles T., and George Foster, *Cost Accounting: A Managerial Emphasis,* 7th Edition, Prentice Hall, Englewood Cliffs, NJ, 1990.

Horngren, Charles T., and Gary Sundem, *Introduction to Financial Accounting,* 4th Edition, Prentice Hall, Englewood Cliffs, NJ, 1990.

Levine, Summer N., ed., *Financial Analyst's Handbook,* Volumes I and II, 2nd Edition, Dow Jones-Irwin, Homewood, IL, 1987.

Morse, Wayne J., et. al., *Management Accounting,* 3rd Edition, Addison Wesley, Reading, MA, 1990.

Short, Daniel G., and Glenn A. Welsch, *Fundamentals of Financial Accounting,* 6th Edition, Richard D. Irwin, Inc., Homewood, IL, 1990.

Sorter, George H., Monroe J. Ingberman, and Hillel M. Maximon, *Financial Accounting,* McGraw-Hill, New York, NY, 1990.

Van Horne, James C., *Financial Management and Policy,* 8th Edition, Prentice Hall, Englewood Cliffs, 1988.

Van Horne, James C., *Fundamentals of Financial Management,* 7th Edition, Prentice Hall, Englewood Cliffs, 1989.

Weston, J. Fred, and Thomas E. Copeland, *Managerial Finance,* 8th Edition, Dryden Press, Chicago, IL, 1989.

INDEX

Accelerated Cost Recovery System
   (ACRS), 109-10, 113, 114
Accelerated depreciation, 105-6
Accounting:
   concepts of, 13-18
      accounting equation, 17-18
      assets, 15-16
      basics, 14-15
      liabilities, 16
      owners' equity, 16-17
   definition of, 3, 9
Accounting equation, 17-18, 19
   and financial accounting, 58-59
Acquisition cost, 45-46
Activity-based costing (ABC), 189-
   91, 195
Adjusting entries, 71
Adverse opinion, 40
Alternative Minimum Tax (AMT),
   178
Amortization, 101-2, 113
Annuities, 160-61, 170
Asset life, and depreciation, 104-5
Assets, 15-16, 18, 20, 26, 214-15,
   249-50
Asset valuation, 45-52, 55
   acquisition cost, 45-46
   for depreciation, 102-5
   future profits, 49, 55
   historical cost, 45-46, 55
   net realizable value, 48, 55
   price-level adjusted historical
      cost, 46-48, 55
   replacement cost, 49-50, 52, 55
   selecting method of, 50-51
Audit:
   auditor's report, 38-43
   and certified public accountant
      (CPA),27-34
   fraud/embezzlement, 36-38
   generally accepted accounting prin-
      ciples (GAAP), 28-34, 42
   management letter/internal con-
      trol, 35-36, 42
   management report, 41, 43
Auditor's report, 38-43

Balance sheet, 19-22, 26, 76-80, 212-19
   current assets, 214-15, 249-50
   current liabilities, 216
   long-term assets, 215-16
   stockholders' equity, 216-19, 250
Book of original entry, *See* General
   journal

Book value per share, 17
Break-even analysis, 95-98
Budgeting:
   budget, definition of, 207
   budget preparation, 198-201
      departmental budgets, 200-
         201, 208
      forecasting, 199-20, 207
      preliminaries, 198-99, 207
   definition of, 196
   flexible budgets, 204-8
   master budget, 197-98, 201, 207
   role of, 196-97
   static budgets, 201-4, 208

Capital budgeting:
   data generation, 151-54
   definition of, 149, 169
   investment opportunities, 150-51
   payback method of analysis, 154-
      56, 170
   time value of money, 156-61
Capital leases:
   criteria for, 173-74
   definition of, 179
   versus operating leases, 172-73
Cash flow information evaluation:
   internal rate of return method
      (IRR),165-68
   net present value (NPV) method,
      161-65,170
   payback method, 154-56, 170
   project ranking, 168-69
Cash flows, statement of, 24-25, 26,
   80-85, 221-25
Certified public accountant (CPA),
   20
   and audit, 27-34
Common size ratios, 247-52
Compounding, 158-59, 170
Computers:
   forecasting programs, 200
   and perpetual inventory, 132
Constant dollar valuation, 46
Consumer Price Index (CPI), 46-47
Contributed capital, 21, 26
Contribution margin pricing, 193-
   94, 195
Cost accounting:
   activity-based costing, 189-91
   cost systems, 186-89, 195
   cost vs. expense, 181-84
   definition of, 194

271

product costs:
  manipulation of, 185-86
  period costs vs., 184-85
  role of, 180
  unit cost, 191-94
Cost-flow assumptions, 134-36, 147
Cost per unit, definition of, 195
Cost systems:
  job-order costing, 187
  process costing, 186-87
  standard costs, 187-89
Credits, 59-63, 71
Current assets, 20, 214-15, 249
Current liabilities, 20, 216
Curvilinear forecasting, 200

Debits, 59-63, 71
Declining balance method of depreciation,106-8
Deferred taxes:
  definition of, 128
  and depreciation, 115-28
  and leases, 176-78
Departmental budgets, 200-201
Depreciation, 100-114, 227
  amortization, 101-2, 113
  asset valuation for, 102-5
    asset life, 104-5
    depreciable base, 104
  comparison of methods, 106-9, 113-14
    declining balance method, 106-8
    double declining balance method, 107
    straight-line method, 106
    sum-of-the-years digits (SYD) method, 108
  and deferred taxes, 115-28
    multi-asset firm, 121-27
    one-asset firm, 116-20
  Modified Accelerated Cost Recovery System (MACRS), 109-13
  straight-line vs. accelerated, 105-6
Depreciation recapture, 117
Disclaimer, 40
Discounted cash flow (DCF) analysis, 166-68, 170
Discounting, 159, 170
Double declining balance method of depreciation, 107
Double-entry bookkeeping, 58, 71

Earnings:
  retained, 21-22, 26, 77, 218-19
  stability of, 93-94, 99
Earnings per share, 226

Efficiency ratios, 254-56
  inventory ratios, 256
  receivables ratios, 254-56
Embezzlement, 36-38
Entity, definition of, 14, 18
Equity, 16-17
  stockholders' equity, 16-17, 18, 21, 26, 216-19
Expenses, 22, 77

Federal Depositors Insurance Corporation (FDIC), 5
FIFO, *See* First-in, first-out (FIFO)
Finance, definition of, 3-4, 9
Financial accounting, 57-86
  and accounting equation, 17-18, 58-59
  debits/credits, 59-63, 71
  definition of, 3-4
  double-entry bookkeeping, 58, 71
  financial statements, 74-85
  general journal, 57-58
  journal entries, 58
  ledgers, 73-74
  and recording of financial events, 63-71
Financial Accounting Standards Board (FASB), 31-32
Financial information:
  recording, 57-71
  reporting, 72-86
Financial leverage, 90-94
  collateral factor, 93
  earnings, stability of, 93-94, 99
  leverage decision, 92
  rule of OPM, 92-93, 99
Financial management:
  definition of, 3-4, 9
  goals of, 4-9
    profitability, 5
    viability, 6-9
Financial statements, 19-26, 72, 74-85, 211-26
  balance sheet, 19-22, 76-80, 212-19
  goodwill, 15-16, 250
  income statement, 22-24, 76, 219-21
  notes to, 25-26, 225-43
  and SEC, 28
  statement of cash flows, 24-25, 80-85, 221-25
  See also Audit
First-in, first-out (FIFO), 135, 136-44, 148, 231-35
  definition of, 148
Fiscal year-end, 20, 26
Fixed assets, 20, 249

Flexible budgets, 204
    price/quantity variances, 205-7
    variance/volume variance, 204-5
Fraud, 36-38
Full disclosure, 34
Fundamental accounting equation,
    17-18, 19
    and financial accounting, 58-59

General journal, 57-58, 71
Generally accepted accounting prin-
    ciples (GAAP), 28-34, 40-41,
    45, 173, 212
    conservatism, 32, 42
    consistency, 34, 42
    cost, 33, 42
    definition of, 31, 42
    full disclosure, 34, 42
    going concern, 32
    matching, 32-33, 113
    materiality, 33-34, 42
    objective evidence, 33, 42
Goodwill, 15-16, 250
Gross margin, 219

Historical cost, 45-46, 55
    price-level adjusted historical
    cost, 46-48
Hurdle rate, 161-63

Income statement, 22-24, 76, 219-
    21, 250-511
Inflation, 133-34
Intangible assets, 15, 21
Internal control, auditing of, 35-36
Internal rate of return method
    (IRR), 165-68
    variable cash flow, 166-68
Inventory costing, 129-48
    cost-flow assumptions, 134-36, 147
        comparison of FIFO/LIFO, 136-
        44
        first-in, first-out (FIFO), 135, 148
        last-in, first-out (LIFO), 136, 148
        specific identification, 134-35,
        147
        weighted average (W.A.), 135-36
    and inflation, 133-34
    inventory equation, 129-30
    inventory methods, 130-33
        periodic method of inventory,
        131
        perpetual method of inventory,
        131-33
Inventory process, 181-82, 194
Inventory ratios, 256

Investments, definition of, 20-21
Investment tax credit (ITC), 178

Job-order costing, 187, 195
Journal, 57-58, 71
Journal entries, 58
    adjusting, 71
    posting, 76

Last-in, first-out (LIFO), 136-44,
    148, 227-35
    conformity rule, 145-46
    liquidations, 146-47
    switching to, 144-45
    who should use, 146
Leasing:
    accounting issues, 172-74
    capital leases, 173-74
    operating vs. capital leases,
    172-73
    management considerations, 174-75
    tax considerations, 176-78
Ledgers, 73-74
Leverage, 89-99
    financial leverage, 90-94, 98
    operating leverage, 94-98, 99
Liabilities, 16, 18, 20, 26, 216
    valuation of, 52-54, 55-56
LIFO, *See* Last-in, first-out (LIFO)
Liquidity, 6, 8
Liquidity ratios, 252-54
Long-term assets, 20, 215-16
Long-term cash obligations, 52, 55-56
Long-term liabilities, 250

Management letter, 36, 42
Management report, 41, 43
Managerial accountant, role of, 4
Manufacturing inventory process,
    181-82, 194
Margin ratios, 259-60
Master budget, 197-98, 201, 207
Matching, 32-33, 113
Materiality, definition of, 226
Modified Accelerated Cost Recovery
    System (MACRS), 109-13,
    114, 116-18, 121, 176-77
Monetary denominator, 14, 18
Money, time value of, 156-61, 170
Multi-asset firm, deferred taxes
    for, 121-27, 128

Net cash flow, definition of, 169-70
Net present value (NPV) method,
    161-65, 170
    calculations, 163-65

hurdle rate, 161-63
Net realizable value, 48, 55
Nonmonetary obligations, 53-54, 56
Notes to financial statements, 25-26, 225-43
  significant accounting policies, 228-37

One-asset firm, deferred taxes for, 116-20,128
Opening paragraph, auditor's report, 38
Operating income, 219
Operating leases, 172-73, 179
Operating leverage, 94-98
  break-even analysis, 95-98
Opinion letter, *See* Auditor's report
Opinion paragraph, auditor's report, 38-40
Owners' equity, *See* Stockholders' equity

Paid-in capital, 21, 26
Par value, 217, 226
Payback method of analysis, 154-56, 170
Periodic method of inventory, 131, 147
Perpetual method of inventory, 131-33, 147
Posting entries, 76
Preferred stock, 217, 218
Price-level adjusted historical cost, 46-48, 55
Price variances, 205-7
Process costing, 186-87, 195
Product costs:
  manipulation of, 185-86
  period costs vs., 184-85, 194
Profitability, 5, 9
Profitability ratios, 259-64
  margin ratios, 259-60
  return on investment (ROI) ratios, 260-64

Qualified opinion, 40
Quantity variances, 205-7

Ratio analysis, 244-65
  benchmarks, 246-47
  common size ratios, 247-52
  efficiency ratios, 254-56
  liquidity ratios, 252-54
  profitability ratios, 259-64
  solvency ratios, 256-59
Raw materials inventory (RMI),
181-83, 194
Receivables ratios, 254-56
Replacement cost, 49-50, 52, 55
Required rate of return, *See* Hurdle rate
Retained earnings, 21-22, 26, 77, 218-19
Return on investment (ROI) ratios, 260-64
Revenues, 22, 77
Rule of OPM, 92-93, 99

Scope paragraph, auditor's report, 38
Securities and Exchange Commission (SEC), 20, 27
  and financial statements, 28
Short-term cash obligations, 52, 55
Solvency, 6, 8
Solvency ratios, 256-59
Stability of earnings, 93-94, 99
Standard costs, 187-89, 195
Statement of cash flows, 24-25, 26, 80-85, 221-25
Static budgets, 201-4
Stockholders' equity, 16-17, 18, 21, 26, 216-19
  valuation of, 54-55, 56
Straight-line depreciation, 105-6
Sum-of-the-years digits (SYD) method of depreciation, 106, 108

Tangible assets, 15
Taxes, 222-24
Temporary accounts, 76
Time value of money, 156-61, 170
Total variance, 204, 208

Uniform Price Code (UPC), 132
Unit cost, 191-94
  definition of, 195

Valuation:
  of assets, 45-52
  of liabilities, 52-54
  of stockholders' equity, 54-55
Variances, 204-8
  line-item analysis of, 203-4
Viability, 6-9
Volume variance, 204-5

Weighted average (W.A.), 135-36
Working capital, 24
Work in process (WIP) account, 181-85, 194